Cannibal Joyce

THE FLORIDA JAMES JOYCE SERIES

UNIVERSITY PRESS OF FLORIDA

Florida A&M University, Tallahassee
Florida Atlantic University, Boca Raton
Florida Gulf Coast University, Ft. Myers
Florida International University, Miami
Florida State University, Tallahassee
New College of Florida, Sarasota
University of Central Florida, Orlando
University of Florida, Gainesville
University of North Florida, Jacksonville
University of South Florida, Tampa
University of West Florida, Pensacola

CANNIBAL JOYCE

Thomas Jackson Rice

FOREWORD BY SEBASTIAN D. G. KNOWLES

UNIVERSITY PRESS OF FLORIDA

Gainesville Tallahassee Tampa Boca Raton Pensacola
Orlando Miami Jacksonville Ft. Myers Sarasota

Copyright 2008 by Thomas Jackson Rice
Printed in the United States of America on acid-free paper
All rights reserved

13 12 11 10 09 08   6 5 4 3 2 1

A copy of cataloging-in-publication data is available from the Library
of Congress.
ISBN 978-0-8130-3219-1

The University Press of Florida is the scholarly publishing agency
for the State University System of Florida, comprising Florida A&M
University, Florida Atlantic University, Florida Gulf Coast University, Florida
International University, Florida State University, New College of Florida,
University of Central Florida, University of Florida, University of North
Florida, University of South Florida, and University of West Florida.

University Press of Florida
15 Northwest 15th Street
Gainesville, FL 32611-2079
http://www.upf.com

For my children: Andrew, Jennifer, Carrie, and Katie

Contents

Figures

Foreword

Ronald Reagan will be remembered for many things, but the one that sticks out in my mind is his fondness for jellybeans. Our fortieth president shared a sweet tooth with another world leader, King Edward VII: in "Lestrygonians" the latter is revealed on his throne, "sucking red jujubes white." The comfits of the king are clearly meant to be discomfiting: the king and his empire are bleeding the colonies white, draining the blood from the red areas of the map. At the end of "Circe," the king's at it again: a red jujube turns white in his phosphorescent face as he "*levitates over heaps of slain.*" Edward VII is a cannibal: his colonization, in Rice's excellent phrase, is colonic.

The connection of presidential jellybean and imperial jujube has been made possible by Rice's brilliant exploration of Joyce's digestive capacity. No one is better in this business than Rice at the precise overview, the detailed and comprehensive analysis of a particular theme. If you or I were to be set the topic of the cannibal theme in Joyce we might think of the return of Stephen's mother, the Eucharist, and the limerick on the Reverend Mr. MacTrigger. Perhaps we might include Swift's "A Modest Proposal" and the near-anagram of Caliban, and say something about Joyce's cannibalization of earlier literature in "Oxen of the Sun." But only Tom Rice would show us that Gabriel Conroy derives his name from a Bret Harte novel that begins with an account of the snowbound Donner party. Only Rice would connect the cannibal trope in fairy tales to the ogres, trolls, and witches of *Dubliners*, would give us the etymology of cannibalization (from World War II) and cannibal (from 1492) and make both relevant to Joyce, would find traces of vampirism in Stephen's villanelle, would call *Finnegans Wake* a literary and linguistic incorporation that is intended to be the reader's breakfast. Everything from Shylock to seedcake is thrown into the maw, until suddenly all of Joyce is about consumption. When Rice arrives at the moment of truth in the Gresham Hotel, as Gabriel asks his innocent question about the nature of Michael Furey's death—"Consumption, was it?"—we reach, like Gabriel, the last moment of our innocence, and our souls swoon with the new possibilities of Rice's reading.

Rice has other fish to fry: *Cannibal Joyce* is not just a study of alimentary aspects in Joyce's writing, but an investigation of all the ways in which Joyce can be considered an agent of cultural transfer. Joyce's detachment from his native language as a Berlitz instructor in Pola and Trieste allowed him to manipulate and eviscerate the word: Rice shows us how the linguistic instability of *Finnegans Wake* is anticipated in the first pages of *Dubliners*. Language is let loose in *Ulysses*: a punning analysis of adverbial modifiers in "Scylla and Charybdis" valuably underscores the comedy of that episode, and includes the worst pun on Bakhtin's name that I have ever come across. For Rice, *Ulysses* is a mincer: when Stephen minces Mr. Deasy's words, just after the letter-writer has smugly celebrated the fact that "I don't mince words, do I?," we are given both a reading strategy and an essential clue to the Joycean method. *Ulysses*, in its cannibalization of literary and mythological tradition, is a reprocessing of all that has come before. And then Rice turns his attention from language and the literary past to the technological present, and in a series of dazzling essays he places Joyce squarely in the middle of a postwar avant-garde that embraces the new technologies of sound reproduction, photography, cinema, television, and radio. For Joyce, who predicted not only the fall of Finland but the atrophying effects of television on the interpreting mind, the embrace is pythonic: one must consume or be consumed. This is one of the rare books where the subject and the author find their perfect match: the consumption theme is a rich and rewarding approach to Joyce's work, and Rice has given us, in witty and lucid readings of a wide range of texts, a banquet of ideas to savor.

Sebastian D. G. Knowles
Series Editor

Preface

From Cannibalism to Cannibalization

*cannibalize, v. trans. To take parts from one unit for incorporation in,
and completion of, another (of a similar kind). Hence cannibalization,
the removal of a part (of something) for incorporation in something else.*

The verb "cannibalize" first entered the English language in 1943, according
to the *Oxford English Dictionary*, as one of those neologisms, like "snafu,"
that enriched our vocabulary as a result of World War II. The *OED* cites
the *Journal of the Royal Aeronautical Society*'s definition of the term (1947):
"The necessity for removing serviceable parts from one aircraft to service
another. Cannibalisation [. . .] was frequently the only method of maintaining reasonable serviceability" of aircraft during wartime. Judging from the
OED's list of examples, to "cannibalize" does not migrate to peaceful us-
ages—as in the cannibalization of radio parts—until the 1960s. Perhaps its
origin in wartime explains this odd evolution of a term to describe creativity out of a word that most people would associate with inhuman barbarity.
Yet it is also possible to argue that, if the human anthropophagus existed
long before Christopher Columbus gave the word "cannibal" to the world
in 1492 (Lestringant 15–16), so also did forms of creative craftsmanship that
resemble cannibalization exist long before the arrival of this verb. The history of technology, for example, offers countless examples of adaptations
of one kind of device, intended to perform a specific function, to meet the
needs of another machine altogether. As Paul Virilio has noted, in an observation I will return to in my final chapter, Colonel Gatling, inspired by
a steamer's paddle wheel in 1861, "hit upon the idea of a cylindrical, crank-
driven machine gun" (11)—the ancestor of the weapon that redefined warfare on the Western Front—and then Étienne-Jules Marey, inspired by the
Gatling gun, "perfected his chronophotographic rifle, which allowed its

user to aim at and photograph an object moving through space" (11), contributing to the development of motion pictures. These odd pas de deux between military and civilian technology (the internet, the interstate), and between the art of war and art itself through the modern era (see Virilio's *War and Cinema: The Logistics of Perception*), are paralleled by the symbiotic relations between mass culture and "high" culture through the modernist period (see Andreas Huyssen's *After the Great Divide*), a relationship too often obscured by critical focus on the creative adaptations of literary tradition in modernist art, as in the dense texture of allusions in Eliot, Pound, or Joyce. In effect, to call James Joyce's dismemberment, digestion, and reprocessing of the English language, literary topoi and forms, together with his *incorporation* of popular culture into his works, "cannibalization" is neither a category error nor an anachronism.

Joyce took seriously the lessons his Jesuit educators taught him as well as those he learned from his struggles as a young artist attempting to break into the literary marketplace. In his fiction he adapts and literalizes the theological mystery of the Incarnation—the word made *flesh*—to create an art that reciprocates the creator by persistently investing spiritual significance in the *body* of the literary work. Yet Joyce's experience of his contemporary material culture also impressed on him the conviction that if he was to realize his ambitions as an artist, the body of literature must be *consumed*. (No doubt this is why he was fond of the title of the lowbrow literary journal *Prize Titbits*.) Thus in my first chapter I will argue that Joyce's immediate religious, intellectual, and cultural situation as a turn-of-the-century Irishman, and most important, his political formation, led him to conceive of his art as a kind of creative cannibalism that in turn invites its own consumption, and I will trace in his writing his direct and indirect incorporation of the motifs of cannibalism. Cannibalism for Joyce comes to represent both the artist's act of creation (incorporation) and the readers' act of reception (consumption). For the remainder of this study, however, I will turn my attention to three ways his aesthetic of creative cannibalism manifests itself in forms of cultural transfer: in his manipulations of language, in his uses of literary tradition, and in his exploration of new technical possibilities for the art of fiction. Further, within each of these subsections, I will trace how Joyce's artistic practice illustrates his incorporation of mass culture into "high" modernist works of literature, his cannibalization of two forms of unproductive expression as "the only method of maintaining reasonable serviceability" of the work of art.

To be precise, the method of cannibalization is not quite the same thing as Gatling's and Marey's technical adaptations or, say, Edison's successful modification of the Morse telegraph to develop his phonograph, or Julian Schnabel's recycling of broken crockery into works of art. The *OED* definition in this chapter's epigraph emphasizes that the term should strictly apply to taking working parts from one nonfunctioning device of some kind (say, a perfectly good motor from a junked auto), to replace nonfunctioning parts from another device of the *same kind* (say, another auto with an intact body but a "blown" engine), to create a functional unit (a working auto). Thus, one kind cannibalistically incorporates *its own kind*, in order to continue operating, for its enrichment, for its improvement, and ultimately for its survival.

We can see the closest analogue to this form of cannibalization in one of the striking but rarely discussed features of Joyce's use of the English language in his early fiction: his hybridization of words, a stylistic technique that matures into his often-noted exploitation of the portmanteau word by the time he reaches *Finnegans Wake*. In reaction against the worn-out figurative language of contemporary fiction, language that no longer "functions" as it once did, language that no longer impresses the reader with the sense of fresh and original insight, Joyce adopts a strategy of hybridizing two (and sometimes more than two) words that have lost their original vividness to create a compound word that arrests the readers' attention, reanimating the dead language of contemporary prose, particularly the adjectival excesses of late Romantic writing, and returning nonfunctioning words to full serviceability. (His strategy also gives word-processing programs fits, as everyone can attest who has typed Joycean texts—even passages from the early work—and confronted the numerous highlighted "misspellings" identified by their spell-checkers.) Joyce's cannibalization of language begins gradually in *Dubliners*, a work that generally eschews florid language as the young Joyce attempts a style of "scrupulous meanness" (*Letters*, II 134). We find his gestures toward cannibalization in the numerous hyphenated compounds in the *Dubliners* stories, and most especially in adjectival constructions: the "bottle-green" eyes of the "old josser" in "An Encounter" (*D* 27, 26) and the "ever-changing violet" of the evening sky in "Araby" (*D* 30), through the "snow-stiffened frieze" of Gabriel Conroy's overcoat at the opening of "The Dead" (*D* 177), Gabriel's reflections on the "*thought-tormented music*" of Browning's poetry (*D* 192), or his story of the "never-to-be-forgotten Johnny" (*D* 207), and so on.[1] This hyphenation drops away in *A Portrait of the Artist as a Young Man*—announced by the "moocow" of the novel's opening sentence—as Joyce now regularly uses a cannibalized language to reanimate a cliché: Stephen Dedalus is terrified by his father's breakdown at the conclusion of the first chapter's Christmas dinner scene, but he does not look on this scene "with terror in his eyes," nor is he simply "terror-stricken." Rather, Joyce writes, "Stephen, raising his *terrorstricken* face, saw that his father's eyes were full of tears" (*P* 39; my emphasis). Stephen himself comes to relish this very cannibalization of language:

> He drew forth a phrase from his treasure and spoke it softly to himself.
> —A day of dappled *seaborne* clouds.
> The phrase and the day and the scene harmonized in a chord. Words. Was it their colours? He allowed them to glow and fade, hue after hue: sunrise gold, the russet and green of apple orchards, azure of waves, the *greyfringed* fleece of clouds. No, it was not their colours: it was the poise and balance of the period itself. Did he then love the rhythmic rise and fall of words better than their associations of legend and colour? Or was it that, being as weak of sight as he was shy of mind, he drew less pleasure from the reflection of the glowing sensible world through the prism of a language *manycoloured* and richly storied than from the contemplation of an inner world of individual emotions mirrored perfectly in a lucid supple periodic prose? (*P* 166–67; my emphases)

Every page of *Ulysses* features similar cannibalized words from Joyce's own *Wortschatz*, from Buck Mulligan's "dressinggown" (*U* 1.3) at the opening through Molly's memories of the "rosegardens" of Gibraltar at the close (*U* 18.1602). In *Finnegans Wake* the noncannibalized word is the exception, rather than the rule.

 Stephen identifies the rhythms of the sentence and the harmonious relation of signifier to signified—reinforced by the chord-like harmonies, the multiple and compounded "voices," of the cannibalized words: "seaborne," "greyfringed," "manycoloured"—as the stimuli to his swooning response to language. My second chapter will argue that James Joyce shares Stephen's equation of language and music in this passage and elsewhere in *A Portrait of the Artist as a Young Man,* and trace the provenance of this equation to the Pythagorean tradition that grounds both language and music in mathematics. Joyce, like Stephen, was prepared by his intellectual training to perceive language, music, mathematics, and ultimately religious belief, as axiomatic systems, or as the text of *A Portrait* would have it, as "logical and coherent" absurdities (*P* 244), and even approximates this perception as a youthful university student in his academic essay "The Study of Languages." But, as my third chapter will contend, Joyce was equally well prepared to perceive the English language—and by extension all language—as an axiomatic system by his deracinated relationship to his "native" language as an Irishman: "I have not made or accepted its words" (*P* 189). Joyce arrived at his "Saussurian" perception of language as an arbitrary assemblage of signifiers, I will argue, not through an exposure to contemporary linguistic theory, but through his direct experience of the popular cultural phenomenon of Maximilian Berlitz's language training program. His deracinated relation to the English language, as well as his growing sense that language is a *consumable* commodity, were intensified by his experience teaching English by the Berlitz method in Pola and Trieste during the first decade of the twentieth century. Joyce's increasingly denatured relation to English progressively liberated him to disassemble and reassemble language to increase the artistic "serviceability" of words.

The following two chapters of this study—concerning Joyce's appropriations from literary culture—similarly juxtapose the "high" cultural and mass cultural sources of his creative cannibalization of literary traditions. Although my governing conception of Joyce as a literary cannibal is original, in other respects these chapters reflect a long-established understanding of the artist's hybridization of, for example, the naturalist and symbolist traditions, as Edmund Wilson discusses in his essay on Joyce in *Axel's Castle* (1931) and Harry Levin expands in his survey of "the map and the myth" (65) in *James Joyce: A Critical Introduction* (1944). However, the full effect of these critics' analyses of Joyce's fiction, exacerbated by Richard Ellmann's magisterial biography *James Joyce* (1959; rev. ed. 1982), was to "valorize the separation of [Joyce's] art from his material and domestic life" and thus generate "the powerful mythology of Joyce as a modernist artist" in autonomous isolation from and reaction against contemporary mass culture (Norris, *Joyce's Web* 8). So, while my fourth chapter unravels a complex mesh of literary allusions to the "high" cultural tradition—Dante and Browning—in Joyce's "The Dead," my fifth chapter will reciprocate this emphasis by tracing the indebtedness of the most literarily sophisticated chapter of *Ulysses*, the Scylla and Charybdis episode, to the conventions of mass market literature for adolescents in the early decades of the twentieth century.

Critics like Cheryl Herr, R. B. Kershner, and others, have made major contributions to our understanding of Joyce's incorporation of contemporary popular culture in his work, to redress the emphasis on his indebtedness to the long traditions of Western literary culture, and the final section of this study continues this process of unearthing Joyce's creative cannibalization of the "high" modernist literary tradition and the materials of contemporary mass culture to create works that are uniquely of their time, while maintaining their claims to literary immortality. My last three chapters, respectively, trace the impact of emergent forces in contemporary popular culture that, though seemingly tangential, have a direct influence on Joyce's conception of artistic creativity and explorations of the possibilities of fiction, especially in his last two books, *Ulysses* and *Finnegans Wake*: birth control (specifically the condom) and new communication technologies (the phonograph, the film, radio, and television). His reflection of, and response to, contemporary forces that potentially threaten the dissemination of meaning—incorporating and transforming them for his own needs in the body of his work—offer the strongest illustrations of the cannibal's impulse to consume and draw strength from those who would otherwise threaten his own existence, and thus survive to feed others. Moreover, just as this cannibalism originated in his political formation, in these last three chapters I will argue that his cannibalization of literature, popular culture, and ultimately technology increasingly functions as a form of political engagement.

Joyce's aesthetic, however, owes as much to his religious training as to his political formation, and thus the concept of cannibalism that I employ to describe his practices will, like the Roman Catholic doctrine of real presence in the Eucharist that provides one of its sources, appear to border on the literal. In my view, Joyce incorporates, or ingests and digests, the Other (the language of the oppressor, literary tradition, popular literature, the products of contemporary culture), to nourish the *body* of his own creation, conceiving of his writing as a corpus/corpse for the eventual consumption and nourishment of his audience. (We are to understand *Finnegans Wake*, his ultimate expression of this idea, as literally written on the body [see *FW* 185.35–36].) My project, then, might be seen as a contribution to the emergent field of "cultural transfer" studies that, I was pleased to learn as I completed this book, has recently turned to invoking the metaphor of cannibalism to characterize the processes of reception and adaptation of "cultural" artifacts (i.e., intellectual properties) across "cultures," usually defined as distinct linguistic and national entities. While the theory of cultural transfer has, to date, largely focused on literary translation, adaptation, and performance, it draws its inspiration from studies of "ethnology and cultural anthropology, reception theory, translation theory and the study of media cultures" and thus enables a broader definition of cultures to signify differing "social classes, groups, generations, parties, or ethnicities."[2] My present project is itself an example of this cultural transfer, as I have, so to speak, incorporated and digested this theoretical viewpoint from one research culture, to nourish the body of my own study of Joyce, which belongs to the "culture" of literary analysis. In this process of transfer, I have adapted the expansive understanding of "cultures" to subsume discrete entities ("high culture" vs. "mass culture"), or fields of activity (literature, commerce, technology) within a single language community. Cultural transfer theory, in fact, predicts that I would do precisely this, for its purview is "processes of cultural change, adaptation, mediation and interpenetration" that characterize cultures in contact (Lüsebrink and Reichardt 20). Central to these processes is the balance of assimilation and "blockage" that will "ensure that the foreign does not become one's own," similar to the cannibal's conflicting desire to absorb the Other yet fear of becoming the Other: "convinced that it is important to maintain one's own cultural identity, social groups develop strategies against the transformational powers of cultural transfer which allow them to maintain their identities."[3] As I will argue in the following chapters, James Joyce's response to English, the language of the alien, and his mediations among "high" culture, popular culture, and contemporary material culture and technology demonstrate precisely this same dynamic of assimilation and resistance.

Without resistance, however, I want to thank here several individuals whose advice I assimilated and whose assistance helped to make this book possible: Jim LeBlanc and Bill Brockman, the organizers of the 2005 North American James Joyce Conference at Cornell University, who invited me to present in a plenary address the core of my argument that Joyce is a creative cannibal; Sebastian Knowles, the editor of the Florida James Joyce Series, who enthusiastically read a preliminary version of the manuscript, offered me countless suggestions for its improvement, shared with me an "everything-is-illuminated" journey through rural Poland, and saved me there from an unwise encounter with the Belarusian border patrol; my former student Agata Szczeszak-Brewer, who reminded me that Stephen's sow is a cannibal and who persuaded both me and Sebastian to visit her native Poland; my good friend Michael O'Shea, who helped me realize that Kate's tour of the "museyroom" is a kind of Berlitz lesson; and yet another good friend, Ewald Mengel, who introduced me to cultural transfer theory as we wandered through the Wienerwald. For reading the manuscript at various stages, I thank Mark Sibley-Jones and Roy Gottfried, and for answering questions along the way, Erin Giordano and Khristina Westbrook of the Berlitz Languages Corporation, John McCourt and Renzo Crivelli in Trieste, Bill Brockman (again), and John Muckelbauer.

For so generously assisting me in gathering the illustrations for this book, I want especially to thank Steve McVoy of the Early Television Foundation, Dave Arland of the Thomson-RCA Corporation, Leonard DeGraaf of the Edison National Historical Site, Alex Magoun of the David Sarnoff Library, Kate Calloway of the EMI Archives, Angel Vu of the University of California Press, Patrick Scott, director of Rare Books and Special Collections at the Thomas Cooper Library of the University of South Carolina, and once again Sebastian Knowles; and for their valuable technical expertise in helping me prepare the illustrations for publication, I thank Elizabeth Sudduth and Jeffrey Makala, also of the department of Rare Books and Special Collections of the Thomas Cooper Library, and Keith McGraw of the University of South Carolina's Department of Instructional Services.

Earlier versions of portions of this book first appeared in the following publications; I thank their publishers for permission to reprint:

"The Distant Music of the Spheres." Copyright 1999. From *Bronze by Gold: The Music of Joyce*, ed. S. D. G. Knowles, New York: Garland, 1999, 213–28. Reproduced by permission of Taylor & Francis Group, a division of Informa plc.

"Dante. . .Browning. Gabriel..Joyce: Allusion and Structure in 'The Dead,'" *James Joyce Quarterly* 30.1 (Fall 1992): 29–40. By permission of the *James Joyce Quarterly*.

"The (Tom) Swiftean Comedy of 'Scylla and Charybdis,'" *Joyce and Popular Culture*, ed. R. B. Kershner, Gainesville: University Press of Florida, 1996, 116–24. Reprinted with permission of the University Press of Florida.

"Conrad, Condoms, and Joyce," *Twenty-First Joyce*, ed. Morris Beja and Ellen Carol Jones, Gainesville: University Press of Florida, 2004, 219–38. Reprinted with permission of the University Press of Florida.

"His Master's Voice and Joyce," *Cultural Studies of James Joyce*, ed. R. B. Kershner, *European Joyce Studies 15*, Amsterdam: Rodopi, 2003, 149–66. By permission of *European Joyce Studies*.

"*Ulysses* and the Kingdom of Shadows," *James Joyce Quarterly* 40.1–2 (Fall 2002): 161–68. By permission of the *James Joyce Quarterly*.

I thank Brandy Kershner, Christine van Boheemen, Carol Kealiher, and Heather Romans for expediting these permissions.

I also thank Amy Gorelick and Michele Fiyak-Burkley of the University Press of Florida for their assistance as I prepared the manuscript for publication.

Finally, for tolerating their father's penchant for bringing up his most recent enthusiasms at inopportune times, like during dinner, I thank my four wonderful children, to whom I dedicate this book.

Figure 1. The Spitting Cannibal. Engraving from Théodore de Bry, *Americae Tertia Pars* (Frankfurt am Main: Ioannem Wechelum, 1592), 125. Courtesy of Rare Books and Special Collections, University of South Carolina.

I

"Consumption, was it?"

Joyce and Cannibalism

> Do you know what Ireland is? asked Stephen with cold violence.
> Ireland is the old sow that eats her farrow.
> —*P* 203

> Rum idea: eating bits of a corpse.
> —*U* 5.352

Priscilla Walton begins her *Our Cannibals, Ourselves* (2004) by remembering when she saw her "first 'cannibal'" on the "TV program 'Gilligan's Island'" in the 1960s (1). I can place my own arrival at the age of awareness of cannibalism, also via television, both a little earlier and even more precisely. On Sunday evening, 13 December 1959, my family sat down to watch one of our favorite shows, *Alfred Hitchcock Presents*. That evening's episode, titled "Specialty of the House," featured a Mr. Laffler (Robert Morley) who "wants to be a life member of a gourmet restaurant" named Sbirro's, famous for its specialty dish, "Lamb Amirstan." When Mr. Laffler violates restaurant policy by looking into the "off-limits kitchen, he becomes a life member[,] and like all life members, he [himself] becomes the specialty of the house" (*Alfred Hitchcock Presents*). I remember being intrigued by this example of an extremely rare form of anthropophagy, "gastronomic" cannibalism, and for weeks afterward I and my brother would refer to our evening meals as "Lamb Amirstan."[1] This episode of *Alfred Hitchcock Presents* clearly moved cannibalism from the periphery of my awareness to the center of my attention, however briefly. Were I a cultural critic then, instead of a child, I might have paid attention longer and noticed that anthropophagy was pervasive in the popular culture of my youth: elsewhere on TV (as in the famous 1962 *Twilight Zone* episode "To Serve Man"), in popular music about "giant purple people eater[s]," and in countless sci-fi and horror flicks. One of my favorite films, for example, was the B-movie classic *Invasion of the Body Snatchers* (1956), in which alien seed-pods appropriate the bodies of humans within a northern California community and then become soulless and emotionless replacements of their original owners. As a child, I gave little thought to why this story of alien invasion prompted my fear and my fascination, and how it resonated with current Cold War anxieties about invasion and the supposedly dehumanizing effect of communist ideology; nor did I recognize that the film also exploited a traditional representation of imperialism by picturing colonization as an act of literalized incorporation, namely ingestion.

In this chapter, however, I am not concerned with such recoveries of the repressed to expose cannibalism, as both a subject and a trope, in fact as a near obsession of mass culture in the twentieth century. Walton and others have already done this, analyzing the public's conviction that aliens, both extraterrestrial and terrestrial Others, inevitably lust for human flesh and blood, not to mention the public's fascination with the abominations of psychopathic cannibals both real (Jeffrey Dahmer or Andrej Chikatilo) and fictional (Hannibal Lecter), and its morbid interest in notorious cases of survival cannibalism, such as the story of the sixteen Uruguayan survivors of a 1972 plane crash in the Andes that inspired several books and a feature film, *Alive*, in 1993 (Askenasy 101–6, 204–11; Petrinovich 67–73). Even advertising has exploited bad taste to promote good tastes: in a recent television commercial for the Mars candy company, three giant M&M candies, one plain, one peanut, and one crunchy, sit on a couch eating "their own kind"; after being admonished (by John O'Hurley), they exchange their candy packages to resolve the problem. Recent studies have also clarified how other, more sublimated forms of anthropophagy pervade contemporary culture, particularly in our tendency to see diseases that involve either self-consumption or the invasion of alien "life forms," like anorexia nervosa, cancer, or AIDS, in cannibalistic terms (Walton 71–74, 105–20). Computer viruses and worms that consume our operating systems, by analogy, are yet another kind of cannibalism—like eating like—that we might call "technophagy."[2]

Although our vast and varied access to tales and images of cannibalism may separate us from James Joyce and his time, our cultural preoccupation with literal and figurative forms of anthropophagy does not. The illustrations of cannibalism were as pervasive in the late nineteenth-century mass culture of Joyce's youth as they are today;[3] the "camnabel chieftain" or "cannibal king," for example, was a stock character in the "pantomime" (*FW* 362.05, 600.01, 599.36)—especially in the perennially popular adaptations of *Robinson Crusoe*—and assorted cannibals and related anthropophagi proliferated in contemporary popular literature, then as now: witches, vampires, and werewolves (Askenasy 149–53; Lestringant 170–79; Malchow 41–166). Indeed, anthropophagy has been continuously present in Western culture from the time Chronos ate his offspring in a primal example of incestuous cannibalism (endocannibalism), and this presence intensified from the Early Modern era forward, paralleling the rise of imperialism to become the near obsession in the nineteenth century that it remains today. Thus in *Totem and Taboo* (1913) Freud would speculate that the psychic origins of religion and our humanity—"the moment when the human animal became human" (Gay 482)—reside in another primal act of incestuous cannibalism, actual or displaced, although in Freud's scenario the rival sons consume the father (512). It should come as no surprise, then, that the subtext of cannibalism in its manifold forms pervades Joyce's fiction, from *Dubliners* through *Finnegans Wake*, or that we can similarly trace this cannibalism in the psychic origins of Joyce's conceptions of art and the artist.

Like most children, the young Joyce probably first encountered anthropophagy in the safely fantastic world of folklore, particularly in fairy tales, a genre astonishingly invested in cannibalism. Popular tales like "Hansel and Gretel" immediately come to mind, where the children narrowly escape being consumed by an evil witch, or "Jack the Giant Killer" with its blood-lusting Giant and "Irish hero" (*U* 12.176), or "Little Red Ridinghood," in which, at least until recent versions, Red Ridinghood is always consumed by the wolf. (In early versions, Red Ridinghood's grandmother herself is the wolf—a werewolf—while in others the girl joins the wolf in eating her grandmother [Lestringant 77, 85].) As Grace Eckley has shown, Joyce alludes to children's games and lore extensively in *Finnegans Wake*, for instance, varying throughout the motif of the Giant's "Fee, fi, fo, fum" in "Jack the Giant Killer" (95–96), the "most famous war cry in English literature" (Opie and Opie 78, n 1). But traces of the folklore of cannibalism are already evident in his earliest fiction, beginning with the ogre figures of Fr. Flynn in "The Sisters," with "his big discoloured teeth" (*D* 13), and the "old josser" in "An Encounter," who the boy narrator fears could "seize me by the ankles" and drag him down a "slope," the predatory behavior of trolls that hide beneath bridges (*D* 26, 28). The "next-door girls" possibly play their trick on witch-like Maria in "Clay"

(*D* 105), not only because she has "accused [them] of stealing" (*D* 103), but also because they see her as one of those crones notorious for feeding on little children, usually enticing them with sweets like the witch in "Hansel and Gretel," or with cakes like Maria. And, of course, Joyce seems to have been fascinated early by the folklore elements in Homer's *Odyssey* emphasized by Charles and Mary Lamb in their *The Adventures of Ulysses* (1808), which includes accounts of several anthropophagi: Polyphemus the Cyclops, the Lestrygonians, and the ravenous six-headed monster Charybdis.

There would also have been a time when Joyce came to the age of awareness of cannibalism as a fact of life in the world. His own "Specialty of the House" experience perhaps came through some sensational story of survival cannibalism in the popular press, literature, or art, such as accounts of the fate of the snowbound Donner party in the High Sierras during the winter of 1846–47—which inspired the opening section of Bret Harte's significantly titled novel *Gabriel Conroy* (1876)—or of the cannibalism among the survivors of several infamous shipwrecks that captured popular imagination. Chief among these were the losses of the French frigate *Medusa* in 1816, which Géricault immortalizes in his painting *The Raft of the Medusa* (1819), and the New England whale ship *Essex* in 1820, the original of Melville's *Pequod* in *Moby-Dick* (1851; Melville's earlier novel *Typee* [1846] also deals with cannibalism) (Petrinovich 22–40, 53–55). Equally likely and closer to home, young Joyce would have heard the anecdotal accounts of survival cannibalism during the Great Irish Famine of the 1840s, which continued to haunt late nineteenth-century Ireland and, like all famines, reduced some of its victims to anthropophagy (Lysaght 35–37; Kinealy, *Great Irish Famine* 28–29).[4] Such inescapable exposure to cannibalism means that Joyce, like many children who have been raised and educated in the Roman Catholic religion, particularly a child as thoroughly indoctrinated as he, must at some point have stopped at the words "*Hoc est enim corpus meum*" in his missal and realized that they were, according to the doctrine of transubstantiation, a factual statement that the body and blood of Christ are literally present in the Eucharist. The Catholic mass, a "meal," is not simply modeled on, but *is*, by doctrine, an act of ritual or ceremonial cannibalism. This belief that the mass enacts "theophagy" had generated explanation and equivocation among theologians throughout the history of the Church, especially after Innocent III officially proclaimed the doctrine of transubstantiation at the Fourth Lateran Council in 1215 (Kilgour, *From Communion to Cannibalism* 79–85). Early proponents of transubstantiation had already provoked persistent accusations of cannibalism against Christians during the Roman era that resurfaced, directed against Catholics, during the Reformation, and likewise recurred in English characterizations of the Catholic Irish as blood-lusting barbarians (Tannahill 38; Lestringant 65–71; Smart and Hutcheson 68). Whether their own discovery or the result of the accusations of nonbelievers, Catholics in the wake of Innocent III's proclamation seem to have become acutely self-conscious about the associations between the consumption of the Eucharist and cannibalism. As Merrall Price observes, "the doctrine of real presence entailed an awareness on the behalf of a medieval congregation that, on its most literal level, Holy Communion was a form of participatory and often infanticidal anthropophagy" (30). Most Catholics still at some point reach this same awareness, if they are educated in their religion. Nevertheless, in doing so, the young congregant who can see no visible difference between the unconsecrated and consecrated Eucharist will also come to consider the heretical possibility that cannibalism may function as more a metaphor than a reality, much as it did in the charges and counter-charges that permeated the political discourse on British imperial policies in Ireland (Smart and Hutcheson 68–71). Thus Joyce would have been positioned to recognize, as a young Catholic living in a society suffering under English authority, how deeply implicated both literal and figurative cannibalism was with the rapacity of imperialism. One of the most common accusations leveled against the colonized Other by the colonist, *and by* the colonized against their oppressor, has been cannibalism (Arens 13 and passim).[5] Colonialism was imaged as doubly "colonic." In his most mature story in *Dubliners*, "The Dead," Joyce correlates the idea of cannibalism with the fact of colonialism in several ways that return with even more force in *Ulysses*. Further, because Joyce, like his autobiographical counterpart Stephen Dedalus in *A Portrait of the Artist as a Young Man*, ties the sacramental miracle of transubstantiation to the transformative powers of art (*P* 221), bringing with this association the innuendo of cannibalism, so also does the idea of anthropophagy underlie his artistic method of "cannibalization"—as the following chapters will illustrate—in both *Ulysses* and *Finnegans Wake*.

Merrall Price notes the "coincidence of chronology between the beginnings of colonial incorporation and the reification of an encompassing theory of theophagy," through the now official doctrine of transubstantiation, that "manifests itself in a proliferation of late medieval and early modern texts—literary, legal, and geopolitical—that actively explore the idea of the consumption of human flesh by other human beings" (3). Correspondingly, "accusations of cannibalism against the Saracens, or against the allies, appear in crusade literature," as well as several recorded instances of "siege cannibalism" in the chronicles of the crusades, involving Saracens and Christians alike (8). Only in the immediate wake of American exploration and colonization, however, from the early sixteenth century onward, did Europeans begin to see anthropophagy firmly linked to the colonial subject, in the light of the apparent discovery of ritual cannibalism as a defined cultural practice among New World natives. Christopher Columbus, himself, brought them this news, also giving them the new word "cannibal"—a corruption of the Arawak word *cariba* ("bold") into *"caniba"*—that makes its initial appearance in the journal for his first voyage to America "in an entry dated 23 November 1492" (Lestringant 15–16). Although his European readers would argue about its possible causes, suggesting, for example, that the American natives lacked other sources of nutrition, they were not particularly shocked by Columbus's second discovery; the ceremonial practice of cannibalism was immediately comprehensible, if abhorrent:

> The communal aspect of the rite, its relation to the worship of the dead [. . .] and the hope of a substantial benefit to an entire group are all common points of belief between the New World and the Old. An inferior and distorting mirror of the chief sacrament of the Christian religion: this is what [. . . they] saw in the cannibalism of the Cannibals, which could be interpreted, according to taste, either as the repulsive remains of an archaic stage of development, or as a caricature of obviously diabolical inspiration—Satan (known to be a born plagiarist) aping his betters. (Lestringant 9)

The news was, nonetheless, sensational. As Frank Lestringant notes, the "Cannibals came to France in 1517" in a translation from the Italian of Montalboddo's 1507 account of New World explorations, *Mondo Novo e Paesi*, that became a runaway best seller: "it was reprinted at least six times within a few months" (32). Inevitably, living cannibals themselves arrived in France as ethnographic exhibits, to meet and converse with Michel de Montaigne, among others, in Rouen in November 1562 (Montaigne 158–59; Lestringant 1–2, 187–88). Drawing from these conversations in his remarkable essay "Of Cannibals," probably written near the time of its publication in 1580, Montaigne anticipates Rousseau by picturing the inhabitants of the New World as noble beings "in harmony with Nature" (Lestringant 54). "Of Cannibals" subsequently became a partial source for perhaps the earliest portrait of the colonized Other as cannibal in English literature, the anagrammatically named innocent/savage Caliban in Shakespeare's *The Tempest* (1611). (Caliban also makes a few cameo appearances in *Ulysses*.)

Montaigne has several reasons for reversing his readers' preconceptions "Of Cannibals": in part, he is contributing to what Lestringant calls a "well-established literary tradition" of the "unexpected eulogy" for the Other in sixteenth-century French culture (54); in part, he is depicting an idyllic realm that in its "original naturalness" is innocent of the "corruptions," pestilence, and religious warfare "of this side of the ocean" (Montaigne 153, 158); and in part, he is working to subvert the Protestant attacks on Roman Catholics as cannibals during the Reformation. A far more common Catholic response to these attacks, however, was to return them with interest. Considering Protestants in league with Satan and capable of all sorts of demonic perversities, including anthropophagy, Roman Catholics commonly read "Calvinistic" as an encoded term for "Cannibalistic" (Lestringant 38). Of course, each side in this war for religious dominance was both repeating the charges and counter-charges of cannibalism that seem the inevitable accompaniment of imperialism, from the Crusades through the European discovery of the Americas, and redirecting one of the most common themes of Christian anti-Semitism, the widespread myth that Jews practiced blood-sacrifices and consumed Christians, with a pronounced fondness for "Christian baby-flesh" (Walton 11; also see Tannahill 93–96, Price 34–35 and passim). This is what lies behind the "anti-Bloomite" Reverend Alexander J. Dowie's attack on Bloom, the Jew, as a "Caliban!" in the Circe chapter of *Ulysses*, a charge that ironically carries a punishment that promises to reenact his supposed crime: "The stake faggots and the caldron of boiling oil are for him" (*U* 15.1753, 1759–60).

Dowie's indictment of Bloom brings to focus one of the most fascinating features of the discourse on cannibalism during the Early Modern era that carries into our present: although the revisionist anthropologist William Arens has argued in his *Man-Eating Myth* (1979) that there is no indisputable proof that ritual cannibalism has *ever* been a customary practice in any society (21 and passim), and Columbus was himself skeptical of the existence of the cannibals reported to him by his native sources, there is abundant historical evidence that both empowered and threatened social groups insistently *believe* their adversaries to be anthropophagi (Arens 140; Lestringant

17; I. M. Lewis 101).[6] Furthermore, time and again the discourse on cannibalism tells us that the conviction that anthropophagy is practiced by the Other results from the "false projection" of all the self's darkest impulses upon this Other (Horkheimer and Adorno 187; also see Walton 24–25, 33–34). Dowie, an American, ironically attacks Bloom by *calling him an American* and thus projects native American behaviors on him, just as his preferred punishment for Caliban-Bloom seems to express his own relish at the prospect of a feast;[7] similarly, in the autos-da-fé of the Inquisition, the conquistadors' genocidal slaughter of New World natives, and the immolations of witches during the panics of the seventeenth century, the executioners eerily reproduced the preparations for the cannibal banquets that their victims were often accused of.

This dynamic of false projection appears in one of the foundational literary works of British imperialism, Daniel Defoe's *Robinson Crusoe* (1719), which in the words of Neil Heims "shows the justifying fantasy of the Europeans for their brutal consumption of human lives" by displacing this savagery onto the cannibals (191–92). What is perhaps unconscious in Defoe, however, becomes the central irony in Jonathan Swift's "A Modest Proposal" (1729), as he exposes England's rapacious treatment of the brutalized Irish people as anthropophagic: "*I could name a country which would be glad to eat up our whole nation*" (498). And this ironic recognition of the savagery of "civilized" imperial policies remains a constant theme into the years of Joyce's political formation, in both explicit treatments of European imperialism, such as Joseph Conrad's *Heart of Darkness* (1899)—where the representative European Kurtz accepts the sacrificial offerings of "unspeakable rites" and cannibalizes the savages under his dominion (118)—and in more indirect attacks on British imperialism, such as H. G. Wells's early scientific romances. Wells's *The Time Machine* (1895) warns of the internal consequences of the capitalist ideology of colonialism by picturing the privileged class, the consumers of the productive labor of the underclass, becoming those who will be literally consumed by the anthropophagic descendants of the working class in the future.[8] Similarly occupied with current politics through the lens of the future, *The War of the Worlds* (1898) inverts Britain's contemporary dominant position in the world by subjecting the English to colonial conquest by a "higher" civilization of technologically advanced Martians, vampires who ironically emulate British imperialism as they drain the blood of the victims. The most famous vampire fiction of this era, and of all time, Bram Stoker's

Figure 1.1. The Franciscan missionary Bartolomé de Las Casas (1474–1566) was among the first visitors to the New World to recognize, in his *A Brief Account of the Destruction of the Indies* (1552), that the Spanish conquistadors had projected their own brutality upon the Indians, while themselves savaging the natives. Woodcut from an English translation of *The Destruction of the Indies* in *An Account of the First Voyages and Discoveries Made by the Spaniards in America* (London: D. Brown, 1699), frontispiece, plate 8. Courtesy of Rare Books and Special Collections, University of South Carolina.

Dracula (1897) likewise critiques British imperialism covertly, first employing parallels between the Count and the savage Other of imperial discourse, but subsequently developing Dracula as an imperial invader who attempts to establish a colony of vampires within England, as England has done in Stoker's Ireland: Dracula's "aim is total, not partial, control over the people and their environment, much as a colonizer would desire" (Smart and Hutcheson 75; also see Arata 107–32).

Each of these critics of imperialism writes from the vantage point of the outsider *within* but not fully invested in the hegemonic order, in terms of class (Wells), location (Swift, the Englishman, exiled in Dublin), or nationality (Conrad as Polish and Stoker as Anglo-Irish), that allows him to perceive imperial ideology as "political, economic, and cultural cannibalism," projecting its own rapacity on its victims to justify its brutality (Greenblatt 136). But there is a different dynamic at work in the colonial subject: if the imperialist displaces his own innermost desires upon the Other, the subjects of domination may internalize those perceptions of the colonist that justify their subjection, on the one hand effectively alienating them from their own native culture, without earning them a place within the hegemonic order, and on the other hand making any resistance to imperial power an ironic fulfillment of the cultural stereotype of their barbarism. The subject is thus caught in a classic double-bind, and furthermore, as Maggie Kilgour has observed, even the act of internalization is itself a form of oral incorporation ("The Function of Cannibalism" 239): the savage's consumption of a sense of its savagery is savage in itself. The consequence of such internalization is cultural schizophrenia, a disintegration of any sense of a unified identity, self-contempt, and a self-consumption that is written on the psyche if not on the body (Bhabha 46–47).[9] I would argue that this dynamic of internalization and self-consumption is a significant subtext in James Joyce's work, from "The Dead" through *Finnegans Wake*, and that Joyce himself reflects his own internalization of the colonizer's perceptions in his aesthetic in *A Portrait of the Artist as a Young Man* and its realization in *Ulysses* and *Finnegans Wake*.

James Joyce Learns to Spit

A half-century ago Gerhard Friedrich identified Bret Harte's novel *Gabriel Conroy* as the source of Joyce's name for his central character in "The Dead" and his use of snow symbolism in this story (442–44), but Friedrich stops short of drawing any significance from Harte's own source for his novel in the history of the Donner party (Scharnhorst 50).[10] In fact, the anthropophagy in *Gabriel Conroy* is but one of several entry points for discussing the latent cannibalism in Gabriel Conroy. Gabriel does not quite preside as the Cannibal King over a ritual feast at the Misses Morkan's, yet his internal savaging of those whom he honors at the table, together with the "lugubrious" subject of the dinner conversation in "The Dead" (*D* 201), do evoke associations between this funereal scene and the profane rites of cannibalism, particularly in the light of another important literary source for the story. As I will argue in my fourth chapter, at the conclusion of "The Dead" Joyce symbolically places Gabriel among the living-dead in the final canto of Dante's *Inferno*, among those who have similarly sinned "AGAINST THE TIES OF HOSPITALITY" (Ciardi 274) and who spend eternity gnawing upon each other in Dante's invocation of the yet-to-be-named and most inhospitable act of cannibalism. Coexisting and conflicting with his latent cannibalism, however, is Gabriel's status in the story as a "West Briton" (*D* 188), as an Irishman who has internalized the values of imperial England, both appropriating the role of racial superiority to the Irish Other in his patriarchal domination of his wife Gretta and his condescension toward the party guests generally, yet demonstrating his own self-consumption in his recurring feelings of insecurity, stemming from his momentary recognitions that he is not what he wishes to appear, but the Irishman that England had long essentialized as barbaric. Emulating the imperialist, Gabriel justifies his own inferiority by projecting it onto others ("vulgarians" [*D* 220]); but as the colonized Other himself, Gabriel ironically validates the imperialist's assumption that he is, by nature, a savage Irishman. In short, Gabriel is a "symbolic collaborat[or] with the ruling masters of the English colonial empire" (Cheng 135), supporting its governing ideology of superiority and, ironically, its expectations of his own inferiority.

There are abundant ironies, too, in the final scene of "The Dead" when Gretta Conroy tells her husband the story of Michael Furey. Joyce's strategy for alerting his readers to the situational and verbal ironies at this point in the story is to note, twice in quick succession, Gabriel's own unsuccessful attempts at sarcasm as he questions Gretta "ironically," and to follow these by describing him as "humiliated by the failure of his irony" (*D* 219). Any irony in Gabriel's next question for Gretta, then, after she tells him that Michael Furey has died, is not his but Joyce's, for now Gabriel only speaks "sadly": "And what did he die of so young, Gretta? Consumption, was it?" (*D* 220). Gabriel innocuously assumes that a young man who has died "when he was only seventeen" (*D* 219) in Ireland at the end of the nineteenth century probably suffered from pulmonary phthisis (tuberculosis), and his use of the contemporary generic term "consumption" for tuberculosis is entirely natural. Joyce's word choice, however, is not innocent. The general term "consumption," from the Latin *consumo* (destroy, spend, consume), simultaneously carries medical and economic meanings, both of which slip toward its third, alimentary denotation, leading to the parallel between any number of wasting diseases in which the body appears to consume itself and cannibalism, as well as common associations among capitalist economics, colonialism, and cannibalism (one of Marx's favorite tropes for capitalism [Phillips 184–87]).[11] The evidence that Joyce intends such slippage at this moment in "The Dead" comes in Gretta's response to Gabriel's question. Actually, she does not directly identify the cause of Michael Furey's death but alludes to the "greater love" of the Christian sacrifice: "I think he died for me, she answered" (*D* 220). Thus Joyce establishes the ironic contrast between the Christ-like Michael who has been consumed for another's benefit, and the cannibalistic Gabriel who initially, in his "fever of rage and desire" wants to conquer the Other, "to crush [Gretta's] body against his, to overmaster her" (*D* 217), and to consume her sexually, and who finally turns inward, in the story's final paragraphs, toward his own symbolic death by self-consumption, the wasting away of his self: "His own identity was fading out into a grey impalpable world: the solid world itself [. . .] was dissolving and dwindling" (*D* 223).[12]

Underlying the apparent contrast of Michael's sacred self-sacrificial love and Gabriel's profane savage erotic desire—and impulse toward rape that literalizes imperial rapacity (Bauerle, "Date Rape" 114–18)—is their shared relationship to "unification" cannibalism, an anthropophagic ritual that realizes a complete assimilation of the desired Other (Askenasy 126–28).[13] In this rite, which is probably "*the* prototype of sacrificial communion" (I. M. Lewis 99), lover consumes the dying or recently deceased beloved, child consumes parent, or parent consumes child to achieve a full union with the Other, or the cannibal ingests the Other to magically incorporate "desirable characteristics of the consumed"—"[s]trength, courage, sexual potency, health"—often concentrating on "specific body parts [to] bring about the desired enrichment" (Askenasy 107–8; also see Frazer 556–78).[14] The "*reverend Mr MacTrigger*" limerick that Bloom recalls in *Ulysses* (*U* 8.748–83 passim) demonstrates Joyce's familiarity with this ritual as recorded in America, Africa, and Polynesia, and Bloom accurately supposes "the chief consumes the parts of honour" (*U* 8.746), but it is also possible that Joyce knew Strabo's report, in his *Geography* (c. 7–18 A.D.), that the ancient Irish also "reverently ate their dead parents" (Tannahill 7). The important point to emphasize here is that Gabriel's literally erotic and figuratively anthropophagic desire for union with Gretta originates from his own sense of incompleteness, like the cannibal's desire for "enrichment." His lack of a cohesive identity is the condition of the victim of colonial subjection who has been stripped of his own national identity—what Bhabha refers to as the "colonial alienation of the person" (41)—and this leaves him only one option: imitate the master. What Gabriel might say of his self in relation to his assumed West Britonism, Stephen Dedalus thinks of in terms of his relation to the speech of the English dean of studies in *A Portrait of the Artist as a Young Man*: "His language, so familiar and so foreign, will always be for me an acquired speech. [...] My soul frets in the shadow of his language" (*P* 189).

Stephen Dedalus, then, like Gabriel manifests the dis-integrated identity of the colonized subject, both internalizing the colonizer's perspective and ironically fulfilling the expectations of barbarism. Glossing Stephen's (and Joyce's) demythologization of the peasant as the noble savage portrayed by the writers of the Irish Renaissance, Edward Hirsch observes the same "West Britonism" (1124) in Stephen that Molly Ivors descries and decries in Gabriel:

> Many Catholic Dubliners affected English styles, manners, and habits, stigmatizing the Gaelic language and peasant customs as a badge of social inferiority and backwardness. Their insecurity suggests that as colonials they had internalized English attitudes and stereotypes. [...] This Anglicization left the Catholic Dubliners with the painful feeling that they had no identity, that they had lost their native culture without being subsumed by English customs and culture. [...] One way to deal with a debilitating sense of cultural alienation was to turn a Joycean arrogance against Ireland's native culture. (1123–24)

Ultimately for Stephen, in both *Stephen Hero* and *A Portrait*, "the peasant is distanced as a completely different physical type, someone wholly Other" (Hirsch 1127), as, for example, in his diary entry on the old man from the "west of Ireland" who both echoes ancient fears of anthropophagi—"Ah, there must be terrible queer creatures at the latter end of the world" (*P* 251)—and inspires in Stephen an analogous horror: "I fear him. I fear his redrimmed horny eyes. It is with him I must struggle all through this night till day come, till he or I lie dead" (*P* 252). And elsewhere in the novel Stephen twice significantly images the Irish "soul" as both feminine—echoing a convention in imperialist discourse that engenders the Other as female and thus subject to desire and conquest—and "batlike" (*P* 183, 221), that is, "vampiric" (Smart and Hutcheson 70), using a cannibalism trope commonly applied to the Irish by the English, and to the English by Stoker, among many other Irish, in return (Smart and Hutcheson 67–71). Stephen's twin references to the "batlike soul" of his race appear in erotically charged moments, first, while reflecting about the Irish peasant woman who has propositioned Davin and, later, while thinking about E-C- during his composition of his villanelle. On one level they suggest his sexual anxieties, his fear of being consumed by the Other—both national and personal—his fear of emasculation as an artist and as a male that drives his escape from Ireland. Yet the placement of these cannibalistic innuendoes in *A Portrait*, effectively bracketing the long university sequence that culminates in Stephen's discussion of aesthetics, allows us to bridge the difference between the student Dedalus's scholastic theories of art, and those of the mature artist of the novel that contains him. As Stephen attempts to compose his villanelle, he is distracted as he "bitterly" contemplates the "batlike soul" of E-C-, "a figure of the womanhood of her country" (*P* 221)—he has been made intensely jealous by her flirtation with Father Moran (*P* 220)—yet he recovers his inspiration in a "radiant image of the eucharist," concluding his poem with the verse:

> *While sacrificing hands upraise*
> *The chalice flowing to the brim,*
> *Tell no more of enchanted days.* (*P* 221)

This image invokes the moment of consecration, the miracle of transubstantiation in the mass, but it also finds its ground in the doctrine of real presence: the vampirism of the batlike soul is elevated (literally) and transformed into the sacramental cannibalism of Catholicism, an artistic transmutation that functions analogously to the transubstantiation it invokes and expresses the colonized's desire to reconcile at a higher level his divided identity. In a representative movement of cultural transfer, Stephen assimilates theological doctrine yet redefines it in/as an act of artistic transformation. Thus Stephen, in his jealousy of Father Moran, at this moment of inspiration juxtaposes his powers as an artist to those of the priest, and in doing so he defines the aesthetic of the novel that contains him and the priest-like role of the artist who has created him: "a priest of eternal imagination, transmuting the daily bread of experience into the radiant body of everliving life" (*P* 221). Obviously, however, the miracle of this transubstantiation of the mundane into the "body" of art is meaningless unless this body is consumed.

Overtly, as has often been noted, Joyce's aesthetic of transubstantiation is apparent in his investment of significance in the trivial details of the everyday, the "daily bread of experience," so that "the commonest object [. . .] seems to us radiant," as Stephen defines the moment of "epiphany" in *Stephen Hero* (*SH* 213). The fact that this aesthetic rests on an act of ritual cannibalism, however, has immediate practical implications for Joyce's art of fiction. The narrative, technical, and linguistic fragmentation of *Ulysses* and *Finnegans Wake* now appears as a dismemberment of the "body" of literary convention for the reader's anthropophagic consumption, much as the artist himself has fed off the corpse of literary and cultural traditions—"Dead breaths I living breathe, tread dead dust, devour a urinous offal from all dead" (*U* 3.479–80)—assimilated them into his system, and processed them into the body of his text: "Rum idea: eating bits of corpse" (*U* 5.352). (The excremental outcome of this processing will gain emphasis in *Finnegans Wake*.) These acts of figurative anthropophagy nourish and enrich the living consumer of the text, as they have the original text, creating and sustaining "everliving life" through a nutritional recycling similar to what Bloom considers when he reflects on the (less immediate) value of the human corpse in Hades: "It's the blood sinking in the earth gives new life [. . . .] Every man has his price. Well preserved fat corpse, gentleman, epicure, invaluable for fruit garden" (*U* 6.771–73). And it is clear that the more direct recycling of life through cannibalism is near the surface of Bloom's (and Joyce's) mind here, for at the center of this same passage—in the ellipsis of my quotation—Bloom recalls one of the typical anti-Semitic legends of Jewish anthropophagy, "Same idea those jews they said killed the christian boy" (*U* 6.771–72), a variant of which Stephen will recite to him later that night, in Ithaca. Seen in light of this "nutritional" aesthetic, the texts of *Ulysses* and *Finnegans Wake* thus resemble the "spitting" cannibal of New World literature who, in a "song" quoted by Montaigne, faces his own immolation by inviting his consumers to "all come boldly and gather to dine off him, for they will be eating at the same time their own fathers and grandfathers, who have served to feed and nourish his body. 'These muscles,' he says, 'this flesh and these veins are your own; poor fools that you are. You did not recognize that the substance of your ancestors' limbs is still contained in them'" (158). The work of art, then, is brought to life and gives life through consumption. As Joyce internalizes and enacts the empire's projection of anthropophagy upon the Irish, in doing so he re-

Figure 1.2. The image of the spitting cannibal, from Jean de Léry's 1578 account of his sojourn among the Tupinambas, apparently Montaigne's chief source for his account of the spitting cannibal in "Of Cannibals." The cannibal, facing his own immolation, points skyward (or heavenward?) and, speaking directly to the man about to strike the death-blow, in Léry's version boasts "I have eaten your father [. . . .] I have struck down and [eaten] your brothers" (123). Théodore de Bry obviously based his superb, highly detailed copperplate engraving of the spitting cannibal of 1592 on Léry's woodcut (see figure 1), although he used it to accompany a reprinting of Staden's *The True History of His Captivity, 1557*. From Jean de Léry, *History of a Voyage to the Land of Brazil*, trans. Janet Whatley (Berkeley: University of California Press, 1990), 124. By permission of the University of California Press.

imagines cannibalism as a creative and affirmative act, inverting the savage stereotype and contrasting it to the brutal and destructive rapacity of imperialism. Much as Montaigne does in his discussion of the poetry of the "spitting" cannibal, Joyce covertly answers the charge of cannibalism by ennobling the cannibal as the civilized artist: there is "nothing barbarous in this fancy" (158).[15]

Ruminating upon a Rum Idea

By calling Leopold Bloom a "Caliban!" the Reverend Dowie voices the traditional anti-Semitic accusations of cannibalism against the Jews, at the same
time echoing the British imperialist's similar characterization of the Irish.
(Stephen Dedalus alludes to this English conflation of the Irish and New
World savages in his earlier discussion of Shakespeare, by referring to "*Patsy
Caliban, our American cousin*" [*U* 9.756—[my emphasis].) Bloom is the victim of an *Irish* anti-Semitism in *Ulysses* that replicates the dynamic of the
imperialist by projecting its own barbarity on the Other in an Ireland that
gives only lip service to the parallel Israelite and Irish historical experiences of
oppression (e.g., John F. Taylor's "Moses" speech [*U* 7.828–69]); the nation-
alistic Citizen in, and the narrator of, Cyclops are the most brutal characters
in the book. Thus Bloom becomes a "double subject," a victim of the victim,
who internalizes both British and Irish convictions of his inferior status and
ironically fulfills the doubled presumption of his savagery. Dowie is right:
Bloom *is* the cannibal in the text. Yet this ironically connects Bloom to his
creator—and through Stephen to *the* Creator—for both Bloom and Joyce
reimagine cannibalism in ultimately positive ways.

As in the *Odyssey* that inspires it, anthropophagy is never far from the
surface of *Ulysses*. The novel's two openings both begin with images of cannibalism, first with Buck Mulligan's mock consecration of the Eucharist,
"the genuine Christine: body and soul and blood and ouns," despite a "little
trouble about those white corpuscles" (*U* 1.21–23). Stephen's response is his
first word of internal monologue in the novel, "Chrysostomos" (*U* 1.26),
golden-mouthed, ostensibly reflecting Buck's garrulousness as well as his
gold-capped teeth, yet simultaneously invoking one of the most outspoken
proponents of the doctrine of transubstantiation among the Fathers of the
Church, St. John Chrysostom, who also seems to have been one of the early
Christians rumored to practice cannibalism.[16] The second part of *Ulysses*,
correspondingly, opens by describing a carnivorous Bloom who "ate with
relish the inner organs of beasts and fowls. He liked thick giblet soup, nutty
gizzards, a stuffed roast heart, liverslices fried with crustcrumbs, fried hen-
cods' roes. Most of all he liked grilled mutton kidneys which gave to his pal-
ate a fine tang of faintly scented urine" (*U* 4.01–05). True, this menu only resembles a cannibal's feast, for Bloom consumes nonhuman entrails, though
echoing in its conclusion Stephen's devouring of the "urinous offal from all

dead" from the preceding page of the novel. Bloom clearly fails to faithfully observe the dietary rules of both cannibalism and Judaism. Nevertheless, Joyce's text provokes the same disgust with "unclean" meats that readers experience, albeit more emphatically, in graphic accounts of cannibalism. These parallel openings lay the groundwork for the numerous literal and metaphoric allusions to anthropophagy that follow, some of which I have already noted. Significantly, Joyce frequently places these allusions in the context of the consumption of language and art, from Stephen's "vampire" poem in Proteus (*U* 3.397) to Murphy's postcard in Eumaeus, which supposedly depicts "maneaters in Peru that eats corpses and the livers of horses" (*U* 16.470–71), the latter presumably not "fried with crustcrumbs" but nonetheless reminiscent of Bloom's dinner of "liver and bacon" in the Ormond Hotel in Sirens (*U* 11.499). Lotus Eaters introduces the doggerel *"Plumtree's Potted Meat"* advertisement, placed under the obituaries in the morning edition of the *Freeman's Journal* (*U* 5.145, 8.742–44)—which becomes a recurrent motif exploiting the links between cannibalism and sexuality throughout the novel—as well as Bloom's reflections on the "Hokypoky" of the Eucharist (= *hoc est corpus*; *U* 5.362): "Why the cannibals cotton to it" (*U* 5.352). Although the stereotypical cannibal/Jew Shylock and "Patsy" Caliban both enter into Stephen's Shakespeare interpretation in Scylla and Charybdis—Titus Andronicus is strangely absent in this context—the stronger association to anthropophagy in this chapter is Stephen's concept of the androgynous and anthropophagic artist who *feeds* off of his own experience to create, transmuting the incest that haunts him into a creative principle that precisely parallels the creative cannibalism of Joyce's own aesthetic. Furthermore, there are fundamental connections between incest, the sexual consumption of one's own kind, and anthropophagy—observed long before Freud joined these primal taboos—that explain their recurrent conjunction in anti-Semitic discourse and provide Stephen a lever to "[p]rove" that the incestuous/cannibalistic artist Shakespeare "was a jew" (*U* 9.763).[17] Indeed, as the "artist" in the text of *Ulysses*, both drunk and sober, Stephen is haunted by the supreme anthropophagic creator: "The ghoul! Hyena!" and the "corpsechewer" (*U* 15.4182, 4214), his "omnivorous" God who "can masticate, deglute, digest and apparently pass through the ordinary channel with pluterperfect imperturbability such multifarious aliments as cancrenous females emaciated by parturition," namely his mother, May Dedalus (*U* 14.1287–89). The novel's ultimate conflation of cannibalism and art appears in Stephen's recitation to Bloom of the legend of the "ritual murder" of "*Little Harry Hughes*" in Ithaca (*U* 17.844, 802), typical anti-Semitic propaganda that stops just short of Little Harry's "immolat[ion]" and consumption in the "strange habitation, [...] a secret infidel apartment" of the Jew (*U* 17.836–37). To strengthen the anthropophagic innuendoes here, Joyce plays on the word "host" in a series of three Ithacan questions, applying the term to Harry Hughes as "host (victim predestined)" to be a sacrificial body, to Stephen as "host (reluctant, unresisting)" the same threat of Jewish perfidy, as he sits in Bloom's "strange habitation," and to Bloom as "host (secret infidel)" who, by his hospitality, betrays the anti-Semitic stereotype (*U* 17.838, 841, 843). All that is "consumed" in Bloom's kitchen is "Epps's *mass*product, the creature cocoa" in a parody of the ritual cannibalism of the Eucharist (*U* 17.800, 369–70; emphasis mine). Stephen is safe, because Bloom's carnivorous appetites are only metaphorically anthropophagic, and his cannibalism is otherwise fully internalized in the form of self-consumption.

As we have seen, Bloom eats unclean meats, meals "fit for a [cannibal] prince" (*U* 11.359): a pork kidney for breakfast in Calypso and liver for dinner in Sirens, two acts of consumption that the text emphatically connects: "Leopold cut liverslices. As said before he ate with relish the inner organs, nutty gizzards, fried cod's roes" (*U* 11.519–20). For lunch in Lestrygonians, however, he eats only a gorgonzola cheese sandwich, an innocent collation, perhaps, were Bloom not simultaneously thinking about cannibals and reconstructing the limerick concerning the consumption of "*the reverend Mr. MacTrigger*," mentioned above, when he orders his meal (*U* 8.745 ff.); had he not earlier this morning *ruminated* on "cheesy" corpses and the anthropophagy of rats in Hades—"Ordinary meat for them. A corpse is meat gone bad. Well and what's cheese? Corpse of milk" (*U* 6.779, 981–82); and did he not "relish" the "feety savor" of his sandwich (*U* 8.818–19). With his sexual appetites, however, Bloom's internalization of the double English/Irish projections of savagery upon the Irish/Jew produces a cannibalism of self-consumption. As the Nausicaa episode shows and the Junius voice of Oxen of the Sun states, he is "his own and his only enjoyer" (*U* 14.914–15); he may devour Gerty MacDowell with his eyes, so to speak, but Joyce juxtaposes his masturbation in Nausicaa to the ritual of Benediction, to emphasize that the Eucharistic experience is entirely internalized rather than incorporated by the congregation and Bloom. Bloom's onanism is a form of cannibalistic self-consumption, particularly in light of the beliefs that

masturbation would inevitably lead to wasting diseases and self-destruc-
tion voiced in religious tracts and popular culture through the nineteenth
century; in any era, however, it would be difficult to argue that this is "creative" cannibalism. Rather, as Scylla and Charybdis develops the model of
Shakespeare's creative cannibalism, the other two chapters of *Ulysses* that
invoke anthropophagi in their titles, Lestrygonians and Cyclops, are where
Joyce shows the creative potential in the positive transmutation of Bloom's
self-consumption.

Lestrygonians abounds with references to cannibalism, many of which
I have already cited, that culminate perhaps in the disgusting spectacle of
feeding in the Burton restaurant (*U* 8.650–96), yet anthropophagy is present from Bloom's opening confusion of himself—"Bloo .... Me?"—with the
sacrificial victim, in the YMCA handout "Blood of the Lamb" (*U* 8.8–9).
At this point in *Ulysses* his understandable self-absorption on this particular day most explicitly turns toward self-consumption, indeed to extended
rumination. Today we would probably diagnose Bloom's problem as clini-
cal depression: "No-one is anything. This is the very worst hour of the day.
[. . .] hate this hour. Feel as if I had been eaten and spewed" (*U* 8.493–95).
Immediately before these lines and, ostensibly, their cause, the text describes
a "heavy cloud hiding the sun slowly" (*U* 8.475)—sunlight has similarly altered Bloom's mood in Calypso (*U* 4.218–42)—but a few passages after these
lines, Bloom experiments with parallax to obscure the sun himself: "The tip
of his little finger blotted out the sun's disk" (*U* 8.566), to make the point
clear that Bloom's sense of desolation—like his wife's imminent infidelity—is
self-generated. He is eating and spewing himself, like the "ravenous terrier"
that eats its own "knuckly" vomit (*U* 8.1031–32). In fact, the bulk of cannibal
references in the text carry the connotation of self-consumption, from Nosey
Flynn "snuffling" up his "dewdrop" (*U* 8.804, 983) and "a drowsing loafer
[. . .] gnawing a crusted knuckle" (*U* 8.1066–67), to Bloom's wondering "who
was it used to eat the scruff off his own head? Cheapest lunch in town" (*U*
8.872–73).

Joyce's alimentary model for Lestrygonians may explain the chapter's
abundant references to consumption, and its title allusion to a race of anthropophagi in Homer may likewise account for the cannibalistic nature of
many of these references, but neither explains why this episode also contains
the most detailed information about the Blooms' past sexual life that the
reader receives in *Ulysses*. One obvious explanation is that, as "is well-known,

eating and sexuality are closely related modes of intimate social interaction that readily flow together, both literally and metaphorically" (I. M. Lewis 102). What is less often emphasized is that the more literal this connection of appetites, the more it shades into cannibalism: "Consumed with desire, the lover eagerly seeks to devour the object of his passion[. . . .] In the contemporary Western world this equivalence or concurrence of the two modes of commensality—eating and sex—is appropriately reflected in the striking similarity in style and format between gourmet sex manuals and cookbooks" (I. M. Lewis 102). Thus Bloom's problem—familiar enough in criticism of *Ulysses*, but rarely phrased in this sense—is that he is eating himself up when he should be consuming his wife. Yet, at the same time, in Lestrygonians Joyce gives Bloom the opportunity to turn his self-consumption toward a creative vision of sexual consumption that equally suggests both the elevated communion of the Eucharist and its origins in the ritual of unification cannibalism, when Bloom recalls his first lovemaking with Molly on the hill of Howth—a memory that Molly reciprocates in the concluding passage of *Ulysses*—as he savors the bread, wine, and "feety" cheese of his cannibalistic lunch in Davy Byrne's (*U* 8.819):

> Ravished over her I lay, full lips full open, kissed her mouth. Yum. Softly she gave me in my mouth seedcake warm and chewed. Mawkish pulp her mouth had mumbled sweetsour of her spittle. Joy: I ate it: joy. Young life, her lips that gave me pouting. Soft warm sticky gumjelly lips[. . . .] Wildly I lay on her, kissed her: eyes, her lips, her stretched neck beating, woman's breasts full in her blouse of nun's veiling, fat nipples upright. Hot I tongued her. (*U* 8.906–09, 913–15)

On one level, this memory transubstantiates the chapter's motifs of consumption, redeeming through love the disgusting recycling of the already eaten—stout contaminated with rat vomit or the terrier's "cud" (*U* 8.47–49; 1031)—and elevating Bloom and Molly's exchange of chewed seedcake to a sacramental communion. Further, this passage emphasizes a moment of nearly literal oral incorporation of the Other, focusing on the taste of the Other ("Yum," "sweetsour"), the Other as edible ("gumjelly lips"). Molly is giving her "Young life" to her lover. As Stephen will shortly do in the next chapter, Scylla and Charybdis, Bloom reimagines cannibalism as an affirmative and creative act, for it would seem that more than just *seed*cake passed

between Bloom and Molly on this afternoon on which she got him to pro-
pose to her, and that her own ecstatic "yeses" would suggest that this moment of consumption was also the consummation of their sexual relations (*U*
18.1607–09; see *U* 17.2277–78).

Ironically, Bloom's ennobling of the savage happens only in memory and
is, in this respect, symptomatic of his continuing self-consumption, in the
context of cannibalistic consumption (his lunch). His anthropophagic masturbation in the Nausicaa episode, followed similarly by extended *rumination*, further frustrates any attempt to argue that Bloom's vision of creative
cannibalism in Lestrygonians, or his sermon on love in Cyclops, prove that
he has transcended his self-destructive internalization of savagery, although
many readers will continue to believe that some sort of positive transformation has taken place in him during his day. Unfortunately, however, because
Bloom's final words in *Ulysses* stop short of (apparently) his somnolent final
request to Molly, just as the legend of *Little Harry Hughes* stops short of his
immolation earlier in Ithaca, we will never know precisely what he has in
mind when he "ask[s] to get his breakfast in bed" (*U* 18.01–02).

With the exception of "His Majesty the Alaki of Abeakuta," who drinks
from "the skull of his immediate predecessor"—a characteristic detail in
many descriptions of the cannibal—the Cyclops chapter is surprisingly free
of even indirect references to anthropophagy (*U* 12. 1515, 1527–28), for the
Lestrygonians and Scylla and Charybdis chapters have already removed
cannibalism from the context of violence that dominates this episode in
which virtually every other form of brutality and persecution comes into
both the conversation in Barney Kiernan's pub and the text's interpola-
tions. Thus the references to ritual sacrifices in Cyclops, in the interpolated
descriptions of a hanging and a boxing match, and the narrator's remarks
on a lynching in Georgia (*U* 12.525–678; 12.960–87; 12.1321–28), occlude
suggestions of cannibalism to emphasize the sacramental, if ludicrous, nature of the sacrifice: the hangman Rumbold, for example, prepares "two
commodious milkjugs [. . .] to receive the most precious blood of the most
precious victim" (*U* 12.623–24). On the other hand, this is the only episode
in the novel that contains a supposed embodiment of an anthropophagus
per se, the Citizen-as-Cyclops in Joyce's schemas, adding irony to the con-
frontation between the two vastly different characters that are nonetheless the same: the persecuted Irishman persecutes the Jew, while both are
anthropophagi. The difference between the Citizen and Bloom as cannibal

figures is that the former remains trapped in the dynamic of the colonized, brutally reprojecting his own brutalization upon an Other, making himself the counterpart of those who have subjected him, much like the beaten Farrington who beats his son in the *Dubliners* story "Counterparts." Bloom, however, assumes the sublime and ridiculous features of the messiah-victim, like the other victims of ritual sacrifice in the episode, because from his perspective as the "double-subject" he has both fully directed inward the projections of savagery he has internalized and already recognized the affirmative and creative possibilities of consumption of the Other in the Lestrygonians episode. He may eloquently reject "Persecution," "Force, hatred, history, all that" in the concluding pages of Cyclops (*U* 12.1417, 1481), but in doing so, Bloom is simply giving voice to his earlier transubstantiation of the ethos of "Eat or be eaten. Kill! Kill!" into creative consumption in Lestrygonians (*U* 8.703).

The most compelling evidence of cannibalism in the Cyclops episode, however, is found in the chapter's form rather than its content, where Joyce cannibalizes two voices—one of which in turn cannibalizes various forms of discourse: guidebooks, mythology, news reporting, legal documents, graffiti, and so on—a chiasmic method that appears early in the book, in Aeolus (headlines and text), and recurs in successive narrative styles in Nausicaa and the questions and responses of Ithaca. In other words, particularly after the paired anthropophagic chapters Lestrygonians and Scylla and Charybdis that establish the creative possibilities of cannibalism, Joyce's own text increasingly illustrates this creative principle, incorporating multiple voices or, in the musicalization of style for Sirens, the linguistic-embryological model for Oxen of the Sun, the animated parody of inanimate style in Eumaeus, and the fluid "feminine" voice of Penelope, cannibalizing a variety of discourses. Circe, in effect, cannibalizes and recycles all elements of the novel that precede it, much as *Finnegans Wake*, as Kim Devlin has argued, incorporates all that has come before it in Joyce.

The Self-Consuming Artifact

Joyce himself implies that the *Wake* cannibalizes his earlier works when he alludes to his literal consumption of his own books, an act of bibliophagy, midway through his text: "And trieste, ah trieste ate I my liver [livre]" (*FW* 301.16) (see Knowles, *Dublin Helix* 110, 154–55). Consequently, Joyce's last book recycles, literalizes, and intensifies the anthropophagic themes already discussed. Indeed, cannibalism pervades *Finnegans Wake* to the extent that much of what has already been written about Joyce's final novel—even the common rejections of the *Wake* as "indigestible"—suggests an underlying recognition of the anthropophagy that permeates the book through its persistent incest theme (sexual cannibalism), its inclusion of the Freudian patricidal paradigm, its continuing exploration of the psychic dynamics of colonialism, and its fixation on the body of HCE, as well as the overarching associations of the "wake" itself with the cannibal feast: "But, lo, as you would quaffoff his fraudstoff and sink teeth through that pyth of a flower-white bodey behold of him as behemoth" (*FW* 7.12–14). In other words, HCE is the fraudulent foodstuff of the Eucharist, wine to be quaffed and floury bread—the staff of life—to be eaten, as well as the "stuff" of Freud's primal father, a monstrous bogeyman. Of course, although HCE is the victim of consumption, he is also a consumer; like the primal father or, indeed, like the spitting cannibal, HCE is himself an anthropophagus who "has an eatupus complex" (*FW* 128.36). Campbell and Robinson nonetheless assert that the "theme of eating is always associated in *Finnegans Wake* with the eating of the god: the consuming of the life substance of the father by his sons and retainers" (196), and if this is so, it might explain why, in his many and shifting identities throughout the text of the *Wake*, HCE often proves to be, well . . . a highly edible creature. Among his most prominent roles, HCE is an egg, suggesting his potential for rebirth (*ricorso*), but he is also clearly a Humpty Dumpty who will fall again and again, and become breakfast, a morning meal for his mourners: "And even if Humpty shall fall frumpty times [. . .] there'll be iggs for the brekkers come to mournhim, sunny side up with care" (*FW* 12.12–15). Similarly suggestive of the cycle of renewal is HCE's recurrent role as a salmon, the "honourable Master Sarmon" (*FW* 615.18), combining a progenitor that leaps at Leixlip and into the Anna Liffey, and the figure of the patriarch: "they saw him shoot up her sheba sheath [vagina], like any gay lord salomon [Solomon]" (*FW* 198.03–04). Elsewhere, among the countless epithets for HCE in the opening section of I, 6 (*FW* 126.10–13), he resembles other Finn-ed creatures, a "herring" or a "tarpon," for example, and even "fash and chaps" (*FW* 136.26–27, 137.11). The point is not simply that HCE assumes the forms of "Breakfates, Lunger, Diener and Souper" (*FW* 131.04),[18] but that through these identities he is consumed, again and again, by others in the book, like the "Four" who seem to be suffering from ingesting bad carp or crab (*FW* 392.05, 11; 397.25)—despite "saying their grace before fish" (*FW* 384.16)—and most significantly, like Shem, the Freudian patricide and son of Solomon, or "(sowman's son)" (*FW* 169.14), whose "lowness creeped out first via foodstuffs" (*FW* 170.25–26). Shem limits his diet to the body of the father—eggs and fish: "Rosbif of Old Zealand! he would not attouch it" (*FW* 171.01–02). In his "cookerynook" Shem "brooled and cocked and potched in an athanor, whites and yolks and yilks and whotes" (*FW* 184.17–19), to prepare egg dishes, from the exotic ("oves and uves à la Sulphate de Soude" [*FW* 184.29]) to the mundane ("Frideggs" [*FW* 184.32]). For fish, predictably, he "preferred [. . .] salmon tinned [HCE], as inexpensive as pleasing, to the plumpest roeheavy lax [ALP] or the friskiest parr [Shaun] or smolt troutlet [Issy] that ever was gaffed between Leixlip and Island Bridge" (*FW* 170.26–29). Best of all, Shem combines eggs and fish for his "sowtay sowmmonay à la Monseigneur" (*FW* 184.30).[19]

What remains to be said, however, is that Joyce also incorporates his aesthetic of creative cannibalism into this last portrait of the artist Shem (James), who is both the "cannibal Cain" (*FW* 193.32) and the self-consuming "somatophage" (*FW* 171.03) in the *Wake*, and who transcribes the text "over every square inch of the only foolscap available, his own body," for his own and the readers' consumption (*FW* 185.35–36). Shaun's portrait of "Shem the Penman" (*FW* I, 7; viz. 125.23) stresses the degree to which the artist "self exiled in upon his ego" is consumed *with* himself: "all over up and down the four margins of this rancid Shem stuff the evilsmeller [. . .] used to stipple endlessly inartistic portraits of himself" (*FW* 184.06–07; 182.16–19); yet Shaun's accusation of *somatophagy* emphasizes that Shem is consumed *by* himself as well, as the inescapable consequence of writing on one's body. Of course, Shaun attacks Shem for being an onanist like Bloom, "his own and his only enjoyer" (*U* 14.914–15), for playing only with his "*hand*some present of a selfraising syringe and twin feeders" (*FW* 188.29–30; emphasis mine), yet his charge of self-cannibalism finally involves a literal self-consumption. Shem, the image and likeness of his creator, and Shem's art, like the book with its tail in its mouth that contains him, represent "self-consuming artifacts" in a literal sense not quite contained in a conception of literature fathered by a somewhat different Fish. The *Wake*'s final description of itself as generated by a mechanical-digestive process and intended for the readers' consumption as a meal, breakfast in fact, makes this cycle of the cannibal that is cannibalized explicit, in a rare moment of relative clarity as the book approaches its peroration:

> Our wholemole [whole-*meal*] millwheeling vicociclometer, [. . .] autokinatonetically [self-motion] preprovided with a clappercoupling smeltingworks exprogressive process, [. . .] receives through a portal vein [i.e., digestive process] the dialytically [i.e., dialysis] separated elements of precedent decomposition for the verypetpurpose of subsequent recombination so that the heroticisms, catastrophes and eccentricities transmitted by ancient legacy of the past, type by tope, letter from litter, word at ward, [. . .] all, anastomosically [i.e., connected blood vessels, and "stomach-ally"] assimilated and preteridentified paraidiotically [almost-privately], [. . .] may be there for you, Cockalooralooraloomenos, when cup, platter and pot come piping hot, as sure as herself pits hen [pen] to paper and there's scriblings scrawled on eggs. (*FW* 614.27–615.10)

Thus, as a massive work of literary and linguistic incorporation, ultimately intended for the readers' digestion, *Finnegans Wake* becomes the cannibal facing its own cannibalization. Like Montaigne's spitting cannibal, the *Wake* invites its own consumption, affirming that its readers will ingest that which is "common to allflesh, human only, mortal," in its fleshly "integument" that has absorbed and transubstantiated "all marryvoising moodmoulded cyclewheeling history [. . .] transaccidentated through the slow fires of consciousness" (*FW* 186.01–06). Further, if the book is the unconscious ruminations of a dreamer—one standard model for reading the *Wake*—it may equally be seen as this dreamer's broken-down and only partially digested, incorporated experience of the world. Consequently, the readers' task is to digest the "chewed" and "mumbled" contents of the body *in* and *of* the *Wake*, the "[m]awkish pulp" that passes from its mouth to ours (*U* 8.907–08). The challenge to our digestion is precisely the same that Bloom sees redeemed by love in *Ulysses*. Our desire to incorporate *Finnegans Wake* into ourselves depends on whether we view the book as a Eucharistic host, to be consumed in a cannibalistic ritual of communion, as a revolting "halfmasticated gristle" like that mumbled and spit "back on his plate" by a toothless patron of the Burton restaurant in Lestrygonians (*U* 8.659–60)—a foil for the artist Stephen, the "Toothless Kinch" (*U* 3.496) in *Ulysses*—or as *both*, like the flesh of our "own fathers and grandfathers" spit at us by the cannibal artist (Montaigne 158).

Joyce's Mumbling

It comes as no surprise, then, that Joyce the cannibal was drawn to an art of creative cannibalization as he stylistically fuses language, for example, as I described in my preface, so that his words enact a linguistic assimilation and digestion of their own kind. Such manipulation of words, which matures into parodic-travesty of language itself in the later stages of *Ulysses* and throughout *Finnegans Wake*, results from several interrelated factors in Joyce's intellectual formation that I will trace in the next two chapters: his growing conception of language as an arbitrary axiomatic system—and thus susceptible to manipulation, deformation, and "play"—and his fundamentally alienated relation to the English language, a relation that Stephen Dedalus voices in chapter five of *A Portrait of the Artist as a Young Man*, resulting from his, like Joyce's, heightened linguistic self-awareness as an Irishman deprived of his native language, speaking that of his oppressor: "I cannot speak or write these words without unrest of spirit" (*P* 189). M. M. Bakhtin excellently distinguishes the naïve native-speakers of a language who perceive their "own language [. . .] as the sole and fully adequate tool for realizing the word's direct, objectivized meaning" (61), from those individuals who stand at a remove from the language they speak and have thus developed a heightened linguistic consciousness, perhaps through an alienation from their given language, such as Joyce's from English, perhaps as a consequence of bilinguality or polylinguality, such as Joyce increasingly acquired living in the polyglossic community of Trieste, or perhaps from teaching a language to others, as Joyce did for over a decade as he began his writing career. Joyce's linguistic awareness, developing from these triple sources of detachment from an English language that had been politically imposed upon him—this "language, so familiar and so foreign, will always be for me an acquired speech. I have not made or accepted its words" (*P* 189)—thoroughly positioned Joyce to see the "distance [. . .] between language and reality" that Bakhtin defines as a "linguistic consciousness" which enables "the creating artist [. . .] to look at language from the outside, with another's eyes, from the point of view of a potentially different language and style. It is, after all, precisely in the light of another potential language or style that a given straightforward style is parodied, travestied, ridiculed. The creating consciousness stands, as it were, on the boundary line between languages and styles" (60). Joyce's creating consciousness inhabits precisely this boundary line, and his ambivalent relation to the languages and styles of the Other exemplifies the balance of adaptation and resistance found in the act of cultural transfer. The following chapters will demonstrate Joyce's full internalization of the imperialists' projection of cannibalism upon his kind that, "transaccidentated through the slow fires of" his linguistic "consciousness" (*FW* 186.03–04), emerges in a creative cannibalization of languages, of styles, and ultimately of cultures, a most articulate kind of mumbling (i.e., both "to bite or chew with toothless gums" and "to babble" [*OED*]).

PART I

Cannibalizing Language

2

The Distant Music of the Spheres

Language as Axiomatic System

> Perhaps when a man considers the arts, he may fancy that mankind
> need number only for minor purposes—though the part it plays
> even in them is considerable. But could he see the divine and the
> mortal in the world process—a vision from which he will learn both
> the fear of God and the true nature of number—even so 'tis not any
> man and every man who will recognize the full power number will
> bestow on us if we are conversant with the whole field of it—why,
> for example, all musical effects manifestly depend upon the numera-
> tion of motions and tones—or will take the chief point of all, that
> 'tis the source of all good things, but, as we should be well aware, of
> none of the ill things which may perhaps befall us. No, unregulated,
> disorderly, ungainly, unrhythmical, tuneless movement, and all else
> that partakes of evil, is destitute of all number, and of this a man
> who means to die happy must be convinced.
>
> —Plato, *Epinomis* 977e–978b

Toward the end of his evening at the "Misses Morkan's annual dance" (*D*
175) Gabriel Conroy, standing in the darkness at the foot of a staircase, gazes
upward at "A woman," his wife Gretta, "standing near the top of the first
flight, in the shadow also." Gretta, he quickly realizes, is "listening to something"—something he cannot hear—"Gabriel was surprised at her stillness
and strained his ear to listen also. But he could hear little save the noise of
laughter and dispute on the front steps, a few chords struck on the piano
and a few notes of a man's voice singing" (*D* 209). Gabriel remains standing
"still [. . .], trying to catch the air that the voice was singing and gazing up at
his wife" (*D* 210). Gabriel compensates for his failure "to catch the air" by
weaving in another kind of air a fantasy of his wife and this scene composing
something like a late nineteenth-century genre painting: "If he were a painter
he would paint her in th[is] attitude. [. . .] *Distant Music* he would call the
picture if he were a painter" (*D* 210). More like the literary critic he is than the

aspiring painter he is not, Gabriel attempts to *read* this scene: he sees his wife "as if she were a symbol of something. He ask[s] himself" the quintessential question of literary criticism: "what is a woman standing on the stairs in a shadow, listening to distant music, a symbol of[?]" (*D* 210).

Other critics have followed Gabriel's lead, and there is no shortage of directions we could take for reading this passage in "The Dead": tracing Gabriel's egoistic projection of his own desires upon his wife, or seeing here a foreshadowing of Gretta's unknowable otherness to Gabriel, or connecting Gretta's physical distance from Bartell D'Arcy's rendition of "The Lass of Aughrim" to her temporal distance from Michael Furey's singing of the same song (*D* 218), or perhaps juxtaposing the relation of Gabriel to Gretta here to that of the young boy in "Araby," who gazes similarly upward toward Mangan's sister, from the shadows, earlier in the collection (*D* 30). Rather than pursue any of these leads, however, I would like to take a different direction in looking at this often-discussed moment in *Dubliners* and trace not only the interesting cannibalization of the literary, pictorial, and musical arts working in this intensely visual scene, but also argue that these conjunctions emerge from a mathematical substratum in this story and in Joyce's early aesthetic that he continues to cannibalize for, and interrogate through, *A Portrait of the Artist as a Young Man*, *Ulysses*, and *Finnegans Wake*.

Gabriel, we know, is fond of himself and fond of his coinages, so he resurrects his "distant music" phrase a few minutes after this staircase scene, and four pages later in the story, as he recalls a love letter he had written to Gretta: "Like distant music these words that he had written years before were borne towards him from the past" (*D* 214). However, more than another sign of Gabriel's egoism is involved in Joyce's repetition of the term "distant music" here; words are not just the stuff of a particular kind of musical art: song, vocal music; words themselves *constitute* music for Gabriel, metaphorically perhaps, and for Joyce, both literarily and literally.

I have long wondered, and well before my students ever asked me this, why does anyone read "The Dead"? It is a very peculiar story, an apparently pointless narrative slice of Dublin life until the readers discover its true direction only in the final few pages. What keeps these readers reading? What sustains the readers' involvement in the story while they await its point? My best answer to this question is that Joyce's stylistic virtuosity, his extraordinarily skillful stimulus of visual and auditory responses through language—and one is tempted to add the full range of bodily sensations, comprising tactile, olfactory, and gustatory responses as well—gives "The Dead" a quality of felt life that belies its title and ultimately a living "body" for its readers' consumption. We experience something of Joyce's synesthetic technique in the staircase scene, when he evokes Gabriel's auditory sensation of music faintly heard by rendering this intensely visual moment through words, words that are themselves distantly musical, through onomatopoeias like "noise," through alliterations like "stood still," "singing," "she," "symbol," and "something," and especially through pervasive assonance like "gazing" and "grace," or once more "symbol" and "something" (*D* 209–10). We find even better examples of this synesthetic method which Mary Reynolds, arguing the influence of Dante's similar "linguistic virtuosity" on Sirens, describes as "the close 'fit' of acoustic and semantic properties [. . .] in Joyce's prose" (94), in those wonderful two paragraphs that immediately precede Gabriel's after-dinner speech in "The Dead."

In the first of these paragraphs, Joyce exploits a variety of auditory devices—alliteration, assonance, consonance, onomatopoeia, phonetic intensives ("nudge," "unsettlings," "pushed"), even punctuation ("A pause followed," followed by a *comma*)—to make his visual description *audible* (note my emphases):

> The raisins and almonds and figs and apples and oranges and chocolates and sweets were now passed about the table and Aunt Julia invited all the guests to have either port or sherry. At first Mr Bartell D'Arcy refused to take either but one of his neighbors nudged him and whispered something to him upon which he allowed his glass to be filled. Gradually as the last glasses were being filled the conversation ceased. A pause followed, broken only by the noise of the wine and by unsettlings of chairs. The Misses Morkan, all three, looked down at the tablecloth. Someone coughed once or twice and then a few gentlemen patted the table gently as a signal for silence. The silence came and Gabriel pushed back his chair and stood up. (*D* 201)

One might say that in this marvelous paragraph, bracketed by the parallel sequences in space (the cornucopia of fruits and sweets) and in time (Gabriel's rising), the "noise of the wine" is the least audible sound present, even if the filling of D'Arcy's glass *is* "allowed." Within a "rectangular" block of text, framed like a painting by unbroken parallel "lines"—unpunctuated sequences in space and in time—the reader experiences the distantly musical, auditory dimension of a represented, visual real, "the ineluctable modality of the audible" contained within the "[i]neluctable modality of the visible" (*U* 3.13, 01).

And the next paragraph continues to exploit these same auditory techniques: with the company "<u>patting</u>" their hands "in encouragement," Gabriel leaning "his <u>t</u>en <u>tr</u>em<u>bl</u>ing fingers on the <u>t</u>a<u>bl</u>ecloth," and "<u>s</u>kirts <u>s</u>weeping again<u>s</u>t the <u>d</u>rawing-room <u>d</u>oor" (*D* 202), as Joyce emphasizes the sensory access for character and reader alike to what he calls, in *Finnegans Wake*, the "morphomelosophopancreate[d]" world (*FW* 88.09).

But in what sense can I claim that Joyce's verbal music in "The Dead," his conjunction of the literary, the pictorial, and the musical arts in the narration of such intensely visual scenes as Gretta on the staircase or Gabriel rising to speak, emerges from a mathematical substratum? For an answer to this question we must turn to *A Portrait of the Artist as a Young Man*, where Joyce, no less fond of a coinage than Gabriel, resurrects once again the phrase "distant music."[1] At the beginning of chapter 3, just before the announcement of the religious retreat, Stephen Dedalus sits in his classroom at Belvedere College solving an algebraic equation. As he works his way through his mathematics assignment, expanding and canceling out terms and exponents, or "indices" as exponents were then called, Stephen transforms the solution of a mathematical problem into a vision of an Aubrey Beardsley-esque fin-de-siècle design, accompanied by the silent music of, perhaps, Richard Strauss's *Salome*, and strangely invoking astronomical images:

> The equation of the page of his scribbler began to spread out a widening tail, eyed and starred like a peacock's; and, when the eyes and stars of its indices had been eliminated, began slowly to fold itself together again. The indices appearing and disappearing were eyes opening and closing; the eyes opening and closing were stars being born and being quenched. The vast cycle of starry life bore his weary mind outward to its verge and inward to its centre, a *distant music* accompanying him outward and inward. (*P* 102–03; my emphases)

While the repetition of the key phrase "distant music" ties this passage interestingly to "The Dead," what actually fuses the paragraph's curious concatenation of images together is Joyce's embedded allusion to the classical quadrivium, his union through Stephen of arithmetic (algebra), geometry (design), astronomy (stars), and the curious fourth partner of these three, music. Of course, what both Joyce and the Boethian quadrivium acknowledge is the traditional recognition, as old as the school of Pythagoras, of the intimate welding of music, mathematics, and the heavens.

"[L]egend-veiled Pythagoras" (Kline, *Culture* 40) (b. 569 B.C.), the inventor of the *gnomon* (James 29–30), recognized that both music and nature share a common language: mathematics.[2] The later Pythagorean school expanded this discovery into a cosmology that supported the union of mathematics, music, and astronomy of the medieval quadrivium, and which survived in the idea "that music was the sound of mathematics, no less" (J. Barrow, *Artful* 199), long after the new Copernican cosmology of the Renaissance finally silenced the fabled Pythagorean music of the spheres in the sciences, or "untuned" the sky as John Dryden and John Hollander put it, by the beginning of the nineteenth century.[3] Pythagoras's discovery of the mathematical language of music not only has survived, but still flourishes because we can as readily demonstrate the numerical ratios that account for musical tones on any stringed instrument today, as Pythagoras is reputed to have done on the day of his miraculous discovery of the octave, one morning in the sixth century B.C., after hearing the harmonious sound of hammers ringing on the anvils of his neighborhood blacksmith (Levenson 21–22). (This was the original "harmonious blacksmith," I presume.) More than this, by the early nineteenth century the French mathematician Joseph Fourier could demonstrate through Newtonian physics that "all sounds, vocal and instrumental, simple and complex, are completely describable in mathematical terms" (Kline, *Culture* 287). To my knowledge, however, only Plato, in his *Epinomis*, dared to assert that mathematics is also the language of language, at least until the early twentieth-century surge of interest in logical systems among Russell, Whitehead, and Wittgenstein, and more recently in the linguistic theories of Noam Chomsky.[4] What I want to suggest is that Stephen Dedalus, as well as the early James Joyce, invokes something resembling the Pythagorean astronomical concept of the celestial, unheard, distant music of the spheres as the goal toward which all literature aspires. And if, in Pater's formulation, all art aspires toward the condition of music, the language of these arts is, as it is for music itself, ultimately mathematical.[5]

Or better yet, invoking Plato's *Epinomis*, Joyce might argue that, could they "see the divine and the mortal in the world process," humankind would recognize that "the part [number] plays [. . . in the arts] is considerable" (977e). In other words, Joyce aspires toward the harmonious Pythagorean ideal of oneness, the Monad (James 77), by seeking a union of mathematics—as in the

A Figure wherein may be seen the Composition of the whole frame of the World.

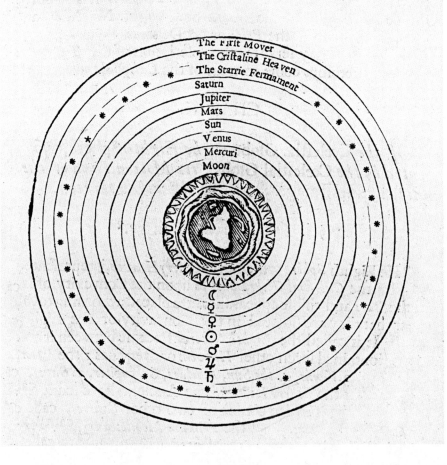

Figure 2.1. The concentric spheres of the Ptolemaic cosmos, from Joseph Moxon's *A Tutor to Astonomy and Geography*, 4th ed. (London: S. Roycroft, 1686), 12. Courtesy of Rare Books and Special Collections, University of South Carolina. Cicero explains the relationship of Pythagoras's octave to Ptolomy's nine spheres in his *Scipio's Dream*, the conclusion of *De republica* (first century A.D.): "a concord of tones separated by unequal but nevertheless carefully proportioned intervals, [is] caused by the rapid motion of the spheres themselves. The high and low tones blended together produce different harmonies. Of course such swift motions could not be accomplished in silence and, as nature requires, the spheres at one extreme produce the low tones and at the other extreme the high tones. Consequently the outermost sphere, the star-bearer, with its swifter motion gives forth a higher-pitched tone, whereas the lunar sphere, the lowest, has the deepest tone. Of course the earth, the ninth and stationary sphere, always clings to the same position in the center of the universe. The other eight spheres, two of which move at the same speed, produce seven tones [that, together with the earth, equal the eight tones of the Pythagorean octave . . .]. The ears of mortals are filled with this sound, but they are unable to hear it. [. . .] the sound coming from the heavenly spheres revolving at very swift speeds is of course so great that human ears cannot catch it; you might as well try to stare directly at the sun, whose rays are much too strong for your eyes" (quoted James 63–64). Rather than counting the earth as one of the spheres, like Cicero, Moxon (1627–91), lexicographer, mathematician, and Royal Hydrographer for Charles II, pictures nine spheres orbiting the earth—as the center of the universe—the first seven associated with the moon and six known planets, the eighth with the starry firmament and crystalline heaven, and the ninth the *primum mobile*, the first mover or the unmoved mover, sometimes associated with God. Other versions, such as Dante's *Paradiso*, placed God outside the spheres, in a region called the Empyrean or Highest Heaven.

quadrivium of arithmetic, geometry, astronomy, and music—with *language*, the trivium of grammar, dialectic, and rhetoric. This oneness derived from seven would be the harmonious union experienced by the guardians and musicians of the spheres, the angels, in the Christian adaptations of "Pythagoras's vision of the musical cosmos" (68) which Jamie James (53–75) traces from the conclusions of Plato's *Republic* ("The Myth of Er") and Cicero's *De republica* ("Scipio's Dream"), through Clement of Alexandria's *Exhortation to the Greeks* and St. Augustine's *De musica*, to Boethius's *De institutione musica* which "remained a standard text for the teaching of music theory at Oxford until 1856" (75).[6] Or as Joyce himself echoes this idea in his precocious undergraduate essay "The Study of Languages": "as mathematics and the Sciences of Numbers partake of the nature of that beauty which is omnipresent, which is expressed, almost noiselessly [as a "distant music"?], in the order and symmetry of Mathematics, as in the charms of literature [. . .] so does Literature in turn share in the neatness and regularity of Mathematics" (26).

This ideal Monad imbedded in Stephen's mathematics class in chapter 3 of *A Portrait* also lurks within Joyce's later description of Stephen's awakening on the morning he composes his villanelle, a waking touched by the distant music of another Gabriel, "Gabriel the seraph":

> Towards dawn he awoke. O what sweet music! [. . .] He lay still, as if his soul lay amid cool waters, conscious of *faint* sweet *music*. [. . .] A spirit filled him, pure as the purest water, sweet as dew, moving as music. But how faintly it was inbreathed, how passionlessly, as if the seraphim themselves were breathing upon him! (*P* 217; my emphases)

Elsewhere I have discussed the quadrivial images drawn from geometry, astronomy, arithmetic, and music that work within this villanelle scene, as geometrical "rays of rhyme" and the image of the "ellipsoidal ball" of the earth inspire the numbers of Stephen's song for his *trivial* language exercise in grammar, dialectic, and rhetoric (*P* 218) (Rice 74–77). Yet this quadrivial imagery represents only part of the story, four-sevenths to be exact, of the harmonious union of the four modes of mathematics and three elements of language within the Monad of the distant music of the spheres, the "faint sweet music" breathed upon Stephen by "the seraphim." Thus the Joyce of *Dubliners* and *A Portrait* creatively cannibalizes both the language of mathematics and the language of literature as equivalent vehicles for encoding, for representing the "visible world," "beauty," "realities." As Stephen claims in *Stephen Hero*, employing the metaphor of bodily incorporation, the artist "alone is capable of absorbing in himself the life that surrounds him and of flinging it abroad again amid *planetary music*" (*SH* 80; my emphases).

We might be tempted, like Madden in *Stephen Hero* (*SH* 81), to regard Stephen's or Joyce's formulation as some sort of woolly mysticism, some vestige of late nineteenth-century romanticism. As Stephen tells Madden, however, "there's nothing mystical" (*SH* 81) in his ideas that the literary work aspires to the "planetary music" of the spheres and that critics, like the astronomers of old, "verify their calculations in accordance with" the "poetic phenomenon [when it] is signalled in the heavens" (*SH* 80). These ideas are inherently classical, located in the unbroken tradition from Pythagoras, through Plato, Boethius, Dante, and the Renaissance *Musici*—Stephen's preferred music, by the way—and well into the eighteenth century, and they correspond directly to Stephen's distinction, moments earlier, between the classical and the romantic tempers. Unlike the "spiritual anarchy" of the romantic or mystic tempers, "The classical temper on the other hand, ever mindful of limitations, chooses rather to bend upon [. . .] present things and so to work upon them and fashion them that the quick intelligence may go beyond them to their meaning which is still unuttered" (*SH* 78). This striving for the unuttered, the unutterable, the ineffable, which of course resides in Stephen's later conception of the epiphany, that moment when the mind apprehends the inarticulable yet "eternal [image] of beauty" (*SH* 213), is the straining to grasp the inaudible distant music of the spheres, or better yet, to attune oneself, one's own "instrument," to this music. Through the limited medium of language—comprising grammar, dialectic, and rhetoric—the artist strives after either or both the structural and verbal *articulation* of "universal beauty," as Stephen says in *A Portrait of the Artist* (*P* 211), spatially or geometrically defining the "esthetic image," temporally or musically apprehending "the rhythm of its structure" (Aquinas's *consonantia*, after Hucbald's tenth-century *The Principles of Harmony*, possesses both musical and intellectual connotations [James 80–81]), to approach the astral union of Thomistic-Platonic-Pythagorean *claritas*: "the supreme quality of beauty being a light from some other world, the idea of which the matter is but the shadow, the reality of which it is but the symbol" (*P* 212–13). And this symbol, this material form given to the idea, may of course equally be an object, a word, a musical note, a number, a geometrical figure, an algebraic equation, or a mathematical *symbol*, any one of which may be a concrete element of the universal of the Monad, a whole always greater than the sum of its parts.

In suggesting that the apprehension of beauty involves not just a straining to grasp the inaudible distant music of the spheres, but also an attempt to attune oneself, one's own "instrument," to this music, I am referring to the Pythagorean trinity of the musical orders, formalized by Boethius as a hierarchy descending from the *musica mundana* (the music of the spheres proper), to the *musica humana* (the similarly inaudible music generated by living organisms), and down to the *musica instrumentalis* (the lowest order, the audible sounds produced by the voice or the musical instrument) (James 74). When the young boy in "Araby" then, in his "confused adoration" of Mangan's sister, claims that his "body was like a harp and her words and gestures were like fingers running upon the wires" (*D* 31), Joyce alludes to the classical concept of the *musica humana*, while his boy seems merely to be voicing a romantic cliché for the sensitive, responsive self. The distinction between Joyce and the boy is the difference between a classically based conception of the vital "relationship between [the self] and the cosmos" (James 182), a harmonic relation inherent in the hierarchical orders of music in the Pythagorean system, and a romantically inspired reduction of the self to the inferior condition of the instrument, a reduction which, with its consequent focus on the impact of nature upon the autonomous individual of bourgeois liberalism, erases the classical emphasis on the integration of the individual into the cosmic harmony.[7] (Compare the integration of the individual within a cosmic order in *Die Zauberflöte* with the triumph of the individual against the constraints of an oppressive, imposed order in *Fidelio*.) The "great emotional outpouring that overwhelmed the expressive arts in the nineteenth century," Jamie James writes, "brought about the virtual exile of the great theme of cosmic harmony" (184); the "focus on the human in the [music of the] Romantic age," evident both in the new "concentration on the performer and composer as personality, and in the scope of the music itself," is consistent with generalized cultural shifts in "scale and emphasis [...] from the cosmic to the human" (192) seen not only in music and literature (compare Pope's universalizing impulse in his "Essay on Man" with Wordsworth's autobiographical account of the "Growth of a Poet's Mind" in his *Prelude*), but in the development of early nineteenth-century science, mathematics, philosophy, and political and economic theories.

When the boy conceives of his body as a harp in "Araby," Joyce, I would argue, both reflects the classical conception of the *musica humana* and treats with irony the romantic reduction of the *musica humana* to the *musica instrumentalis*; this reduction, moreover, involves the characteristically romantic anthropomorphic transformation of a cosmic "reality" in the harmonious Pythagorean system into a metaphor for the self, or simile to be exact, a mere literary "instrument." Joyce is exploiting and scrutinizing the romantic sensibility from the vantage of the classical temper. In effect, Joyce writes *Dubliners*, or at least "Araby," from the vantage of Stephen Dedalus's aesthetic.

Accordingly, in *A Portrait of the Artist as a Young Man* Stephen pursues the harmonious ideal of the Monad "in the real world," one among the many "unsubstantial image[s] which his soul so constantly beheld" (*P* 65); Joyce, however, now simultaneously exploits and distances himself from this obsolete idea of the distant music of the spheres in *A Portrait*, maintaining his often-noted equivocal relationship to both Stephen and Stephen's ideals. The Pythagorean union of language, music, and mathematics, then, fully disintegrates as Joyce moves into *Ulysses* and *Finnegans Wake*. What most interests me in the moves Joyce makes in incorporating the Pythagorean tradition of music into his texts, and particularly in his evolving sense of the relations among language, music, and mathematics, is that rather than reenacting the historical sequence, he simply o'erleaps the cultural transition from classic to romantic, shifting from the classical temper of his early work, to equivocation in *A Portrait*, and then to the modernist, indeed postmodernist, viewpoint embodied most memorably in Leopold Bloom's reflection on music in Sirens:

> Numbers it is. All music when you come to think. Two multiplied by two divided by half is twice one. Vibrations: chords those are. One plus two plus six is seven. Do anything you like with figures juggling. Always find out this equal to that. Symmetry under a cemetery wall. [. . .] Musemathematics. And you think you're listening to the ethereal. But suppose you said it like: Martha, seven times nine minus x is thirtyfive thousand. Fall quite flat. It's on account of the sounds it is. (*U* 11.830–37)

Initially, in this passage, it appears that Bloom merely rehearses the ancient conviction that mathematics is the language of music, but on a closer examination this impression rapidly dissolves, much as it does for Bloom at the end of this paragraph (he ends by refuting his opening premise, asserting that music is not all or only "Numbers"). Likewise, a moment's reflection will tell us that Bloom's calculations are all haywire here: "Two multiplied by two divided by half" is not "twice one," but eight; "One plus two plus six" is not "seven," it's nine. But is Bloom deliberately miscalculating? His errors could very well be intentional, according with the skepticism of his next remarks about mathematics, followed by his similarly skeptical response to the games of language: "Do anything you like with figures juggling. Always find out this equal to that. Symmetry under a cemetery wall." I would argue that Bloom's skeptical awareness of the games played by mathematics, language, and music, despite some incoherence, dimly reflect the turn-of-the-century recognition that all representational systems—mathematical, cosmological, linguistic, and musical—and, by extension, all cultural systems—scientific, religious, political, and economic—are simply "axiomatic" systems, logical and coherent in their own right perhaps, but essentially unrelated, part of no Pythagorean hierarchy, and ultimately distinct from any existential reality they may be supposed to represent.[8] A similar recognition, as I argued in an earlier work, *Joyce, Chaos, and Complexity*, explains why Joyce o'erleapt the cultural transition from classic to romantic in his literary development, as he shifts from the classical temper of his early work to the modernist, indeed postmodernist, viewpoints of *Ulysses* and *Finnegans Wake*.

In the sundering of these systems of representation in *Ulysses*, Joyce sustains his interest in the music of language, in Sirens, for example, but at the expense of some of the referential value of language (a direction *Finnegans Wake* further pursues). And like Bloom, Joyce now seems to discount mathematics, literally dis-*counting* the mathematical language of music within the Pythagorean tradition, to attend to that other language of music: its words, the lyrics of the song, which become a constant source for play or allusion, as in the L-O-S-S acrostic of "Love's Old Sweet Song" in *Ulysses* (e.g., *U* 5.157–60) and the title of *Finnegans Wake*, to cite only two obvious examples.[9] Mathematics now, rather than the language of music or the language of language, becomes for Joyce largely either a resource for metaphor, as in the geometrical patterns of Ithaca and the "Night Lessons" chapter of the *Wake* (II, 2), for example, which establish an alternate language for ciphering and deciphering, or an end in itself in the number, as in his use of numerology, for instance, which intensifies through *Ulysses* and the *Wake*.[10] Mathematics, music, language—and now, increasingly, *languages*—thus become separate but equal axiomatic systems of representation in Joyce's last two books. Once unified by the common language of mathematics, these systems Joyce now reduces to numbers in another sense: they become mere "counters" in the game of representation.

As modernist works, *Ulysses* and *Finnegans Wake* reflect Joyce's recognition that all language systems—including mathematics, music, and language itself—are imperfect human constructions; as postmodernist works, *Ulysses* and *Finnegans Wake* reflect Joyce's realization that all these referential systems are, as human constructions, arbitrary and equivalent. Yet, does not this second recognition return Joyce, in a way, to Pythagoras's position, much as his intensified interest in numerology—an important feature of Pythagorean mysticism (Kline, *Culture* 77–78)—brings him closer to the ancient Greeks? Rather than seeing Joyce's realization that all referential systems are arbitrary and equivalent as a thoroughgoing skepticism, I would argue that Joyce implies the possibility, once again, that these disjecta membra may, at another level, compose a complex harmony, a union yet unheard but sought by the readers of the *Wake*, like the harmony of the legendary "lost *chord*" (*U* 11.407; my emphasis) which, as a word representing both musical and mathematical concepts, implies the very union sought. If so, Joyce finds himself in the company of other twentieth-century artists, like Arnold Schoenberg, Paul Hindemith, and Karlheinz Stockhausen, all of whom sought the ideal of a cosmic harmony, a creative reintegration emerging out of disintegration, a music of the spheres (James 214–30, 238–41).

Rather than a representation of entropic disintegration, *Finnegans Wake* provides a model of the anti-entropic, self-organized complex system that will progressively evolve toward an emergent order through its readership (Rice 112–40). This cosmic harmony may seem far beyond our grasp, yet lest we fall to the skepticism of the heretical schoolboy of chapter 2 in *A Portrait*, let us remember that as much in the Pythagorean tradition as in orthodox Catholicism, our search will be flawed not by the "[im]*possibility*" of our "*ever approaching nearer*" this harmony, but by the "[im]*possibility of ever reaching*" the distant music of the spheres (*P* 79).

The intellectual sophistication of Joyce's conception of language and the august company he keeps in pursuing a creative reintegration out of disintegration—or in more visceral terms, pursuing an art of creative cannibalization—are but half of the story of his evolving understanding of language, contemporaneous with but entirely independent of the ideas of the "founder of modern linguistics" Ferdinand de Saussure, who, through his posthumously published *Course in General Linguistics* (1910), is the acknowledged "forefather" of the disciplines of structuralism and semiology (Macey 342). The other half of the story, traced in the following chapter, finds both Joyce's "alienation from his language"—a detachment that frees him to dismember, digest, and creatively reprocess "the image of language, the image of the direct word" (Bakhtin 63, 59)—as well as his conception of language as an arbitrary axiomatic system, amplified and reinforced by his experiences in the humbler company of his students in the Berlitz schools of Pola and Trieste.

3

"Mr. Berlicche and Mr. Joyce"

Language as Comestible

> by the beerlitz in his mathness
> —*FW* 182.07

From the opening paragraph of "The Sisters," the initial story in his first major work of fiction *Dubliners,* to the last page of *Finnegans Wake,* James Joyce, among many other concerns, trains his readers to converse in a foreign language.[1] Joyce's instructional methodology is intriguing and original for its time. From a very broad overview, we can readily extract the primary features of this method from his work and, with a modest substitution of terms—"instructor" for "author," "students" for "readers"—distill the general principles of the "Joycean Method" for language acquisition into a kind of handbook:

The instructor (a) conducts *all* lessons exclusively in the language that his students have come to him to learn. He accomplishes this (b) by introducing these students to basic vocabulary in the initial lesson, although these words may sound as "strangely in [their] ears" as "the word *gnomon* in the Euclid and the word *simony* in the Catechism" (*D* 9). He encourages the students to repeat aloud and to continue rehearsing these newly acquired words, perhaps modeling for them how they should "Every night" say "softly to [themselves] the word[s]" they have learned (*D* 9). To enhance the students' growing comprehension, the instructor (c) begins by focusing on concrete topics; he reserves more abstract matters for later lessons. He does this by developing sample conversations and narrative situations that, ideally, may be as universal as the experiences of death, friendship, and first love, although the students' initial vocabulary might not be adequate to reach full expression concerning these topics. Gradually and progressively he leads the students through sample experiences they can "relate" to: meeting someone, attempting to purchase some object, planning travel, attending an entertainment, conducting a business transaction, making holiday visits, speaking to public gatherings, and so forth. Further, (d) the instructor demands that the students enter into conversations with him as soon as the first lesson. The best strategies for initiating this dialogue are to put "difficult questions" to the students, "asking [them] what one should do in certain circumstances," or to give them "unfinished sentences" to complete (*D* 13, 11). By the third lesson, even when the instructor is "talking to himself," the students will be able to "interpret these signs" and assign meaning to them (*D* 33). Although the instructor's language has an underlying grammatical and syntactical system, (e) he does *not* attempt to explain such subjects within his lessons. The students gradually come to grasp the structural principles of the language by experiencing them in discourse, rather than by studying them in isolation. The more advanced students will eventually wish to become familiar with these structures. There are abundant guides, handbooks, and schemas for study.

After his students have mastered the initial series of model situations and conversations, the instructor (f) introduces them to a more extended series of experiences featuring, for example, himself as a young man—a central character with whom they might identify. Initially, this narrative only modestly taxes the students' acquired vocabulary; however, as the lessons proceed, their difficulty gradually increases. Thus the instructor acquaints the students with the unique features of the language culture under study: familial relationships, religious customs, social and political conditions, and art and literature. Once the students complete these lessons, the instructor then (g) leads them into the technically more difficult dimensions of the language they are learning: the past perfect tense perhaps ("Happy. Happier then" [*U* 8.170]), the "imprevidibility of the future" imperfect (*U* 17.979–80), and the subtle use of the subjunctive mood for conditional circumstances (though saving the "imperfect subjunctive" for the last lessons of all [*FW* 468.09]), but he continues to illustrate these through a series of narrative situations. The instructor, however, moves on to a new central figure for these narratives. The former character "no longer interest[s]" him or his students "to the same extent" because he "has a shape that can't be changed" (Budgen 107). The instructor effects a transition between the narratives by having the "old" central figure encounter the "new" one. Given the practical concerns of most students who undertake the study of a foreign language, the instructor wisely generates a narrative concerning a businessperson. This strategy also offers wonderful opportunities to introduce a variety of encounters and a multitude of styles for expression. Toward the last stages of this section of the course, the attentive students grasp that the language they are learning is a coherent, axiomatic, but purely *arbitrary* system of signification, and that languages are, per se, equivalent systems, perhaps upon "the inward reflection of there being more languages to start with than [are] absolutely necessary" (*U* 16.351–53). These realizations prepare them for the final stage of their course during which the instructor (h) helps the students understand that learning one foreign language has prepared them to learn many, by particularly emphasizing the *incestuous* familial relationships among various languages in both sound and sense, the preponderance of cognates, and the facility that one might gain, through continued study, in moving among several constantly mutating language systems. Not incidentally, this emphasis by the instructor (i) "insure[s]" that the language-learning center gains a kind of "immortality," keeping its students "busy for three hundred years" and profiting from their tuitions (Ellmann, *James Joyce* 521, 703).[2]

In this opening I have summarized what Lorraine Weir calls "the Joyce system as a pedagogy" (11), to emphasize only half-facetiously what my title may already have given away: this "Joycean method" of language acquisition closely approximates the Berlitz Method of language study. It would seem that James Joyce's admirers have always known that he earned a modest living as a Berlitz instructor in Pola and Trieste, after leaving Ireland permanently in 1904. Alessandro Francini Bruni's 1922 memoir of Joyce, "the first intimate look at the man as well as the first to have received separate publication," chiefly concerns their shared Berlitz experiences (Potts 5), and Richard Ellmann's *James Joyce* devotes several pages to Joyce's on-again off-again negotiations to begin and resume his Berlitz careers. It would also seem that, among Joyce's critics, "Silence with a yawn or two [has] accompanied this thrilling" fact (*U* 16.1664); with the exception of a delightful brief essay by Roy Gottfried and a few suggestions by Hugh Kenner, no one seems to have thought much about the possible significance of Joyce's Berlitz teaching for his art. Similarly, the Berlitz phenomenon, now over 130 years old, has entered into and become such an omnipresence in contemporary consciousness that it has attained precisely the condition of *invisibility* that makes the study of popular culture fascinating.[3] Although there never has been a Berlitz school in every neighborhood, every local bookstore has a generous selection of the modern Berlitz corporation's phrase books, travelers' guides, self-study texts, instructional cassettes, and CD-Roms for language study. It would be only a slight exaggeration to say that the Berlitz Method is something no one talks about because, one way or another, everyone already knows about it. And among Joyce's readers, only Gottfried and Kenner have occasionally caught the echo of his early Berlitz teaching experience in the works, in his cannibalization of the Berlitz *First Book of English* for some details in *Ulysses* (Gottfried, "Berlitz Schools Joyce" 223–38), or for the scrupulously mean style of *Dubliners* (Kenner, *Colder Eye* 188–89) and the model conversations of *Ulysses* (Kenner, *Ulysses* 123–24).

As often the case with mass cultural phenomena—those features of contemporary life that "everyone knows about" but no one seems to comment on—there is very little available information on Berlitz's patented language learning method, on the texts and instructional guides that a turn-of-the-century Berlitz teacher like Joyce used, or on the eponymous Mr. Berlitz himself ("Mr. B" to Francini Bruni ["Joyce" 9]). Yet if Kenner is correct in assuming that Joyce's employment as an English language instructor "forced him to confront anew, idiom by idiom, 'this language, so familiar and so foreign,'" though he offers "no sign that he valued his Berlitz experience at the time" (*Colder Eye* 188), it makes sense to gather whatever historical material we can concerning Mr. Berlitz and his method to assess, as well as we can at this remove, what the impact of Joyce's teaching career on his fiction might have been.[4] I want to argue that Joyce's Berlitz career had at least three significant consequences for his work: (1) prompting his articulation of the pedagogical model for language acquisition within and among his fictions; (2) reinforcing his increasing convictions that language is a "currency" and that his literary works are "commodities" for *consumption* (Osteen, *Economy of* Ulysses 2, 28); and (3) stimulating his ultimate realization that language in itself, as a currency, as a "medium of exchange," has no absolute value (Osteen, *Economy of* Ulysses 17).

Described as a "Pioneer Linguist" who grew up in the Black Forest region of southwestern Germany in his *New York Times* obituary (7 April 1921), Maximilian Delphinus Berlitz seems actually to have been born as David Berlizheimer in Würzburg, on 14 April 1852, as recent genealogical investigations have suggested. The official biographies, however, claim that Berlitz was the son of an artisan, a clockmaker, who in turn "descended from a long line of teachers and mathematicians"; young Maximilian himself followed this line by studying for the profession of language teacher. "He emigrated to the United States in 1872 and arrived prepared to teach Greek, Latin, and six other European languages according to the strict traditionalist grammar-translation approach" (wbc).[5] If his grandson Charles Berlitz is to be believed, M. D. Berlitz continued this preparation and eventually "spoke fifty-eight languages" (ix). After a few years of private tutoring and part-time clock repair, and a one-year stint as a public high school teacher in Westerly, Rhode Island, Berlitz joined the faculty of Warner Polytechnic College in Providence, in 1877. Soon finding himself "at once owner, dean, principal, and only faculty member" of this institution, he fell ill from overwork. In desperate need of assistance, according to the Berlitz corporation's official version, Berlitz hired a Frenchman, Nicholas Joly, only to discover on his arrival that Joly "spoke no English": "Casting about desperately for a way of using Joly, Berlitz told him to try pointing at objects and naming them and to act out verbs as best he could" (wbc). After a six-week convalescence, Berlitz returned to work expecting "to face the wrath of his neglected students. Instead, Berlitz found the students engaging in lively question-and-answer exchanges with their teacher, in elegantly accented French. The characteristic solemnity of the formal classroom had vanished. More important, the students had progressed further than any ever had under six weeks of his own tutelage" (wbc). Out of this episode, Berlitz formulated his "innovative teaching technique"—which, had he not "a boundless entrepreneurial spirit" (*Berlitz* 4), he might have called the "Joly" Method—that would keep students "active and interested" by "replacing rote learning with a discovery process" (wbc).[6]

In the following year, 1878, M. D. Berlitz opened his first language school in Providence, "catering to the well-to-do, who could afford the luxury of foreign travel, as well as to those whose interests were purely intellectual" (wbc). The Newport crowd presumably provided Berlitz a steady clientele, and he soon realized that he had discovered a hot commercial opportunity. He opened a Boston location in 1881 and, in the next few years, founded language centers in Washington, D.C., and New York, where he moved himself with his headquarters in 1886. Berlitz quickly realized that his "product"—language acquisition for an increasingly general public—was "new, and a new business structure was needed to deliver it" (*Berlitz* 1). This innovative structure was the franchise. Berlitz thus continued to expand by licensing his language-school model and instructional method to other entrepreneurs, so there were more than 100 Berlitz schools in the United States and Europe by 1900, making the Berlitz corporation "one of the first multinational companies and one of the world's first franchise-type organizations" (wbc).

Always a shrewd businessman and a genius at self-promotion, he especially capitalized on self-advertising and publicity. Berlitz, who was evidently a superb language teacher with "a great flare [sic] for showmanship" (*Berlitz* 16), took various model classes and learning demonstrations on the road. By the turn of the century, he and his "Method" began to receive world recognition, winning two gold medals for "his innovative approach to language learning" at the Paris Exposition in 1900, special prizes at the Lille and Zurich Expositions (both 1902), the "'Grand Prize' for excellence in language teaching" at the 1904 St. Louis World's Fair, and numerous other exposition awards and medals (London [1908], Brussels [1910], Turin [1911], Gand [1913], Beirut [1921], Marseilles [1922], and Philadelphia [1926]) (wbc).

M. D. Berlitz garnered additional distinctions, and his corporation continued to expand through his later career. At the time of his death in 1921, he was an "officer of the Legion of Honor of France and a Commendator of the Civil Order of Alfonso XII of Spain," and the *New York Times* calculated the number of Berlitz schools, worldwide, at 300 (7 April 1921). (The *Times* fails to mention that Berlitz taught English to Kaiser Wilhelm II or that, in gratitude for his services, the "Sultan of Morocco granted him a tribal emirate" [*Berlitz* 16–17].) Despite retrenchment and near collapse during the Depression years, the Berlitz company held on and, by the 1940s, fully recovered and began diversifying, publishing their first "self-teacher" guides.[7] The decades from the 1960s to the present have seen the Berlitz corporation continue to expand and diversify. In 1966–67 Berlitz became a subsidiary of Macmillan, Inc., which in turn was taken over by the Maxwell Group in 1988. Berlitz went public on the New York Stock Exchange in 1989 ("BTZ"), and has been owned since 2001 by the Benesse Corporation. As of early 2007, the Berlitz Web site claims there are now "more than 450" language centers "in over 60 countries" (wbc).

M. D. Berlitz's story of successful entrepreneurship is one of many in late nineteenth-century American culture. He seems to have recognized early the possibilities of transforming language itself into a commodity to package and deliver to the buying public, of developing an effective corporate structure to distribute this "product," and of realizing the commercial opportunity for tie-in sales of instructional materials. (From 1889, when M. D. Berlitz began publishing the "'Berlitz Method' series" of print instructional materials, until the 1930s, the company "relied on book sales as its principal source of revenue" [*Berlitz* 22, 35].) First in Providence and, shortly after, in most major east coast cities in the United States, Berlitz was uniquely positioned to recognize a market for efficient language acquisition among a newly prosperous clientele that was, in turn, able to take advantage of increasingly safe and affordable transatlantic transport for world travel. Perhaps because of his own European origins, he was also prescient enough to capitalize on the increasing desire for language training abroad, and for English in particular, among the military, businesspeople, and a middle class that, as students in the "University of life" like Leopold Bloom (*U* 15.840), valued self-improvement.[8] To expand throughout Europe, what he needed was qualified teachers, especially for the English language. As Joyce observed to his brother Stanislaus, whom he encouraged to apply for a European assignment in 1904, the "Berlitz school[s . . .] cannot get English teachers to come abroad" (*Letters*, II 69). Somewhat earlier in Paris, in December 1902, James Joyce had himself applied for and was offered a position as a language instructor at the École Berlitz; and although Joyce decided against taking this job, he was to apply again, first in Zurich, then in Trieste, and finally in Pola where he joined the staff of a new school that opened in the fall of 1904. In March 1905 he transferred to the school in Trieste, where he remained on the faculty until his departure for Rome in July 1906. He briefly resumed teaching at the Trieste school after his return from Rome in March 1907, then established himself as an independent teacher (Ellmann, *James Joyce* 113–14, 176, 184–85, 194, 254–55, 262–63).[9]

M. D. Berlitz was also a characteristic fin-de-siècle American entrepreneur in his recognition that with language learning, as with other "industrial" processes, time was money. To Berlitz, language was a commodity either to be accumulated as capital ("fifty-eight languages"), or to be packaged for distribution, sale, and consumption. What he patented, however, was not the commodity itself—an impossibility—but the process for its timely acquisition. His Method was a kind of linguistic "Taylorism," a means of learning that maximizes the efficiency of distribution by ignoring the technicalities of grammar and the rules of syntax, abandoning the drudgery of translations, and thus making readily available a commercially desirable product: competence in a foreign language. Individuals would be capable of carrying on basic conversations in everyday situations in the shortest possible time.[10] His theory, in a nutshell, was that "the best way to learn a foreign language is by listening and repeating just as a baby learns its mother tongue":

The principles he laid down were deceptively simple. Only the target language would be spoken in class, starting with the first greeting by the teacher. Emphasis would be on the spoken word, with students learning to read and write only what they had already learned to say and understand. There would be no formal grammar instruction; instead, students would absorb a grammatical system naturally, by using it. Above all, to develop fluency, students would have to learn to think in the new language, not translate—to associate new words with objects and ideas, rather than with the distractingly familiar words of their mother tongue. Teachers would have to constantly encourage students to speak the language being taught, employing a barrage of questions to be answered and a quickly expanding vocabulary. And, most importantly, each Berlitz teacher would have to have a native command of the language being taught. While the unique system of instruction developed by Berlitz has been refined, enriched, and modernized throughout the years, these elements remain at the heart of all Berlitz language instruction. (wbc)

Alessandro Francini Bruni, the director of the Pola school in 1904 and later Joyce's colleague in Trieste, offers a less sanguine, contemporary European view of M. D. Berlitz's entrepreneurial genius: "Was Berlicche crazy or had we been tricked? We had been tricked. No crazy person had ever been cleverer—he had found the magic key for making a successful enterprise out of nothing" ("Joyce" 9). Sounding very like the Reverend Alexander Dowie, as parodied at the conclusion of Oxen of the Sun (*U* 14.1580–91), Francini Bruni expresses an extravagant contempt for Berlitz's "American" brand of linguistic Taylorism, dubious recruitment of "professors," and corporate evangelism:

He [Berlitz] had managed to patent an American-style gimmick for filling skulls with modern languages and then making these languages come out through the mouth sounding like a big belch. Then using American high pressure, he gathered an army of stray dogs from every place imaginable and unleashed them on the surface of the globe, saying to them "*Ite in civitates*"—run around, break your neck, bruise your feet, your ankles, your shins, and your ass; go wherever you want, but ballyhoo my business like the devil. Tell all the baboons in Europe that my remedy is better than all those sticking plasters that have ruined their corns and their souls, that my method is the real panacea for ignorance. Nothing to those who do not pay, understand! ("Joyce" 9)

"Just you try it on" indeed (*U* 14.1591). It seems that Joyce shared Francini Bruni's skepticism about Berlitz's "American-style gimmick" to maximize the efficiency of language instruction, although he expresses himself more moderately in describing his work to Grant Richards: "I am employed to teach young men of this city the English language as quickly as possible with no delays for elegance" (*Letters*, II 131).

Joyce's few comments on his Berlitz career mix dislike for the language school atmosphere ("Honestly it is awful" [*Letters*, II 87]), contempt for some of his colleagues (*Letters*, II 93), and pride in the "praise" of his "genteel pupils" (*Letters*, II 94). Evidently, his "teaching was arduous and long" (Ellmann, in *Letters*, II 63), yet Joyce clearly found satisfaction in drawing several genuinely distinguished students: "noblemen and signori and editors and rich people" (*Letters*, II 94). In the 28 February 1906 letter to Grant Richards cited above, he drops the fact that one of his pupils is a baroness (Baroness Ralli) (*Letters*, II 131), and, as Richard Ellmann notes, it was the quality of his students and their approval of his teaching that persuaded the resistant director of the Trieste school, Almidano Artifoni, to rehire Joyce on his return from Rome in the spring of 1907: "he was particularly reluctant to lose such prominent pupils as Count Sordina, Baron Ralli, and Roberto Prezioso [editor of *Il Piccolo della Sera*], who were devoted to Joyce" (*James Joyce* 255). Silvio Benco, one of Joyce's contemporary acquaintances, recounts the general opinion in Trieste that this Irishman "was a marvel at teaching English" (50). Francini Bruni, however, who worked with him and who probably imports his own disdain for Berlitz, portrays him as an aloof, arrogant, and unhappy teacher in his two memoirs of Joyce. "We [. . .] had exceptional students," and the faculty "were all moderately friendly with each other" ("Recollections" 39), Francini Bruni recalls, yet to Joyce the school was "a dark depressing cloud [. . .] to freedom" ("Joyce" 30). Obviously, not every pupil was distinguished: "The students [were] vain and dull apes of every imaginable kind: coquettish women, cashiers about to abscond, single girls with no hope of ever being otherwise, officers as ignorant as donkeys, jobless waiters, ship's officers ready to embark, and more. [. . .] They competed in murdering the language" ("Joyce" 8).[11] Francini Bruni describes Joyce's "cool

and collected" contempt of the school administration—"He had the noncha-
lance of a bored dandy" ("Joyce" 11–12)—as well as his irreverent adaptation
of the Berlitz method, quoting several typical examples of Joyce's classroom
practice of using "instructive examples drawn from everyday life" to generate
English conversation, such as "'Mr B. is an insatiable sponge. His teachers
have had their brains soaked up. And their flesh? These crucified ones are
hung on the pole, reduced to skin and bones. I offer myself to my students as
an example of the giraffe species, thus teaching zoology objectively, according to the methods of my boss'" ("Joyce" 26–27). Perhaps Joyce, as Francini
Bruni says, "in no time shook the dust of the [Berlitz school] from his heels"
("Joyce" 30), yet this dust, like so much else in Joyce's formative experiences,
clung to him. Joyce creatively cannibalized his teaching experience and "the
methods of [his] boss" for his fiction, not only to refine his prose style and
dialogue, as Hugh Kenner maintains, but also to convert Berlitz's model for
instruction into his own original method for training his readers.

One of the most commonplace observations among his critics is that Joyce
teaches his readers how to read his works.[12] In *Dubliners,* for example, he fo-
cuses his first three stories on a young boy who gradually comes to understand
his world, as the readers do, in terms of the vocabulary—paralysis, gnomon,
and simony—introduced on the first page (in a paragraph Joyce added to
"The Sisters" only in the Berlitz year 1905). Each story culminates in a conversation exercise of sorts, as the young boy and readers puzzle themselves to
discern, with increasing acuity, the meanings of the words spoken by Eliza in
"The Sisters," the old josser in "An Encounter," and the shopgirl in "Araby."
In the balance of the story collection, Joyce continues to elaborate upon his
basic vocabulary and emphasizes throughout the often tortuous problems
of communication, from Eveline's muteness to Gabriel's disastrous conversations with women. *A Portrait of the Artist as a Young Man,* which Joyce
began as he ended his Berlitz career in the late summer of 1907 and largely
completed, while still teaching English in Trieste, by 1911, similarly opens by
introducing a vocabulary in its first one-and-a-half pages that will provide
an interpretive basis for the rest of the book.[13] (Stephen Dedalus, like the
boy in "The Sisters," also worries over the meanings of words throughout
the novel.) As many readers have recognized, moreover, Stephen's *conversation* with Lynch in chapter 5, provides a "grammar" of sorts for grasping the
"language" of Joyce's novel, much as his discussion of Shakespeare in *Ulysses*
clarifies the author's own relationship to his art. True, Joyce was further re-

moved from teaching, and Trieste, by the time he completed *Ulysses,* yet the Berlitz "discovery process" paradigm remains subtly and pervasively present in the text (wbc). According to the Berlitz method, the pupils will learn a language by speaking, by emulating a native-speaker; in *Ulysses,* the readers will learn how to read the novel in the act of reading, by emulating a text that recurrently reads itself: "Who ever anywhere will read these written words? Signs on a white field" (*U* 3.414–15).

The opening three chapters of *Ulysses* miniaturize the novel's overall movement from accessibility to complexity and provide a heuristic roughly comparable to the opening triad of *Dubliners,* while the next three episodes reinforce this heuristic through repetitions that both parallel this opening and establish the book's and its readers' strategic juxtapositions of its convergent central characters. Characters in a work of fiction and writers as well—Bloom actually does more writing on this day than Stephen and, as Fritz Senn has observed, is equally concerned with "righting" his world ("Righting *Ulysses*" 6)—Stephen and Bloom also perform the roles of readers in the book, in effect actively modeling reading for their readers in these opening episodes. In Nestor, for example, the readers observe Stephen give his pupils an indecipherable riddle and then proceed to assist Sargent with his ciphering: "Across the page the symbols moved in grave morrice, in the mummery of their letters" (*U* 2.155–56). In the next episode, Proteus, Stephen ciphers and attempts to read the riddle of himself. (As Mallarmé has said of Hamlet, quoted later, we can say that Stephen "*se promène, lisant au livre de lui même* [. . .] *reading the book of himself*" [*U* 9.114–15].) Bloom, in his perusal of Milly's letter in Calypso, models the slow, careful, and close reading and rereading, attentive to both what is stated and what is implied, that the book that contains him demands. Altogether, he reads this letter four times (*U* 4.280–82, 394–415, 427), and Milly's letter is neither the first nor certainly the last text that Bloom reads critically, or "gravely" (*U* 4.191), within the text that contains him. Hugh Kenner contends that these early episodes, very like the introductory lessons "in the kind of course Joyce gave for years at the Trieste Berlitz," generate "a sort of collective vocabulary out of which, it seems, anything at all can [. . .] be composed" by the time he reaches the fifteenth chapter, Circe (*Ulysses* 123). I agree, but I would add that we see an even greater influence of Joyce's exposure to the Berlitz method in his "total immersion" of the readers—without grammar or guide, transition or translation—into the alien language of his text (wbc). The readers' experience of *Ulysses,* then, is remarkably similar to that of the Berlitz students who learn a foreign language *as a text* that "repeatedly defines itself, instructs us in its semiotic operations, specifies its genre, provides models of the relationship between its micro- and macro-structures, gives us practice lessons in decoding" (L. Weir 39).

To this point I have used this term "language" figuratively to signify Joyce's ordering of his fictional worlds according to rules as a "grammar," and his use of thematic/symbolic patterns as a "vocabulary" that his readers only acquire through a Berlitz discovery process in the act of reading. But Berlitz's innovations, recall, were twofold: both patenting a process for language acquisition and, correlatively, transforming language itself into a commodity for distribution and acquisition. Correspondingly, with *Finnegans Wake* we can drop these quotation marks because, in this work, Joyce is immediately concerned with language per se, with language as commodity, with the "reduction of various expressive media to their primitive economic directness." In the *Wake*, as Samuel Beckett further observes, Joyce's "writing is not *about* something; *it is that something itself*" (16, 14). And although most distant in time from his Berlitz career, *Finnegans Wake* is also the clearest illustration of the "Joycean Method" of language acquisition. The readers must approach the *Wake* much as the beginning Berlitz students enter the foreign language classroom, sans dictionary, sans interpreter, sans everything. Better yet, we might describe the readers' plight as that of students who enter a kind of Berlitz school-without-walls, a "Tower of Balbus" (*FW* 467.16) where "the air [is] filled with the languages of Babel" (Francini Bruni, "Recollections" 39). One and many voices are speaking and even, in the first lesson, pointing at objects: "This the way to the museyroom. [. . .] This is a Prooshious gunn. This is a ffrinch. Tip. This is the flag of the Prooshious, the Cap and Soracer. This is the bullet that byng the flag of the Prooshious. [. . .]" (*FW* 8.09–13). Cognates help make some of this language comprehensible, illustrating the Berlitz principle that "a person who speaks English," for example, "already has a knowledge, though he may not realize it, of thousands of foreign words" (Berlitz x). Yet the readers, like the Berlitz students, can only learn this language from within, for if one of the longest-standing convictions about *Finnegans Wake* is that it "is about *Finnegans Wake*" (Tindall, *A Reader's Guide to James Joyce* 237), we can equally say that much of the language of the *Wake* is about its language: "*Finnegans Wake* is a text preoccupied with its own condition of being, its own textuality and performance system" (L. Weir 13). It only seems appropriate that many readers of *Finnegans Wake* have independently arrived at what the Berlitz schools suggest as one of the best ways to learn a foreign language: "to pair off with someone else, or to organize a small group" (Strumpen-Darrie and Berlitz v–vi).

But the greatest impact of Joyce's experience as a Berlitz teacher on this, his culminating work of fiction, was his early realization "of the arbitrary nature of the linguistic sign" (Norris, *Decentered Universe* 3). As an Irishman "doomed to express [himself] in a language that is not [his] own" (Francini Bruni, "Joyce" 28), Joyce discovered himself in Trieste, a strikingly multilingual environment, in the peculiar situation of having *no native language*. Like Stephen in *A Portrait*, Joyce had been alienated from the English language of the colonial occupiers of Ireland: "His language, so familiar and so foreign, will always be for me an acquired speech. I have not made or accepted its words" (*P* 189). He had to be alive to the irony of his personal circumstances that forced him doubly into the role of poseur: first, he had *not* "Graduated with highest honors from Cambridge University" as advertised by the Berlitz school ("Joyce" 10), and second, and most important, technically he was *not* the "native" speaker that the Berlitz rules stipulated. Joyce's deracinated relationship to the English language, exacerbated by his rootless existence as an Irishman in Trieste, surely intensified his recognition of what might only dawn slowly upon the native speaker who stands in an unmediated relationship to his own language: that this language is a logical and coherent, yet arbitrary network of signifiers, simply a medium of exchange or a "currency" with no absolute value in itself, which merely spans the "incertitude of the void," rather than resting upon any ground of originary signifieds (*U* 17.1015). (Already in *A Portrait*, Stephen likens language both to a "net" and to a currency to be "forge[d]" [*P* 203, 253].) In Bakhtin's terms, Joyce's Berlitz experience refined his "Linguistic consciousness" to the point that he was free to cannibalize the words of the language from which he had become progressively "alienated" (60, 63). The Berlitz proscription on translation, moreover, simply reinforced Joyce's recognition that no language is ultimately translatable into some *ur*-language that is somehow absolute or true. In this light, Derek Attridge notes how Joyce's linguistic experimentation in the *Wake* exposes "thoroughly the myths of a monosemous language and a preexisting structure of meaning [. . . .] There is no escape from its insistence that meaning is an *effect* of language, not a presence within or behind it, and that the effect is unstable and uncontrollable" (194, 197). And if, as Margot Norris contends, *Finnegans Wake* reflects "that intellectual shift which locates meaning in relationships and structure rather than in content"—that language is a medium of exchange lacking absolute value in itself—a shift generated by the publication of Ferdinand de Saussure's *Course in General Linguistics* "in Paris in 1910," which nonetheless "appears to have gone unnoticed by contemporary writers" (*Decentered Universe* 3), I would argue that "Mr. Jinglejoys'" experience teaching *beurla* (English) at the "beurlads scoel" allowed him to achieve and sustain this same intellectual shift through independent means (*FW* 466.18, 467.25).

While Joyce's understanding of language as an arbitrary axiomatic system liberates him to cannibalize words, initially and modestly fusing the words of English and subsequently moving toward the revolutionary cannibalization and massive cultural transfer of multiple languages within the portmanteau vocabulary of *Finnegans Wake*, his fictions illustrate a similar transfer, incorporation, and fusion of the alien bodies of "high" and popular literary cultures, as we will see in the next two chapters. As he has arrived at his conception of language equally from his intellectual training and his practical experience as a teacher, so also does Joyce incorporate both the "high" culture of world literary tradition—invoking, for example, the epic journey of Odysseus for the title of one book—and the world of mass culture—invoking, for example, a popular music hall song for the title of another book—to create fictions that cannibalize worlds as well as words.

PART II

Cannibalizing Literature

4

Consuming High Culture

Allusion and Structure in "The Dead"

> May I trespass on your valuable space. That doctrine of *laissez faire* which so often in our history. Our cattle trade. The way of all our industries. Liverpool ring which jockeyed the Galway harbour scheme. European conflagration. Grain supplies through the narrow waters of the channel. The pluterperfect imperturbability of the department of agriculture. Pardoned a classical allusion. Cassandra. By a woman who was no better than she should be. To come to the point at issue.
> —*U* 2.324–30

Readers familiar with *Ulysses* will instantly recognize this paragraph from the Nestor episode as the text of the first half of Mr. Garrett Deasy's letter on the foot-and-mouth disease, although it is quite clearly *not* the text *as written* by Deasy. Deasy assures Stephen Dedalus "I don't mince words, do I?" (*U* 2.331), immediately following this very "minced" version of his letter's opening. I will return to this passage and consider the implications of Joyce's mincing of text in my final chapter. For the present, however, let us consider the readers' likely response to the assortment of sentence fragments, undeveloped allusion, and, for most readers, unfamiliar references to mid-nineteenth-century Irish politics and economics in Deasy's letter. The first-time reader of *Ulysses* could be pardoned a "classical" confusion at this early point in the novel. What has happened to Deasy's letter is that it has filtered rapidly through the reading mind of Stephen, a reader much better placed than the reader of *Ulysses* to anticipate and absorb what Deasy has to say; Stephen's attention is only momentarily arrested by the substantives and the stylistic quirks (clichés, circumlocutions) of the letter—and these are all that remain in *Ulysses*'s text. The reader is challenged to fill the gaps, to complete the sentences, perhaps to research the references, to note the "classical allusion," and thus to digest and create a plausibly coherent narrative out of this minced text. In effect, this is what the reader has to do throughout *Ulysses*; so, reading Mr. Deasy's letter becomes an exercise in the necessary strategies for reading the novel that contains it, much as the famous letter becomes a model of the text within the text of *Finnegans Wake*.

To borrow Brook Thomas's term, the reader of *Ulysses* is compelled to make the "ghosts" of the book materialize, filling its *Leerstellen*, those inevitable gaps that exist in a text. In *James Joyce's* Ulysses: *A Book of Many Happy Returns*, Thomas describes how such absences become a form of "presence" in Joyce's novel. Through a Brunonian reconciliation of opposites, Thomas argues that Joyce's "art of writing [. . .] seems to have the power to turn absence into presence, sundering into reconciliation, escape into return" (97), and proceeds to show how Stephen, Joyce, and the readers are mutually engaged in this process, turning and returning to the text, fashioning meaning by filling the gaps in texts. *Leerstellen* such as when exactly did Molly say "at Four"? what happened at the Westland Row station? and who moved the furniture in Bloom's parlor? have provoked more than one analysis of *Ulysses*. But it is also clear that this process of identifying and materializing the ghosts of a text applies to Joyce's earlier fiction as well, and, as Wolfgang Iser has argued, to the reading of all texts. Conspicuous absences abound in *Dubliners*, for example, absences that constitute a kind of presence. The readers are irresistibly drawn to these gaps, challenged to fill them, to make an absence a presence, and thus to complete the exasperatingly unfinished sentences of the stories. Interpretations of *Dubliners* routinely do this: completing Old Cotter's sentences one way or another in "The Sisters," speculating about what the "old josser" (*D* 26) actually does in "An Encounter," paraphrasing the subtext of the boy's apparently inconsequential conversation with the shopgirl in "Araby," examining Frank's possible motives in "Eveline," explaining what Corley and the slavey have been up to in "Two Gallants," describing Farrington's abject apology to Mr. Alleyne, or identifying the "soft wet substance" (*D* 105) touched by Maria in "Clay." For the most part, the readers complete the "parallelogram" of these "gnomonic" texts with ease (see D. Weir 343–60); however, with the growth of Joyce's artistry in "The Dead" there comes a multiplication of the gaps in the text and an increase in their complexity and suggestiveness: what has occasioned Lily's bitterness? why does Miss Ivors leave the party? what happens during the intervals between the story's three parts? what was the real nature of Michael Furey's relationship with Gretta? on what day or date does the Morkan party take place? and so on. Of course, a major ghost in the story, Michael Furey himself, is made a presence in the final pages of "The Dead"; at least two other ghosts in the conclusion that have materialized in Joyce criticism are the Ibsen of *A Doll's House*, or *When We Dead Awaken*, and the Dante of the *Inferno*.[1] Yet one remaining ghost among the many that haunt "The Dead" is Robert Browning, and one remaining gap in the story is the quotation from Browning's poetry that Gabriel Conroy promises us, but never provides. Browning too hovers as an absent presence in the conclusion of "The Dead" and, more important, the identification of Gabriel's unused Browning quote fills one very basic gap in the story: connecting the ostensible climax of Gabriel's evening, his after-dinner speech, with the actual climax of the tale, Gabriel's concluding vision of "the region where dwell the vast hosts of the dead" (*D* 223).

A simple and fairly satisfactory way of explaining Browning's ghostly presence in "The Dead," at least by name, *is* his name. Together with Mr. Browne and the brown goose of the dinner table, Browning's name contributes to the murky atmosphere of "brown imperturbable faces" (*D* 29) that Joyce associated with Dublin and the Dubliners. Yet I am convinced that there is a more significant absence here, in this case the missing quote from Browning's poetry rather than the man himself, constituting a kind of presence for Joyce (or one is tempted to say a "substantial absence"). This absence is doubly emphasized by Gabriel's two references to his unused quotation (*D* 179, 192). Applying the reading strategies of *Ulysses* to *Dubliners* is always a hazardous business, though Joyce's critics have long done so; but I suggest that applying the strategies of *Ulysses* criticism to the exploration of what Joyce might have intended with Gabriel's Browning quote leads us into a plausible network of associations that not only clarify what Joyce and Gabriel had in mind, but also provide an intriguing justification for the ghostly presences of both Browning and Dante in the concluding paragraphs of "The Dead." Moreover, this constellation of associations among Gabriel, Browning, and Dante shows that Joyce has advanced appreciably toward the sophisticated, structural use of allusion that we find in *Ulysses*.[2]

John Feeley, in a 1982 issue of the *James Joyce Quarterly*, has already made one attempt to fill the gap of Gabriel's Browning quote, plausibly identifying some appropriate verses he might have chosen from Browning's last volume of poetry, *Asolando* (1889), and noting a variety of thematic relationships between this book of poems and Joyce's story (87–96).[3] Although *Asolando* has one major advantage as a nominee, namely that it was published on the day of Browning's death, 12 December 1889, and would thus contribute to the funereal symbolism of "The Dead," there are several problems with Feeley's argument that weaken his point: he sees Gabriel paraphrasing *Asolando* during his speech, rather than directly quoting the poetry; moreover, these paraphrases do not jibe with Gabriel's proposed placement of the quote in conjunction with the judgment of Paris, as indicated by his list of his speech's headings on page 192. Also, Feeley speculates that Gabriel has probably reviewed *Asolando*, in the *Daily Express*, for what turns out to have been the *American* publication of Browning's *Poetical Works* (1894–1903), a reissue of the 1888–89 British edition (95 n 1). Basic to Feeley's argument is his assumption that the action of "The Dead" takes place in January 1904. While internal evidence would support the 1904 date for the story, several other details in "The Dead" suggest a second time setting for its action.[4] As Richard Ellmann notes in his biography of Joyce, the character of Gabriel Conroy is a composite of three figures, Joyce himself in his egoism, Constantine Curran in his insecurity, and John Joyce in his role in the Morkan family (*James Joyce* 246–47). Indeed, the basic situation of "The Dead," with Gabriel presiding at table and presenting his after-dinner speech, as Joyce's father did annually for his aunts and cousin at their house at 15 Usher's Island, and staying with his wife at the Gresham Hotel while the young children remained at Bray, as Joyce's parents did, and giving his speech, as Stanislaus has noted, in "good imitation of his father's oratorical style," all confirm that an earlier time-setting, the late 1880s, coexists with the 1904 setting in the story (*James Joyce* 245). If this is so, Gabriel's purported review of Browning's poetry would probably have been an essay on a recently published late volume, a far more plausible occasion for a review than the American reissue of a British collected edition. One likely candidate for Gabriel's review, which is appropriate to "The Dead" in several ways, is Browning's penultimate volume of poems: *Parleyings with Certain People of Importance in Their Day*, published in 1887.

Browning's *Parleyings* consists of a prologue, an epilogue, and seven dialogues with the dead, conversations with those who, while long departed, have exerted a continuing influence on the thought of Robert Browning (such as the poet Christopher Smart, the artist Francis Furni, the philosopher Bernard de Mandeville, or the musician Charles Avison). Browning's *donnée*, the livingness of the dead, would have certainly appealed to Joyce, who was intrigued by the tendency of the dead to rise again: "That the dead do not stay buried" not only in "The Dead," is, in Ellmann's words, "a theme of Joyce from the beginning to the end of his work" (*James Joyce* 244). That Browning is covertly present and uncharacteristically autobiographical in *Parleyings*, facts that his first reviewers missed altogether, also might have appealed to Joyce, since he maintains a similarly ghostly presence in his supposedly objective fiction.[5] Though it might be presumptuous to suggest this, it is also possible that Joyce was drawn to *Parleyings* by its notorious obscurity; one of its first reviewers, describing his exasperation with the volume, sounds remarkably like the initial reviewers of *Ulysses* and *Finnegans Wake*: "Mr. Browning, who often amuses himself by writing in a cipher to which he alone has the key, has seldom propounded to his disciples a more hopeless puzzle."[6] Gabriel, if he has in fact reviewed *Parleyings*, is a more tolerant, though not necessarily more enlightened reader. Confusion becomes a ground for approbation: "*One feels that one is listening to a thought-tormented music*" (D 192).

Yet the most compelling reasons for suggesting that Gabriel's Browning quote could have come from *Parleyings* are the thematic affinities between Browning's prologue to his volume, titled "Apollo and the Fates," and Joyce's "The Dead." In his prologue Browning establishes a metaphor for the structure of *Parleyings*, much as he does with his ring-metaphor in the opening and closing books of *The Ring and the Book*, by recounting the story of how Apollo tricked the three malign sisters, the Fates, into granting a new lease on life to his favorite, Admetus. Essentially, this prologue prepares the reader for Browning's resurrection of long-dead figures, as he confers a poetic life-in-death on the subjects with whom he parleys in the volume. In Browning's prologue the Fates impose one condition upon Apollo before they will grant his wish and stay the shears of the third sister, Atropos, to extend the life of Admetus: Admetus must find an inhabitant of Thessaly, his kingdom, who will sacrifice his or her life in his stead, one who will "die for [his] sake" (D 222), as Michael Furey has died for Gretta. However, the parallels among *Parleyings*, "Apollo and the Fates," and "The Dead" go beyond the similar notions of life-in-death and self-sacrifice. Like Gabriel, Admetus of the Apollo legend is a sublime egoist, confident that all of his subjects would sacrifice their lives for the sake of their king.[7] But neither parent, nor friend, nor citizen proves willing to die for his sake. Ultimately, Admetus must sacrifice his wife, Alcestis, in order to live. While this hardly seems generous of him, Admetus does have his good side too. He is remarkably dedicated to the ancient law of hospitality (his unquestioning acceptance of the disguised Apollo into his household is what won him the favor of this god). Moreover, on the day of

Alcestis's funeral, he graciously receives Hercules as a guest, disguising his grief; in return for his hospitality, Hercules, when he learns the truth of the situation, combats Death on Admetus's behalf and returns a living Alcestis to him. Thus, the legend of Admetus, Apollo, and the Fates offers a number of striking parallels to the background circumstances, present situations, and possible futures of Gabriel and Gretta Conroy in "The Dead." The death of the lover for another's sake, the extension of life by suspending the shears of Atropos, the egoism of the husband, the sacredness of the law of hospitality, and the promise of resurrection to those obedient to this law, all tie into Joyce's themes in "The Dead."

In Gabriel's speech, as we have it in *Dubliners*, he is playing fast-and-loose with his mythology as he rises to his peroration. Like his creator, Gabriel cannibalizes a variety of mythological figures and motifs for his speech. First, he correlates his aunts and Mary Jane to the benign figures of the Graces, calling them the "Three Graces of the Dublin musical world" (*D* 204), then he slides, by association, into an allusion to the Judgment of Paris, a judgment not of the fairest of the Graces, but of the fairest of three goddesses—Hera, Athena, and Aphrodite: "I will not attempt to play to-night the part that Paris played on another occasion. I will not attempt to choose among them" (*D* 204). At this point, I suggest, as indicated by his outline of "the headings of his speech" (*D* 192), Gabriel would have cannibalized the three fair Graces, by a similar kind of association, with their dark antitheses, the Three Fates, those whom Joyce calls "the aged sisters" in *Ulysses* (*U* 14.392). Further, this allusion would incorporate a quotation from Browning's "Apollo and the Fates."[8]

Why, then, does Gabriel suppress his Browning reference? There are at least four plausible answers. First, he may have concluded, after the (to him) pedestrian dinner conversations he has just heard, that his Browning quotation would truly "be above the heads of his hearers" (*D* 179). Second, he may have decided, as the dinner conversation had so recently been chilled by a turn to the "lugubrious" (*D* 201), that invoking the legend of Apollo and the Fates to express the wish for extending the lives of his "Graces," or particularly the life of Aunt Julia whose health seems most fragile (though Gabriel calls her one "gifted with perennial youth" [*D* 204]—a typical mythological boon), might introduce the chilling shadow of death inappropriately into his speech. Significantly, Gabriel "hasten[s] to his close" immediately after glimpsing the smiles and tears of his aunts (*D* 205). Third, as sensitive as Gabriel is to self-exposure, he could easily feel that associating his aunts with the malign figures of the Fates, even in a complimentary context, would betray his private opinion of them: they are only "ignorant old women" (*D* 192). Fourth, and most telling, Gabriel may have suppressed his reference to the legend because, like Admetus, he is convinced that he is generally loved, while being himself incapable of love. Only later in this evening will Gabriel discover the existence of a love that will sacrifice life itself for the sake of the loved one, in the example of Michael Furey.

So, there are a number of thematic parallels that support the identification of Browning's "Apollo and the Fates," from *Parleyings*, as a probable source for Gabriel's Browning quotation, as well as several ironic implications, evident to Gabriel, that explain his decision not to use the quote. But a further twist in the allusion to the Fates, apparent to Joyce rather than to Gabriel, adds strength to this identification. While the three Fates—Clotho who spins, Lachesis who weaves, and Atropos who cuts the threads of man's destiny—are frequently referred to in Western literature, the story of Atropos staying her shears at the request of a god is a much less common source of mythical allusion. One significant use of this legend that Browning possibly had in mind and that Joyce certainly knew, at the time he was writing "The Dead," appears in Canto XXXIII of Dante's *Inferno*. As Joyce formed his initial conception for "The Dead" during his several months' stay in Rome, in 1906–7, he was also renewing his acquaintance with Dante's *Commedia*, possibly stimulated by his and Dante's shared "hostility to the temporal power of the Church," a hostility reawakened in Joyce by his "marked dislike of Rome" (Reynolds 27).[9] Written within what Mary Reynolds calls the "second stage" of Joyce's developing knowledge of Dante, "The Dead" shows direct traces of Dante's influence, particularly in the symbolic setting of its last scene, locating Gabriel, by his vision of the snow immuring the "living and the dead" (*D* 214), in the ninth circle of the *Inferno*, the lake of ice called Cocytus, the setting of its final Cantos (26, 156).[10] The damned in the ninth circle are punished by being imbedded in a lake of ice, so placed that they may cannibalize one another, gnawing each other's heads. In the third round of the ninth circle, called Ptolomea, one additional unique feature about the damned emerges: those consigned to Ptolomea are not yet dead on earth; they are thus condemned to a living death while their corporeal selves, back on the surface, have been taken over by demons. (Joyce, incidentally, would have relished this detail because Dante has the opportunity to damn his living acquaintances by this quite untheological stratagem.) Friar Alberigo explains to Dante how this damnation-in-life has come to be. Dante has recognized the Friar as one of the living and wonders if Alberigo has died suddenly, in the time since he began his descent into the Inferno: "'What! Are you dead already?' I said to him" (l. 121). Through Alberigo's reply, Dante invokes the mythical parallel to the legend of Apollo and the Fates:

> "[. . .] How my body stands in the world
> I do not know. So privileged is this rim
> of Ptolomea, that often souls fall to it
> before dark Atropos has cut their thread."
> (ll. 122–25) (Ciardi 278–79)[11]

It is not just this second, perhaps coincidental reference to Atropos, however, that pins down the connection between Gabriel's suppressed Browning quote and the Dante-esque conclusion to "The Dead"; one more fact makes the relationship between Gabriel's speech and his condition of living-death, frozen in the drifts of "faintly falling" snow (*D* 224), most convincing: those condemned to the third round of Cocytus, Ptolomea, are damned for their treachery "AGAINST THE TIES OF HOSPITALITY" (Ciardi 274). Through an ironic reversal of the allusory context, Dante cites a legend concerning the sacrifice of one's own life for another's sake and the reward of a return to life for hospitality, to reinforce his condemnation of those who have betrayed their loved ones and committed crimes against hospitality: Friar Alberigo, for example, is damned for having taken long-nursed vengeance against his brother, Manfred, by inviting Manfred and his son to a banquet where he had them both murdered.[12]

Gabriel too has sinned against hospitality, though less egregiously than Friar Alberigo: Gabriel's modification of his speech to include a few phrases commending the Irish virtue of hospitality, ironically taking a most inhospitable vengeance on a guest, Miss Ivors, condemns him to the Ptolomean punishment of death-in-life that juxtaposes the life-in-death of Michael Furey. As theologians would tell us, and Joyce would know, his crime is not diminished by the fact that his insult misses its target. Sin lies as much in intention as in accomplishment. Further, Joyce magnifies Gabriel's guilt by emphasizing that he recognizes the solemn obligations of hospitality, by his own words. He has sinned in a grievous matter, in full knowledge, and with full consent of his will. He has sinned mortally.[13]

Gabriel has earned his frigid, Ptolomean situation at the end of "The

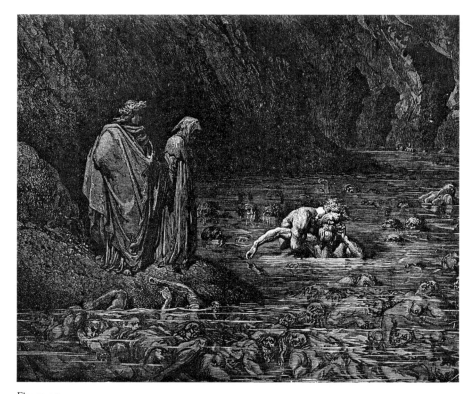

Figure 4.1.

> [. . .] I saw two souls together
> in a single hole, and so pinched in by the ice
> that one head made a helmet for the other.
> As a famished man chews crusts—so the one sinner
> sank his teeth into the other's nape
> at the base of the skull, gnawing his loathsome dinner.
> (ll. 124–29) (Ciardi 271)

Gustav Doré's etching depicts Virgil and Dante observing Count Ugolino cannibalizing Archbishop Ruggieri, among the damned imbedded in the frozen lake of Cocytus, at the conclusion of Canto XXXII of the *Inferno*. From *Dante's Inferno*, trans. Henry Francis Cary (Chicago: Thompson, 1901), 153.

Dead," not simply for his failure to "pass boldly into that other world, in the full glory of some passion" (*D* 223), but specifically for his after-dinner speech, hypocritically praising hospitality. This connection between Gabriel's speech and the conclusion of "The Dead," a structural use of allusion worthy of the author of *Ulysses*, has never been noticed. Nor would this connection be convincing, were it not reinforced by Dante's and Browning's parallel allusions to the role of Atropos, suspending death, from Alberigo's tale in *The Divine Comedy* and from the legend of "Apollo and the Fates" in *Parleyings with Certain People of Importance in Their Day*. Materializing the "ghosts" of "The Dead," therefore, not only draws Gabriel together with Dante, via the poetry of Robert Browning, but also draws our attention to the most prominent "ghost" of all in the tale, sharpening our awareness of the artist who spins, weaves, and determines the fabric, Joyce himself.

Identifying a specific source from Robert Browning, even under erasure, may expand our awareness of how Joyce cannibalizes literary and mythological traditions into his texts in ways that anticipate his techniques in *A Portrait of the Artist as a Young Man*, *Ulysses*, and *Finnegans Wake*, yet it also confirms the long-established view of his indebtedness to Western "high" culture valorized by Joyce critics as early as (if not before) Valéry Larbaud's pre-publication lecture on *Ulysses* on 7 December 1921—"The reader who approaches this book without the *Odyssey* clearly in mind will be thrown into dismay" (258)—and T. S. Eliot's praise of the same novel's use of classical myth to "manipulat[e] a continuous parallel between contemporaneity and antiquity" (201) in his 1922 review "*Ulysses*, Order and Myth," and echoed by countless critics in their wake. Indeed, although this chapter offers a useful insight into Joyce's early development of his structural use of allusion and sustains my argument that cannibalism is never far from this author's matter as well as his method—for the allusion to Dante's Cocytus adds one more example to the suggestions of cannibalism in "The Dead" that I note in my first chapter—my discussion of the Browning quote simply provides yet another illustration of the intersections between Joyce's fiction and high culture that preoccupied scholars' discussions of Joyce through the second half of the twentieth century. As we shall see in the concluding chapters of this study, however, my emphasis here on Joyce's early and sustained provocation of the readers' active involvement in making the meanings of his texts has much in common with the more recent turn in Joyce studies toward understanding the political subtext of his works. Joyce does not simply empower an underclass of readers long disenfranchised in traditional fiction by subverting all forms of "privileged discourse," as MacCabe nicely argues (27; also see 1–12, and passim), but this empowerment expands and matures in Joyce's later fiction as he reacts increasingly against the threatened usurpation of individual subjectivity in modern culture, most especially but not exclusively by political totalitarianism.

Nevertheless, my primary focus in this chapter on how James Joyce consumes the body of world literary culture to nourish his own creative works, though cast in the novel form of a metaphor of cannibalism, remains well within the range of traditional readings of his fiction. Indeed, given the dozens of "Joyce and..." studies that have appeared over the years, from Fr. Noon's *Joyce and Aquinas* (1957) to Fargnoli and Gillespie's Joyce and "Zola" (237), the penultimate entry in their *James Joyce A to Z* (1995), and works published before and since, there seems to be little need for me to further demonstrate here his cannibalization of high culture. We could look again at his creative reprocessing of English literary styles from the Anglo-Saxon era to the near present in the Oxen of the Sun episode of *Ulysses*, but Robert Janusko's *The Sources and Structures of James Joyce's "Oxen"* (1983) has covered this ground thoroughly and well, not to mention Weldon Thornton's superb *Allusions in Ulysses* (1968), which also takes care of the rest of the novel. Larbaud seems to have started the ongoing conversation about Joyce's incorporation of Homer into *Ulysses*, in his 1921 lecture, two months before the book was officially published, and William Schutte has written the necessary book on *Joyce and Shakespeare* (1957). Don Gifford, in addition to complementing Thornton's work with his Ulysses *Annotated* (rev. ed. 1988), has similarly tracked the literary allusions in *Dubliners* and *A Portrait of the Artist as a Young Man* in his *Joyce Annotated* (2nd ed. 1982), while James Atherton's indispensable *The Books at the Wake* (1959) is a model study of Joyce's central and tangential literary allusions in his last book. Roland McHugh's *Annotations to* Finnegans Wake (3rd ed. 2006) supplements Atherton with additional glosses for every page of the *Wake*, and dozens of articles and notes continue to fill the gaps for this and the earlier books, all, in effect, offering forensic identifications of the membra disjecta of Joyce's cannibalistic consumption.

Joyce, the first reader of his own work, participates in this process of identifying his sources, for instance, with his titles for *Ulysses* and *Finnegans Wake* that acknowledge his consumption of both classical literature and popular culture. As my remarks on Joyce's somatophagy in *Finnegans Wake* at the conclusion of my first chapter suggest, moreover, there is yet another way of thinking about his relation to "high" culture, if we accept that this term applies to his own works. Throughout the *Wake*, for example, Joyce incorporates allusions to all of his previous works—to name but a few instances—from the lost childhood poem "Et tu, Healy!" (*Et Cur Heli!* [*FW* 73.19]), through each of the stories in *Dubliners* (*FW* 186–87), *Ulysses*—"his usylessly unreadable

Blue Book of Eccles" (*FW* 179.26–27)—and even the "epical forged cheque" of the *Wake* itself (*FW* 181.16), all but the first of these concentrated in the "Shem the Penman" chapter (I, 7), a cannibalizing rewrite of "a poor trait of the artless" *as a Young Man* (*FW* 114.32). More broadly, throughout the *Wake* Joyce ruminates at least three primary features of *Ulysses*, the idea of the voyeur-observed for HCE's "crime" (viz. Bloom in Nausicaa), the cycles of rises and falls, and rising again (viz. Bloom's nighttown sequences in Circe, or the Daedalian-Icarian patterns in *A Portrait*), and the husband and wife in bed, which in turn reminds us that *Ulysses* itself cannibalizes the conclusion of "The Dead." *Ulysses* consumes much more than this, incorporating numerous characters from *Dubliners* and, obviously, Stephen Dedalus from *A Portrait*, who is himself a cannibalization of the young boy of the opening three stories of *Dubliners*. It would not be difficult to argue that the second half of *Ulysses* cannibalizes its own first half, like the somatophage, finding inspiration for its technical experiments in Bloom's musical interests (thus Sirens), abrupt flights of fantasy (e.g., Hades, thus Cyclops), sentimentality (thus Nausicaa), evasiveness (thus Oxen of the Sun; see chapter 6 below), interests in the drama (thus Circe), inarticulateness (thus Eumaeus), and scientific musings (thus Ithaca). The style of Penelope, to complete the rota, owes at least part of its inspiration to Martha Clifford's letter that has accompanied Bloom, like his constant thoughts of Molly, through most of the day and that Bloom has just laid to rest in the sideboard, moments before coming to rest himself.

But Joyce's fondness for consuming the body of "high" culture only accounts for part of his appetite. His simultaneous cannibalization of popular and often ephemeral literature, which has drawn the attention of more recent critics, such as R. B. Kershner in his *Joyce, Bakhtin, and Popular Literature* (1989), has alerted us to the greater extent of this author's capacity for incorporation. The next chapter, thus, reciprocates this chapter's focus on "high" cultural sources to identify Joyce's indebtedness to some of the literature that readers below Gabriel Conroy's "grade of culture" (*D* 179) would have found readily available and accessible.

5

A Taste for/of "inferior literary style"

The (Tom) Swiftian Comedy of Scylla and Charybdis

> "How do you know if there's an elephant in your refrigerator?"
> "You can smell the peanuts on his breath."
>
> "I've just had a frontal lobotomy," Tom said absentmindedly.

In the late spring of 1963 two new forms of verbal humor, sampled above, were making the rounds at suburban cocktail parties: elephant jokes and another more literate and witty kind of wordplay called the "Tom Swiftie." Both of these joke fads became so popular that they gained the notice of the national press.[1] While the Tom Swiftie has, alas, long since departed, the elephant joke has remained a staple form of humor, as long-lived as its subject, to be rediscovered by each generation of elementary-school children, together with "knock-knock" jokes and variations upon "moron" jokes. Frank Kermode testifies to its longevity by planting an elephant joke in the unlikely context of his discussion of hermeneutic criticism in *The Genesis of Secrecy*: "how [do] you fit five elephants in a Volkswagen?" The answer is "two in the front, three in the back" (24, 149). Such logical analysis of an illogical, physical absurdity delights the child and may amuse an older audience as well.

However, the Tom Swiftie appealed chiefly to the literate adult because its effectiveness, as its name suggests, resided in the hearer's awareness of a literary model for its humor: the novels about Tom Swift (among many other heroes and heroines) featured in the so-called Series for Young Americans published throughout the twentieth century in the United States by the Stratemeyer syndicate and Grosset and Dunlap. The Tom Swiftie is pure verbal play, relying on a syntactic paradigm familiar to veteran readers of these enormously successful series, and of much uninspired writing: the use of post-position adverbs to modify a reported speech, appropriately. Since these jokes have disappeared from the cocktail party circuit, perhaps to our general relief, there would seem to be little purpose in resurrecting their memory, except to suggest that their demise has something to do with the decline of reading in adolescence; however, Joyce's readers should be intrigued by the similarity between the technique of the Tom Swiftie and the kinds of verbal humor found in the ninth episode of *Ulysses*, Scylla and Charybdis. Joyce's jokes are not simply similar in method; they share the Tom Swiftie's origins in popular literature.

The Tom Swift novels have long been among the most popular of the Stratemeyer syndicate's books. Preceded by several other series, including the "Rover Boys," "Baseball Joe," and the still popular "Bobbsey Twins," the Tom Swift novels began to appear in 1910. Purportedly written by Victor Appleton, the books were in fact composed as a sideline by a stable of New York journalists to the prescriptions of Edward Stratemeyer.[2] "The Perfect Inventor," as he has been described, Tom began his career as inventor modestly enough with *Tom Swift and His Motor-Cycle* (1910), but shortly moved on to more ambitious modes of transport, such as his electric auto (unfortunately *not* named "Prius"), his hybrid dirigible-airplane (called "Red Cloud"), his monoplane "Humming-Bird," his combination plane, auto, and speedboat "Air Monarch," his magnetic-propulsion submarine "Advance," and his anticipation of current stealth-technology, the silent airplane "Air Scout."[3] Tom developed mid-ocean floating airports, color television in 1928, three-dimensional TV in 1934, and X-ray vision by means of his "Television Detector" of 1933. An American Library Association survey in 1926 discovered that an amazing 98 percent of public school children listed the Stratemeyer syndicate books as their preferred reading and Tom Swift as their favorite series of all. But this was to change shortly: in 1927 Stratemeyer launched the "Hardy Boys," with *The Tower Treasure*, and soon after their female counterpart, Nancy Drew. Now dated by his younger competitors, Tom finally grew out of adolescence and out of publication. We do know that he eventually married his teen sweetheart, Mary Nestor, because he fathered a son who achieved lesser celebrity in a second generation of books, the "Tom Swift Junior" series, first appearing in 1954. This set was authored, naturally, by Victor Appleton, Jr., and featured even greater technological wonders: Atomic Earth Blasters, Jetmarines, and Triphibian Atomicars.[4]

The Tom Swiftie joke became a fad in the early 1960s as the subjects of the 1926 Library Association survey, and their children, reached maturity. As the

Figure 5.1. After developing a variety of vehicles in the first five novels of the original series—motorcycle, motorboat, airship, submarine, and electric automobile—Tom began turning his interests toward new communication technologies with *Tom Swift and His Wireless Message* (1911). The books' covers nevertheless retained their original design, emphasizing air, land, and water transport. Courtesy of Rare Books and Special Collections, University of South Carolina.

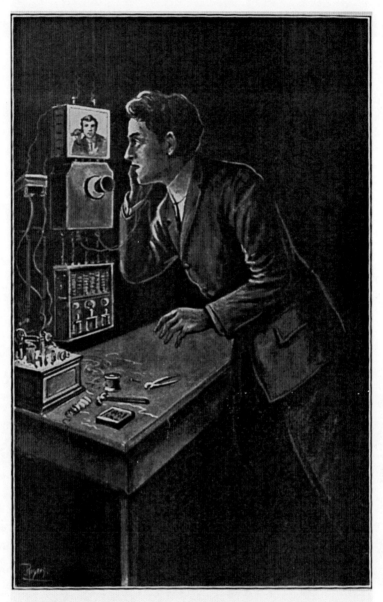

TOM UTTERED A CRY OF JOY, FOR THERE, STARING AT HIM
. FROM THE PLATE, WAS THE FACE OF NED.—*Page* 125.
Tom Swift and His Photo Telephone.

Figure 5.2. Tom had developed a video-telephone by 1914, in the seventeenth novel in the original series, over a decade before Herbert E. Ives of AT&T and other researchers began serious development of this technology (see chapter 8). Victor Appleton, *Tom Swift and His Photo Telephone* (New York: Grosset & Dunlap, 1914), frontispiece.

format of the Swiftie indicates, these generations of the Stratemeyer syndicate's readers had fully assimilated the chief stylistic mannerism of the series and of much popular literature: the recurrent use of post-position adverbs to modify virtually everything characters say. Perhaps "Victor Appleton" used adverbs so generously to enrich his young readers' vocabulary; more likely, he was making a desperate attempt to vary the tedious repetition of "he saids" and "she saids" in the novels, the *inquit* construction for recording direct discourse.[5] In the words of a *Time* magazine reporter, "Tom Swift never simply 'said' anything; he said it 'soberly,' 'thoughtfully,' 'excitedly' (one classic rejoinder: "'Yes, it is an emergency all right,' returned Tom slowly')." This same reporter succinctly defines the strategy of the Tom Swiftie: "Its object [is] to create an adverbial link between what is said and how it is said [. . .] with puns at a premium" ("Games: Season for Swifties" 36). Here are some examples that were making the rounds in the spring of 1963:

"I lost my crutches," Tom said lamely.

"I'm glad I passed my electrocardiogram," Tom said wholeheartedly.

"That was a damn poor chicken dinner," Tom groused.

Many of the jokes, and Leopold Bloom would certainly enjoy these, allude to contemporary advertising:

"Our group had 32% more cavities," said Tom, with a crestfallen smile.

"The pineapple's all gone," Tom said dolefully.

Others, which Molly might find amusing, allude to popular songs:

"Well, I'll be hanged," said Tom duly.

The world of high art is equally well represented:

"You have the charm of Venus," Tom said disarmingly.

Some versions even have a kind of literary allusiveness that Stephen would appreciate:

"You make me feel like a king," Tom said with a leer.

"Enough of your fairy tales," Tom said grimly.

"Accidents are bound to happen," Captain Hook said off-handedly. (Tom needn't always be the speaker.)

"I've been looking forward to this ride," said Lady Godiva shiftlessly.

Two more examples, however, might be as much at home in the world of Joyce's *Ulysses* as in popular literature:

"My wife's not easy to get on with," Tom said shrewdly.

"Get to the back of the boat," Tom said sternly.

The former, if not the latter, of these jokes should sound familiar to most Joyceans, for the Tom Swiftie, which *Time, Life, Newsweek, Reader's Digest*, the *National Observer*, and *Saturday Review* all trace to a word-game played by businessmen in Minneapolis in the early 1950s, is also a principal form of verbal humor in the Scylla and Charybdis episode of *Ulysses*. The shrew joke, for example, comes up early in the dialogue of the chapter:

—A shrew, John Eglinton said shrewdly, is not a useful portal of discovery [. . .] (*U* 9.232)

Notice the resemblance between the Tom Swiftie and Joyce's modification of some other *inquit* phrases during the library discussion:

—What is a ghost? Stephen said with tingling energy. (*U* 9.147)

—Yes, Mr. Best said youngly. I feel Hamlet quite young. (*U* 9.387)

—But Ann Hathaway? Mr. Best's quiet voice said forgetfully. Yes, we seem to be forgetting her [. . .] (*U* 9.240–41)

To Stephen's remark that "Aristotle was once Plato's schoolboy," Eglinton responds:

—And has remained so, one should hope, John Eglinton sedately said. (*U* 9.57–58)

And so the puns run on, in a series of increasingly elaborate variations as the episode proceeds, all in the Tom Swiftie mode:

The quaker librarian came from the leavetakers. Blushing, his mask said:—Mr Dedalus, your views are most illuminating. (*U* 9.326–28).

—The spirit of reconciliation, the quaker librarian breathed. (*U* 9.396)

The benign forehead of the quaker librarian enkindled rosily with hope.
—I hope Mr Dedalus will work out his theory for the enlightenment of the public. (*U* 9.436–39)

The mocker is never taken seriously when he is most serious. They talked seriously of mocker's seriousness. (*U* 9.542–44)

—A myriadminded man, Mr. Best reminded. (*U* 9.768)

Late in the episode Joyce increasingly variegates the paradigm:

—Cuckoo! Cuckoo! Cuck Mulligan clucked lewdly. (*U* 9.1025).

Amused Buck Mulligan mused in pleasant murmur with himself [. . .] (*U* 9.1119)

And these are just a sampling.

The primary effect of Joyce's verbal play, of course, is amusement. After registering the local effect of the jokes, however, the reader may suspect, as a secondary result of the Tom Swiftie, that Joyce could be playing with his *inquit* phrases elsewhere in the novel. (Joyce uses "*inquit*" itself on one occasion [*U* 9.811].) This suspicion is justified. Once recognized as a possibility, variants of the Tom Swiftie, though concentrated in the ninth episode, seem to lurk throughout the text. In fact, Joyce plays with an adverbial modifier on the opening page of *Ulysses*. Recall the latter of the two Swifties that concluded my survey of the genre: "'Get to the back of the boat,' Tom said sternly." One of Joyce's first *inquit* phrases in the book offers a similar pun: mounting the gunrest, breasting the sea, the mock priest and ship-captain Buck Mulligan (who later calls "Kinch ahoy!" [*U* 1.280]), commands the "white corpuscles" of his shaving lather, at line 19, in mixed military and maritime metaphor:

—Back to barracks! he said sternly.

Later in Telemachus we have another Swiftian *inquit*:

—But a lovely mummer! he murmured to himself. (*U* 1.97)

One even suspects Buck of speaking in a French vein when he savages the "ponderous Saxon" Haines:

—God, isn't he dreadful? he said frankly. (*U* 1.51)

Joyce plays with the adjective and adverb "grave" and "gravely" in his *inquit* phrases throughout the Hades episode and joins the Dubliners in one of their favorite puns, noting that when Blazes speaks he is "Boylan with impatience" (*U* 10.486; 11.289, 426). Perhaps the special use of punning modifiers, as in the Tom Swiftie construction, to reflect not just the manner of speech adverbially but the substance of the statement adjectivally, is only appropriate in a novel that begins, as Fritz Senn has noted, with the mixed adjective-adverb "Stately" ("'Stately, plump'" 347–54).

Although occurrences of the Tom Swiftian wordplay can be spotted elsewhere in *Ulysses*, these jokes are most frequent and apparent to the reader in the Scylla and Charybdis episode, so it is there that we should look most closely for further significance in Joyce's verbal comedy. Curiously little attention has been paid to this Tom Swiftian verbal play, so prominent in the library chapter, either in general studies of *Ulysses* or in commentaries on the episode. Most critics who note Joyce's frequent punning tend to view it as a kind of imitative style, an acknowledgment of Shakespeare's love of the double-entendre to accompany a discourse on Shakespeare; Joyce's style is seen as a "composition of tone" to match Stephen's "Composition of place" (*U* 9.163) in presenting his theory. As an added fillip, both Hélène Cixous (564–95) and Brook Thomas (58–61) suggest that play of many sorts is justified in an episode about plays, invoking the same principle, I suppose, that explains why Joyce stages the children's street games in *Finnegans Wake* (II, 1) as a play, "*The Mime of Mick, Nick and the Maggies*" (*FW* 219.18–19). Akin to this, John Houston suspects that the "rare abundance, variety, and freakishness" of Joyce's adverbs in Scylla and Charybdis "perhaps suggests an emphatic style of acting" (92–93). To this we might add that Joyce clearly recognizes one advantage he has, as a novelist, over the dramatist Shakespeare: although the playwright would seem to have the edge on the novelist, not having to struggle against the tedium of the *inquit* construction, Joyce turns the novelist's limitation into a strength, finding an additional resource for humor unavailable to Shakespeare.

The many studies specifically devoted to Joyce's language and style in *Ulysses*, such as Anthony Burgess's *Joysprick* (1973), Roy Gottfried's *Art of Joyce's Syntax* (1980), and Karen Lawrence's *Odyssey of Style* (1981), to name a few, say little at all about the playfulness of Scylla and Charybdis. More interesting remarks, though brief, are to be found in Dermot Kelly's *Narrative Strategies in Joyce's* Ulysses (1988) and Zack Bowen's Ulysses *as a Comic Novel* (1989).

Both critics note what Bowen calls the "flippant tone" of the narration in the library episode (Ulysses 4), and Kelly proceeds to describe the effect on the reader of Joyce's use of "mocking repetition" in his narration: "the narrative appendages have been tailored to reiterate an item from the dialogue in a way that makes one of the simplest fictional conventions seem awkward" (15–16, 19). I will return to this point. On the whole, however, such brief and general comments, though convincing enough, glide over a basic distinction between the overall wordplay of Scylla and Charybdis and the specifically Tom Swiftian play with the *inquit* phrases in the text. While much of the wit in this episode comes through the filter of Stephen's speech or consciousness, most notably the well-known "A.E.I.O.U." and "If others have their will Ann hath a way" puns (*U* 9.213; 9.256–57), the Tom Swiftie jokes work at the level of the episode's narration, quite independently of Stephen's speech or thought. As such, they constitute a kind of play by the emergent narrator-arranger in the text, although David Hayman, who coined the term "arranger," only briefly remarks the role of the narrator here, calling him a "puckish commentator" apropos for a Shakespeare discourse (Ulysses 96). More typical are the conclusions reached by Robert Kellogg and Marilyn French, who both accept and deny the existence of a second voice in Scylla and Charybdis. Kellogg, for example, in his contribution to the *James Joyce's* Ulysses essay collection (1974), states that the "mockery" comes from "Stephen, who shares with the chapter's narrator the attitude of his silent thoughts when they are directed toward his fellow discussants" (148–49). French, in *The Book as World* (1976), sees the narration as essentially still in the novel's "initial style"; ultimately she identifies the narrator's voice as Stephen's: "in this chapter Stephen is so busy composing, watching, and manipulating that it is possible to imagine him composing the chapter itself in which he appears, making himself his own grandfather or at least creator" (110).

While French's approach is intriguing, her argument is driven by a thesis that imposes a pattern of narrative development onto *Ulysses* that the text, finally, will not support. In the library chapter the reader confronts a mixture of the "initial style" and the same antic sensibility, quite separate from Stephen's, that plays with the reader and the text in the earlier chapter Aeolus (in its headlines) and throughout the second half of the novel. John Paul Riquelme is far more accurate in his description of the oscillating relationship between the text and the narration, between the tale and the teller, in Scylla and Charybdis. In fact, Riquelme's discussion of the stylistic playfulness of the episode is by far the best to date, though again brief (193–98). One of the major implications of Riquelme's *Teller and Tale in Joyce's Fiction* (1983), picked up as well in Dermot Kelly's *Narrative Strategies in Joyce's* Ulysses (1988), and implicit in my remarks about the scattered examples of the Tom Swiftie mode of comedy in episodes earlier than Scylla and Charybdis, is that the narrator, the teller, the arranger, or whatever you want to call this voice, is always already present in *Ulysses*. This voice is immanent, not only in the so-called initial style of the book, but also in the earliest surviving drafts of the novel, predating the headlines of Aeolus, for example.[6]

However, there is another implication in Joyce's verbal comedy, at the level of narration, in Scylla and Charybdis. As Dermot Kelly remarks, Joyce's *inquit* phrases make "one of the simplest fictional conventions seem awkward." In effect, the working of Joyce's comedy is precisely analogous, in style as well as in inspiration, with what happens in the Tom Swiftie joke. His puns are a form of play with the pedestrian style of popular literature, a parody of the tired attempt to variegate the style of the *inquit* phrase that leaves the conventions of narration, like the most pedestrian librarian, Lyster, "Swiftly rectly creaking" (*U* 9.969). Joyce's play with the mannerisms of popular fiction "simply lays bare the technique," as Victor Shklovsky observes of Sterne's similar strategies in *Tristram Shandy* ("Sterne's *Tristram Shandy*" 30). Shklovsky would argue ("sternly"?) that by thus exposing the artifice of his art and defamiliarizing the conventions of literature, Joyce promotes the reader's "perception" as an "aesthetic end in itself": *"Art is a way of experiencing the artfulness of an object: the object is not important"* (12). Yet, I would suggest that while Joyce certainly knew the importance of being earnest, his greater debt to Sterne is his jocoserious vision of "the artfulness of an object." By his play with *inquit* constructions Joyce participates in one of the great traditions of the English comic novel, wherein "we find," says Bakhtin, "a comic-parodic re-processing of almost all the levels of literary language, both conversational and written, that [are] current at the time" (301).

Of course, it is highly unlikely that Joyce had the contemporary work of Victor Appleton in mind; the only Swift that inspired his comic imagination was Jonathan Swift, whose spirit flits through *Ulysses* and occupies a major position in the intertextual play of *Finnegans Wake*. But Joyce had more than enough acquaintance with middle- to low-brow fiction of the Stratemeyer syndicate sort, as R. B. Kershner documents in his *Joyce, Bakhtin, and Popular Literature* (1989), not to mention pulp fiction that aims lower in the human anatomy for its appeal. *Ulysses* cannibalizes *both* the matter and style of this literature throughout, much of it real (*Ruby: the Pride of the Ring*[7] and Maria Cummins's *The Lamplighter*), and some of it apparently invented by Joyce for his immediate purposes. Surely "Matcham's Masterstroke" would have been full of tired *inquit* constructions, judging from the style of another of Philip Beaufoy's "Prize Tidbits," "For Vera's Sake":

> "You love another," [Ivan] said fiercely [. . . .] Vera drew herself up proudly as she replied, in a firm tone, "Yes, I do love him [. . .]" (12)[8]

The solitary quotation of fictional dialogue in *Ulysses*, however, comes not from "Matcham's Masterstroke," but from *Sweets of Sin*, "a book of inferior literary style" (*U* 17.733–34) perused by Bloom at the bookseller's in Wandering Rocks. It includes a typical *inquit* phrase: "*You are late, he spoke hoarsely, eyeing her with a suspicious glare*" (*U* 10.614). Just as this passage contains a quotation of a quotation, Joyce's Tom Swiftie technique, by its parody of fictional conventions, involves a kind of implied quotation of a quotation. As Mark Osteen has noted in a different context, the frequent patterns of repetition in Scylla and Charybdis, the text's recurrent quotations of itself, are particularly appropriate for a discussion that relies extensively on the Shakespearian quotation ("Intertextual Economy" 203–4). At the level of the tale, we might add, the quotes are drawn chiefly from "serious" literature; the quotations of the modes of popular literature, however, exist at the level of the teller. Thus, we have one more dimension of the episode's play of antitheses, the Scylla-and-Charybdis polarization of the ideal and the real, in the juxtaposition of quotations from literary art by the tale and from popular literature by the teller. As "high-culture" trickles down into the Bloom chapters, "pop culture" reciprocates by percolating upward into the Stephen episodes, from the Oxbridge high jinks story of the debagging of Clive Kempthorpe (*U* 1.165–71) and the headlines of Aeolus, to the *inquits* of Scylla and Charybdis. Better yet, we might say that the voice of popular literature is repeatedly heard from below stage, or from "beneath" as Shakespeare would have it: "Art thou there, truepenny?" (*U* 9.183; *Hamlet* I, v).

If this Joycean cannibalization of dialogue conventions is always already present in *Ulysses*, is it possible that Joyce has this same effect in mind in his earlier work? The answer is "yes, and no." Although we find little evidence of the Tom Swiftie mode in *Dubliners* and *A Portrait of the Artist as a Young*

Man, we can, nonetheless see the trace of the same motivation that leads Joyce to play with the *inquit* phrase in *Ulysses*. In his earlier fiction Joyce adopts a variety of strategies to erase the *inquit* construction and generally to break out of the traditional methods for recording direct discourse: eliminating quotation marks, for example, and reducing to a minimum the use of adverbs, in the *inquit* phrases in his text as well as elsewhere, to achieve the effect of "scrupulous meanness" in style (*Letters*, II 134). After *Ulysses*, in *Finnegans Wake*, Joyce abandons the *inquit* construction altogether. In *Ulysses*, however, as a part of his move away from the contraction of his early fiction, and toward composition by accretion and expansion, Joyce introduces all sorts of play with the textuality of his text. And the Tom Swiftie wittily contributes to the varieties of self-reference Joyce employs in *Ulysses*. "The *inquit* phrase in fiction will never be the same," we can imagine Joyce chuckling, iniquitously. For, "by such a device the language of the teller calls 'attention to itself,'" John Paul Riquelme might pontificate. And thus "the Tom Swiftie becomes a significant voice in the heteroglossia of *Ulysses*," as Bakhtin would say, antiseptically.

Ulysses, unlike the variety of ephemera it cannibalizes into its text, is now firmly entrenched as a monument of twentieth-century "high" culture—placing first among the century's significant works of literary art in several end-of-the-millennium surveys—but as it recedes further from our present, we are increasingly losing sight of Joyce's determined incorporation of the trivial details and ephemeral matter of his contemporary material culture into this work, and indeed into all his fictions. The two standard volumes annotating *Ulysses*, Weldon Thornton's *Allusions in* Ulysses (1961) and Don Gifford and Robert J. Seidman's Ulysses *Annotated* (1974; rev. ed. 1988), interestingly reflect in their foci and order of publication the original priority given to Joyce's debts to literary tradition among his critics, initially perhaps to legitimate their claims for his artistic achievement, which was followed by the growing recognition of his equal debts to his contemporary material world. (Gifford and Seidman gloss most of the same literary allusions identified by Thornton, as well as a vast number of more topical references in *Ulysses*; Roland McHugh's *Annotations to* Finnegans Wake [1980; 3rd ed. 2006] similarly manages something like a balance of these two orientations.) The following three chapters on Joyce's "adaptation" and "mediation" of the materials of early twentieth-century popular culture—the condom, the emergent technology of sound recording, and the nascent technologies of film, radio, and television—are contributions to this ongoing and, it would appear, never-ending exploration of the artist's contemporaneity (Lüsebrink and Reichardt 20). I do not intend these chapters to make the case for Joyce's debt to mass culture, which has already been fully established, nor could I possibly claim that they exhaust this subject; rather, I offer these chapters as further illustrations of Joyce's method of cultural transfer and incorporation to make two collateral points: first, that his creative cannibalization of the "high" and the "low" is instrumental in Joyce's experimentation with the technical possibilities of fiction, and second, that his cannibalism not only is the consequence of his political formation—as I claim in my opening chapter—but also provides him the basis for voicing, albeit equivocally via strategies of assimilation and resistance, a political viewpoint in his art.

PART III

Cannibalizing Material Culture

6

Condoms, Conrad, and Joyce

> [It's] as if he did not, after all, quite want us to understand his story,
> as if he had, not quite conscious of what he was doing, ended by
> throwing up between us and it a fortification of solemn burlesque
> prose—as if he were shy and solicitous about it, and wanted to
> protect it from us.
>
> —Wilson, *Axel's Castle* 217

Early in *Lady Chatterley's Lover*, a novel that earned its notoriety by speaking frankly and graphically about sex, Lawrence's spokesperson of the moment Tommy Dukes contends "that sex is just another form of talk, where you act the words instead of saying them"—"sex is a sort of communication like speech" (70, 72). But Dukes leaves unspoken the other half of this equation: sex is talk *because* talk is just another form of sex. Typically, for him, in *Lady Chatterley's Lover* Lawrence deconstructs the hierarchies privileging thought over act and oral discourse over sexual intercourse, central to Western philosophical and religious thought, conversely asserting that a sacred communion is imbedded in the profane activity of speech. Lawrence recognizes the hierophany—in Mircea Eliade's terms (11)—already encoded in our language; namely, communication *is* communion, "intercourse" signifies both verbal and sexual exchange, and "conversation" means both speech and cohabitation (via the French *converser*, meaning both "to talk with" and "to live with").[1] While this recognition of the spiritual within the mundane is akin to Joyce's conception of the epiphany, Joyce more immediately exploits an identical double signification of "conversation" for his conclusion to "The Dead" when Gabriel Conroy checks into the Gresham Hotel, expecting "communion" with his wife Gretta. Ironically, before he sleeps Gabriel does have intercourse, but not sex, with Gretta. T. S. Eliot similarly correlates discourse with intercourse throughout *The Waste Land*, associating speechlessness with emasculation, the male lamenting "I could not / Speak" in the hyacinth-girl episode (ll. 38–39, *Complete Poems* 38), for example, or the female imploring her impotent gentleman caller in "A Game of Chess" to "Stay with me. / Speak to me. Why do you never speak. Speak" (ll. 111–12, *Complete Poems* 40), just as he associates garrulousness with promiscuity in the same section's pub scene (ll. 139–73, *Complete Poems* 41–42). Elsewhere in Eliot, J. Alfred Prufrock's problem seems to be that he cannot converse with his beloved, in either sense of the term. That Prufrock's internal monologue, however, is more eloquent than anything he might say ("Shall I say [...]" [l. 70, *Complete Poems* 5]), should remind us that the internalization of speech in the stream of consciousness technique, most clearly in Virginia Woolf, both emphasizes physical isolation and privileges spiritual, bodiless, telepathic, and definitely nonsexual communication. Clearly, this association of speech with sexuality—discourse with intercourse—is a common subtext among the writers of the early part of the twentieth century. I want to argue, however, not only that this subtext is pervasive in modernist writing, but also that thwarted communication, both among characters in these works of literature and between their authors and their audience, comes to represent a kind of prophylaxis. Modern writing may necessarily be "*difficult,*" as Eliot contends, because it reflects the complexity of contemporary life ("The Metaphysical Poets" 65), but much of this difficulty results from what we might call the *condomization* of the text: with the exception of Lawrence, these writers I have cited seem to self-protectively sheathe their texts, shield their words from their audience, not so much from the fear that their words might be made flesh, as from an anxiety that a more direct conversation with the public body might expose their works to some kind of contamination. They seem to want "to protect [them] from us" (Wilson, *Axel's Castle* 217). The Italian anatomist Fallopius, after all, developed the sheath in the sixteenth century as a protection from venereal disease, namely syphilis, not as a means of birth control.[2] Moreover, this figurative condomization of the text approaches the literal in Joseph Conrad's particularly opaque novel *The Secret Agent,* a work which, in turn, exerted an underappreciated influence on Joyce's *Ulysses.*[3]

My principal focus in this chapter is the symptom of textual prophylaxis, rather than its many possible causes, which is fortunate because there are no easy answers here. In part, these modernist authors may be withdrawing from a mass audience that they believed they were never destined to reach, both in reaction against the enormous growths of general literacy and middle- to low-brow literatures aimed at these new readers through the nineteenth century and in a broader rejection of the bourgeois commodification of culture. As Andreas Huyssen remarks, "Modernism constituted itself through a conscious strategy of exclusion, an *anxiety of contamination* by its other: an increasingly consuming and engulfing mass culture" (vii; emphases mine).[4] Yet in part, these writers may also be determined, in principle, to distance themselves from their audience through impersonality, in response to what appeared to them an excessive self-investment in their works by writers in the immediately preceding generations. In part, too, they may be reflecting—to extend Eliot's argument in "The Metaphysical Poets"—the influence of new theories in psychology, physics, and linguistics at the beginning of the century that intensified their sense of the complexity of both the "new" reality and the task of its representation. Certainly, in part, they are responding to the collapse of various structures of authority in recent cultural history by rejecting the role of the "one who knows"—and tells—in their authorship. Nowhere is this more evident than in the prevalence of the ironic mode in modernist writing, the author's prophylactic suppression of intention, which seems to function as both a strategy of detachment from, and an abdication of responsibility for, the horrors their works represent.

There is no greater irony in Conrad's sustained application of the "ironic method" for *The Secret Agent* than his choice of subtitle for the novel, "*A Simple Tale*" ("Author's Preface" 7). Much as in *Heart of Darkness*, Conrad's particularly dense style in *The Secret Agent* makes his tale far from simple, demanding that its first-time readers decode meanings in a work that itself concerns deciphering the subterfuges of international politics. Further, Conrad's disruption of linear chronology—displacing four chapters in time—deceives the readers into misreading the events of the "bomb outrage in Greenwich Park" (144) and then challenges them to reassemble the temporal order in a work that itself concerns an attack on time. Added to this, the readers contend with initially impenetrable dialogues throughout *The Secret Agent*, most memorably the cross-purpose conversations between Adolph Verloc and Mr. Vladimir, between Comrade Ossipon and the Professor, between Inspector Heat and the Assistant Commissioner—which features an eight-page expository interruption in the midst of their exchanges (pages 82–89), one of the novel's several "sudden holes in space and time" (69) that disrupt the reading process, rather like this insertion in my own sentence—and then between Verloc and his wife Winnie, and between Winnie and Ossipon, all of which rely on one or both of the characters' ignorance of the full import or the larger context of what the other is saying. Conrad's readers, too, have a right to complain, as the Assistant Commissioner does to Heat, that the author "shouldn't leave me to puzzle things out for myself like this" (97) and that his method "seems to consist in keeping" them "in the dark" (103). Thus Conrad condomizes his text, imposing prophylactic barriers to complete intercourse both within *The Secret Agent* and between this novel and its readership. But beyond coining the term condomization for Conrad's techniques, I want to make clear that he is himself exploiting both the condom as a governing symbol and as a significant prop for his tale, and the idea of prophylaxis for his central theme.

Like the historically disreputable condom, an invention the English have traditionally credited to the French (the "French Letter") and the French to the English ("*la capote anglaise*") (Himes 194; Kruck 36–37), Conrad's shady central character Verloc has both French and British heritage (22–23). Conrad, in fact, presents Verloc as a kind of human condom, a "mortal envelope" (33, 198) for protection who "exercise[s] his vocation of a protector of society" by acting as a spy amongst revolutionaries (11), a man who has prophylactically "prevented" terrorist plots from reaching their fulfillment and thus thwarted the contagion of the pestilential anarchists (25);[5] Verloc

> surveyed through the park railings the evidences of the town's opulence and luxury with an approving eye. All these people had to be *protected*. *Protection* is the first necessity of opulence and luxury. They had to be *protected*; and their horses, carriages, houses, servants had to be *protected*; and the source of their wealth had to be *protected* in the heart of the city and the heart of the country; the whole social order favourable to their hygienic idleness had to be *protected* against the shallow enviousness of unhygienic labour. (15–16; my emphases)

More than this, Conrad reinforces his prophylactic symbolism by making Verloc a dealer of condoms, a protector of personal as well as social hygiene. Verloc's "ostensible business" (9), his appropriately *prophylactic* cover for his real trade as a double-agent, is a stationery shop in a seedy section of London, which is ironically also a cover, in a second sense, for his trade in sexual goods: the window display of his shop features "photographs of more or less undressed dancing girls" (9), alerting passersby, and Conrad's readers by the third paragraph of the novel, to Verloc's second trade as "a seller of shady wares," unspecified products that prompt Conrad's initial mention of his epithet for Verloc, "a protector of society" (11).

We can grasp Conrad's irony here by revisiting the brief episodes that immediately precede his introduction of this motif in the text. Mr. Verloc customarily sells over his counter "some object looking obviously and scandalously not worth the money which passed in the transaction: a small cardboard box with apparently nothing inside" (10). When Winnie tends the shop, however, male customers evidently intending to purchase such an object, particularly those "of comparatively tender years[,] would get suddenly disconcerted at having to deal with a woman" and instead buy some ridiculously overpriced stationery goods (10). These transactions strongly suggest that Verloc sells prophylactics—small, virtually weightless, and extremely awkward for a young man to purchase from a female—and Conrad reinforces this deduction later in the novel by noting that Verloc supported his household "on the wages of a secret industry eked out by the sale of more or less secret wares: the poor expedients devised by a mediocre mankind for *preserving* an imperfect society from the dangers of moral and physical corruption, both secret too, of their kind" (194; my emphasis). (One of the standard euphemisms for condoms is "preservatives," dating from the eighteenth century [Himes 195; Youssef 227].) We could easily interpret this last passage as referring to Verloc's sale of information to the police and foreign embassies, which it does on one level, for it is difficult to see how condoms could preserve society from *moral* as well as physical corruption. On the other hand, Inspector Heat's earlier comment that Verloc runs the risk of having his wares, "these packages he gets from Paris and Brussels[,] opened in Dover, with confiscation to follow for certain, and perhaps a prosecution as well," implies that he deals in the always highly valued, imported condom (102). As early as the 1770s, for instance, one Mrs. Philips of "No.5, *Orange-court*, near *Leicester-fields*," was circulating handbills announcing that "She defies any one in *England* to equal her goods, and hath lately had several large orders from *France, Spain, Portugal, Italy*, and other foreign places. Captains of ships, and gentlemen going abroad, may be supplied with any quantity of the best goods on the shortest notice" (Grose 10–11). The ultimate irony here, however, is that Conrad seems to have prophylactically obscured the fact of Verloc's condom trade in the novel by muting the explicitness of some of these passages when he revised the serial version of *The Secret Agent*. His description of the object purchased in the transaction I have just quoted, for example, instead of reading "a small cardboard box with apparently nothing inside," was originally the more explicit: "a small cardboard box labelled superfine Indiarubber" in both the manuscript and the serial text of the novel (331).

Mrs. PHILIPS, who about ten years left off bufinefs, having been prevailed on by her friends to reaffume the fame again
upon reprefentations that, fince her declining, they cannot
procure any goods comparable to thofe fhe ufed to vend ;——
begs leave to acquaint her friends and cuftomers, that fhe has
taken a houfe, No. 5, *Orange-court*, near *Leicefter-fields*, one
end going into *Orange-ftreet*, the other into *Cafile-ftreet*, near
the *Upper Mews-gate*.—To prevent miftakes, over the door is
the fign of the *Golden Fan* and *Rifing Sun*, a lamp adjoining
to the fign, and fan mounts in the window, where fhe continues to carry on her bufinefs as ufual.——She defies any one
in *England* to equal her goods, and hath lately had feveral
large orders from *France, Spain, Portugal, Italy,* and other
foreign places. Captains of fhips, and gentlemen going
abroad, may be fupplied with any quantity of the beft
goods on the fhorteft notice.

☞ It is well known to the public fhe has had *thirty-five
years experience*, in the bufinefs of making and felling machines,
commonly called implements of fafety, which fecures the
health of her cuftomers : fhe has likewife great choice of fkins
and bladders, where apothecaries, chymifts, druggifts, &c.
may be fupplied with any quantity of the beft fort.—And
whereas fome perfon or perfons pretending to know and carry
on the faid bufinefs, difcovering the preference given to her
goods fince coming into bufinefs again, have induftrioufly
and malicioufly reported that the *Original* Mrs. PHILIPS is
dead, and that fuch perfon or perfons is or are her fucceffors
(which is entirely falfe and without the leaft foundation), and
hath and doth, or have and do, utter or deliver out in the
name of *Philips,* and as from her warehoufe, a moft infamous
and obfcene hand-bill or advertifement ; the public are hereby
affured, that fuch perfon or perfons is or are a mere impoftor or
impoftors, and that the real original Mrs. PHILIPS lives and
carries on her bufinefs in *Orange-court* aforefaid, and not elfe-
where (as can be teftified by many who daily fee her behind
her counter), and that fhe hath no concern whatfoever in the
bufinefs publifhed by fuch hand-bills of theirs, notwithftand-
ing the impudent ufe of her name thereto affixed ; and neither
prepares or vends, or ever did or ever will prepare or vend,
any other goods than thofe above fpecified. She alfo fells all
forts of perfumes. The following lines are very applicable
to her goods :

> *To guard yourfelf from fhame or fear,*
> *Votaries to Venus, haften here ;*
> *None in my wares e'er found a flaw,*
> *Self prefervation's nature's law.*

Figure 6.1. "Votaries to Venus" in London would evidently "hasten" to Mrs. Philips to
purchase their "machines, commonly called implements of safety." Judging from the "war
of handbills" that occasioned this advertisement (circa 1776), there was fierce competition
in the London condom trade (Himes 199). From Francis Grose, *A Guide to Health, Beauty,
Riches, and Honour* (London: S. Hooper, 1783), 10–11.

Prophylactic imagery proliferates in *The Secret Agent*—coats, cloaks, veils, and most especially Verloc's omnipresent hat—but the more important point is that the novel thematically and structurally reinforces the idea of prophylaxis. The Assistant Commissioner, who like Verloc sees his work in terms of "social protection" (82), decides that the best response for the British government is *no reaction at all* to Mr. Vladimir's scheme for provoking police action and thus prevents Vladimir's plot from having any large national and international consequences. Similarly, Stevie's accidental death, his stumbling with the Greenwich bomb and thereby both blowing himself to bits and absorbing the full impact of the explosion with his body, is an act of prophylactic suppression that also involves the death of the idiot boy, a kind of little man or homunculus.[6] Structurally, Conrad shows the shock of the literally and figuratively abortive terrorist attack climactically moving outward and upward in a series of chapters, until balked by the bulky figure of Sir Ethelred, the Home Secretary. This "great personage['s]" prophylactic decision to suppress an understandable official response (105), in effect, turns the novel and the consequences of the bombing back upon themselves. Correspondingly, after "the police ha[ve] managed to smother so nicely" the affair (230), the balance of the tale traces its rebound shock effects, first on Mr. Vladimir whose awe of "the miraculous cleverness of the English police" leaves him "slightly sick" (171), then on Verloc who is "shaken morally to pieces" (174), and then on his wife: shock "waves [. . .] of the proper length, propagated in accordance with correct mathematical formulas, flowed around all the inanimate things in the room, lapped against Mrs. Verloc's head as if had been a head of stone" (195). These waves then propagate the wife's murder of her husband, the consequent shock of this action upon Winnie, and finally the impact of her suicide upon Comrade Ossipon, within whose hollow interior Conrad leaves the last waves of reaction to reverberate as the novel ends.

Conrad published *The Secret Agent* on 10 September 1907 (Ford, "James Joyce" 6), and Joyce purchased the 1907 Tauchnitz edition for his Treiste library. He probably acquired the novel shortly after its publication, because he apparently used some of the vocabulary in the Verloc-Vladimir conversation in chapter 2 when tutoring his Triestine English students.[7] It is hard to imagine Joyce not being struck, when he read *The Secret Agent*, by the two bedroom encounters between Adolph and Winnie Verloc in Conrad's novel (47–51, 136–38), which resemble his treatment of Gabriel and Gretta Conroy at Gresham Hotel in the recently written conclusion of "The Dead." (Joyce apparently completed this story, coincidentally, on or about 10 September

1907 [Ellmann, *James Joyce* 263–64].) In both Verloc scenes the gas has similarly been turned off, the wife has also preceded her spouse in bed, and the
husband likewise looks upon her recumbent form. In the first of these, Verloc
observes himself, Gabriel-like, in the "looking glass" and shortly after turns
his gaze to the "window-pane" (48). As in the conclusion to "The Dead," the
married couple have verbal discourse rather than sexual intercourse in both
Secret Agent scenes, although with Conrad's pair the conversations are as inef-
fectual as we gather their sexual relations to be. In each, Verloc fails to con-
fide his problems to Winnie (49–50, 137) and is too distracted to make any
response to his wife's attempts at conversation. Most significantly, however,
Conrad describes the quality of Verloc's love for his wife in terms that would
have strongly reminded Joyce of Gabriel's proprietary relationship to Gretta:
"Mr. Verloc loved his wife as a wife should be loved—that is, maritally, with
the regard one has for one's chief possession" (137).

There seems to be no clear evidence for how extensively Joyce might have
revised "The Dead," after completing its initial draft simultaneously with
Conrad's publication of *The Secret Agent*, so it would seem safer to suggest
that he appreciated the novel's treatment of the Verlocs, when he *did* read
the book, than to argue that Conrad exerted any direct influence on the final
scene of Joyce's story.[8] Nevertheless, *The Secret Agent* must have arrested his
attention, and he seems to have kept Conrad's book in mind approximately a
dozen years later when he worked on the final stages of *Ulysses*. There is also
little doubt that Joyce would have understood and appreciated the motif of
prophylaxis in Conrad. Joyce seems to have considered condoms disreputable
(Brown 65), and we have no way of knowing whether he used them himself
either for protection or for contraception (Lowe-Evans 26), but we do know
that he was intensely interested in birth control issues and contraceptive practices when he was writing *Dubliners* and, indeed, throughout his career.[9] He
would have recognized the signals Conrad uses to indicate Verloc's condom
trade. While the sale of prophylactics was not strictly illegal in England (or
the United States, despite the restraints on their trade imposed by the Comstock laws), as it was in Ireland until only recently, it was always a decidedly
shady business, licit or illicit, tainted by the association of condom use with
random promiscuity. Bordellos and prostitutes were, logically, chief sources
for condoms for much of their history, although not necessarily the only
distributors by the beginning of the twentieth century.[10] As James Carens
has discovered, Alec Bannon's reference to a *"marchand de capotes,* Monsieur

Poyntz" in the Oxen of the Sun episode of *Ulysses* is topical (*U* 14.776): apparently young men of comparatively tender years obtained their contraceptives from the "waterproofers and hosiers" S.R. Poyntz & Co. in turn-of-the-century Dublin (346). Leopold Bloom, however, seems to have preferred mail-order prophylactics. In Ithaca we learn that he has "purchased by post from Box 32, P.O., Charing Cross, London, W.C.," both "erotic photocards" and "rubber preservatives with reserve pockets" (*U* 17.1805, 1809, 1804), one of which he carries with him as a kind of back-up for his "Potato Preservative against Plague and Pestilence" (*U* 15.1952).

Joyce, in fact, associates Bloom with the condom at a number of places in *Ulysses*. As both he and Molly remark, he carries his "French letter" in his "pocketbook" (*U* 13.877; 18.1235), with two in reserve that Molly doesn't know about in the locked drawer of the sideboard (*U* 17.1804). Although he has liberated the *Photo Bits* nymph from the indignity of coexisting with ads for contraceptives—"Rubber Goods. Neverrip brand as supplied to the aristocracy" (*U* 15.3256)—elsewhere in Circe he advocates free distribution to the masses of "rubber preservatives in sealed envelopes tied with gold thread" (*U* 15.1571) and is shortly after accused by Theodore Purefoy of "employ[ing] a mechanical device to frustrate the sacred ends of nature" (*U* 15.1741–42). (Yet another eighteenth-century code word for the condom is "machine" [Youssef 227; Kruck 8].)[11] Beyond his personal and perhaps ideological investments in condoms, Bloom's suppression of his habitual "Mr. Knowall" (*U* 12.838) opinions through that most prophylactic of the novel's episodes, Oxen of the Sun, is itself a prophylactic gesture, a form of self-restraint as he, for instance, "enjoin[s] his heart to repress all motions of a rising choler and, by intercepting them with the readiest precaution, foster[s] within his breast [a] plentitude of sufferance" amidst the episode's "tumultuary discussions" (*U* 14.861–63, 849). And I would argue that Joyce's related conception of his own textual prophylaxis in this same episode, his figurative and, as we shall see, *literal* condomization of his text, strongly suggests his unacknowledged debt to Conrad's example in *The Secret Agent*, particularly as he worked on the latest stages of his composition of *Ulysses*.[12]

In the Ithaca episode, for instance, Joyce presents Leopold Bloom's response to the "outrage" at 7 Eccles Street (*U* 17.2196–97), his wife's potentially explosive infidelity, in terms very similar to the official reaction to the "bomb outrage in Greenwich Park" in *The Secret Agent* (144). Rather than return to his home and bed as "an estranged avenger, a wreaker of justice on malefactors, a dark crusader, a sleeper awakened" (*U* 17.2020–22), Bloom decides his best response to Molly's revolutionary gesture is *no reaction at all*, nor any immediate act of "retribution" (*U* 17.2200). Ithaca, furthermore, concludes with condomized intercourse, strictly verbal, between Leopold and his wife, a conversation in which he is as disingenuous as Verloc. If "sex is just another form of talk" (D. H. Lawrence 70), and talk is just another form of sex, neither the talk nor the sex is very good for husband and wife in this scene. Appropriately, this is the point in *Ulysses* where Joyce makes clear that Bloom and Molly have not had "complete carnal intercourse" for "10 years, 5 months and 18 days" (*U* 17.2278, 2282), nor have they enjoyed "complete *mental intercourse*" for "9 months and 1 day" (*U* 17.2285, 2289; my emphases). Like Conrad, in other words, Joyce makes explicit the prophylactic suppression of the "sacred ends" of both sex and speech through the relationship of Bloom and Molly. The Blooms' culminating, cross-purpose conversation, like the dialogues in *The Secret Agent*, challenges both one of its parties, in this case Molly, and of course the readers as well to decipher exactly what her husband has said. (We will never know whether Bloom has "ask[ed] to get his breakfast in bed," as Molly assumes [*U* 18.01–02].) Nevertheless, despite some uncertainties at the end of Ithaca, the readers of *Ulysses* can naturalize this scene and penetrate the author's stylistic and technical sheaths, as in most of the novel, with modest effort. They know with extraordinary precision who is speaking to whom, more or less what each is saying, and when and where they are conversing (as Joyce, for example, scrupulously describes the Blooms' "posture[s]" in bed, "relatively to themselves and to each other" [*U* 17.2311, 2307]). The same cannot be said, however, for much of Oxen of the Sun, the episode that most resists these strategies of naturalization and the episode that is centrally concerned with the frustration of the "sacred ends of nature."

The opacity of Joyce's style in Oxen in the Sun far exceeds anything found in Conrad. More than this, Joyce takes his predecessor's exercise in imitative form a step further, as I will suggest, to use the condom as yet another of the several structural models for this episode. Mary Lowe-Evans's description of the theme of Oxen as "intricate and nearly indecipherable" is only one of the more recent in a long tradition of critical responses to this chapter that seem to echo the complaint of Conrad's Assistant Commissioner: "You shouldn't leave me to puzzle things out for myself like this" (97). Edmund Wilson, for an early example, regrets that "in the maternity hospital, at the climactic scenes of the story, [. . .] Joyce has bogged us as he has never bogged us before" (*Axel's Castle* 216), missing the central point that Joyce has staged, in fact, the prophylactic anti-climax of the narrative thrust of *Ulysses*. Like many readers, Wilson is frustrated by the incomplete intercourse here between author and audience. At the most basic level, Joyce repeatedly thwarts, as he will again throughout *Finnegans Wake*, the readers' natural appetite to know who's speaking to whom, what each is saying, what they look like, or even who sits where in the room; contrast this to the conclusion of Ithaca or to virtually every other scene in *Ulysses*. "Joyce has here half-buried his story under the virtuosity of his technical devices," Wilson complains. "It is almost as if he had elaborated it so much and worked over it so long that he had forgotten, in the amusement of writing parodies, the drama which he had originally intended to stage." Little realizing, it seems, the intimations of contraception and prophylaxis in what he is saying, Wilson concludes his commentary observing that Joyce defrauds his readers by suppressing the climax of his novel—"we [. . . are] dissatisfied with the flatness [. . .] of Dedalus's final meeting with Bloom"—as if he wishes to prevent both insemination and contamination, that is, "as if he did not, after all, quite want us to understand his story, as if he had, not quite conscious of what he was doing, ended by throwing up between us and it a *fortification* of solemn burlesque prose—as if he were shy and solicitous about it, and wanted to *protect* it from us" (*Axel's Castle* 217; my emphases). If the writer's pen is, indeed, the penis, as *Finnegans Wake* maintains, for Oxen of the Sun Joyce's wears a condom.[13]

Benefiting from our access to the author's own intentions for Oxen of the Sun, unlike Wilson in 1931, we now know that this critic, by feeling defrauded, is responding to the episode exactly as Joyce wished. Among the "Correspondences" on the Gorman-Gilbert schema, Joyce identifies the "Crime" of "Fraud" for this episode (Ellmann, *Ulysses on the Liffey* appendix), a motif that embraces Stephen's misrepresentation of the source of his earnings, Bloom's "pelican" piety (*U* 14.921), and much else, but also the crime of birth control. (At the turn of the century, "fraud" was "a common name for contraception" [Lowe-Evans 73].) We also have Joyce's much-quoted 20 March 1920 letter to Frank Budgen, written as he worked on Oxen of the Sun, wherein he identifies his main "idea" as "the crime committed against fecundity by sterilizing the act of coition" and then delightedly outlines, as he then saw it, his exercise in imitative form: the embryological model for the nine stages of the episode's linguistic development (*Selected Letters* 251). In her book *Crimes against Fecundity*, Mary Lowe-Evans excellently surveys the various social, ideological, and ecclesiastical forces that converged to sterilize coition, both literally and figuratively, in early twentieth-century Ireland (53–74), and Robert Janusko thoroughly explores the episode's "Embryological Framework" in his *Sources and Structures of James Joyce's "Oxen"* (39–54). What both overlook, however, is the contradiction between Joyce's main idea of contraception and his purported formal paradigm based upon fecundation.[14] I want to argue that Joyce, while keeping with his plan to structure much of his episode upon the development of the embryo, simultaneously cannibalizes this structure with a patterned association between the episode's progress and the act of sexual intercourse, or more specifically, condomized sex. The pattern begins with the initial penetration of Bloom's entrance into the hospital, intensifies in friction with the episode's debates, has its momentary longueurs in Bloom's reveries, and then climaxes with Stephen's outburst: "Burkes! outflings my lord Stephen, giving the cry" (*U* 14.1391). The virtue of this suggestion is that it helps us better understand Joyce's purpose for the last several pages of Oxen of the Sun, which Janusko believes represent a kind of afterbirth—"The tailpiece [. . .] is probably best considered as the placenta" (53)—whereas I would argue that this swirling mass of ejaculations, fragmentary phrases, and word particles disseminates the unfecundating seeds of conversation, the residue of both verbal and sexual intercourse that remains after the prophylactic sterilization of coition.[15] The artist's pen in Oxen of the Sun, then, is not condomized by "a stout shield of oxengut" (*U* 14.465), but by one of those new and improved condoms of the turn of the century, favored by Bloom, that contain the residue of intercourse in its reservoir tip, a "reserve pocket" at its end (*U* 17.1804).[16]

Joyce's use of a latent (if not yet latex) condom as an objective correlative for the textual prophylaxis of Oxen of the Sun not only resembles the thematic and structural strategies of condomization in *The Secret Agent*, but also replicates yet another fundamental irony in Conrad's book: both authors figuratively employ a mass-cultural product as a shield to protect their works from full communication with, and contamination by, mass culture itself. In doing so, Joyce and Conrad engage in what Andreas Huyssen describes as the "compulsive *pas de deux*" modernism and mass culture have danced "ever since their simultaneous emergence in the mid-19th century" (57). Huyssen's *After the Great Divide*, as well as Peter Bürger's *Theory of the Avant-Garde* and, for Joyce studies, Margot Norris's *Joyce's Web*, have crystallized our awareness of how the "modernist aesthetic" functioned as a prophylactic "reaction formation" to contemporary mass culture: "Only by fortifying its boundaries, by maintaining its purity and autonomy, and by avoiding any contamination with mass culture and with the signifying systems of everyday life can the art work maintain its adversary stance: adversary to the bourgeois culture of everyday life as well as adversary to mass culture and entertainment which are seen as the primary forms of bourgeois cultural articulation" (Huyssen 53–54). Yet, as Norris makes clear and as the dual motifs of contraception and fecundation of Oxen of the Sun also suggest, there is a vital difference between Conrad's and Joyce's embrace of this modernist aesthetic: while *The Secret Agent* illustrates the artist's privileging the autonomy of the work of art as "totally separate from the realms of mass culture and everyday life" (Huyssen 53), Oxen of the Sun and *Ulysses* as a whole are "dramatization[s] and reenactment[s]" of "the oppressive social function of art and texts" implicit in the aesthetic ideal of autonomy (Norris, *Joyce's Web* 147). In other words, Joyce's work both exemplifies and critiques the "autonomy aesthetic" of modernism (Bürger 10), simultaneously embodying "an anxiety of contamination by," and celebrating its conversation with, "its other: an increasingly consuming and engulfing mass culture" (Huyssen vii), as the next two chapters, on Joyce's cannibalization of the technologies of sound reproduction, film, radio, and television, will further illustrate. More immediately, however, if Joyce's condomization of the text of Oxen of the Sun is consistent with the modernist suppression of direct intercourse with the public sphere, his dissemination of the potentially fecundating seeds of discourse at the episode's conclusion (to bear fruit when released in *Finnegans Wake*), together with his imbedded paradigm of fecundation and gestation, parallel the contemporary protest of what Peter Bürger calls "the historical avant-garde," whose aim was to attack the political impotence of the autonomy aesthetic as a crime against fecundity and thus "reintegrate art into the praxis of life, [by] reveal[ing] the nexus between autonomy and the *absence of any consequences*" (27, 22; emphases mine).

There has been relatively little discussion of Joyce's relationship to such avant-garde movements as Dada or surrealism, even though he lived (and composed much of *Ulysses*) in Zurich contemporaneously with Tristan Tzara, Hans Arp, and others, for reasons well articulated by Margot Norris. The "canonization" of Joyce as the preeminent modernist author and the consequent "equation of Joyce with the aestheticism of modernism" (*Joyce's Web* 6)—most notably in T. S. Eliot's praise for his ahistorical "use of Homeric myth in *Ulysses* as 'a step toward making the modern world possible for art'" (*Joyce's Web* 5; Eliot, "*Ulysses*, Order, and Myth" 202)—have totally occluded his investment in the avant-gardist critique of "the detachment of art as a special sphere of human activity from the nexus of the praxis of life" (Bürger 36).[17] And for that matter, there has been no consideration, to my knowledge, of Joseph Conrad's possible response to the turn-of-the-century avant-garde. Nevertheless, I would argue that both *Ulysses* and *The Secret Agent* share one final important similarity, as well as a strong contrast, in their reflection of the avant-gardist attacks on the late nineteenth- and early twentieth-century bourgeois institution of art "as a social realm that is set apart from the means-end rationality of daily bourgeois existence" (Bürger 10). In radical resistance to the idea of autonomy in fin-de-siècle aestheticism and an emergent modernism, the avant-garde sought to reintegrate "art into life praxis," to close "the gap separating art from reality," and thus to "make art productive for social change" (Huyssen 8). In short, the avant-garde attempted to conjoin art with "political and social revolution" (Huyssen 12).

For a renowned political novel, *The Secret Agent* is strangely apolitical in its messages that the best action is inaction and that the masses are well served by remaining in ignorance of the causes and import of the Greenwich bombing. In fact, Conrad's book is equally if not more concerned with the political as a metaphoric substitute for the aesthetic, to make a case for the detachment of art from the public sphere of action. To see this clearly, it helps to recognize that "[t]hroughout the 19th century the idea of the avantgarde [was] linked to political radicalism," finding "its way into socialist anarchism and eventually into substantial segments of the bohemian subcultures of the turn of the century" (Huyssen 4–5). In this light we can see that Conrad demonizes the Professor both as the "perfect" political anarchist (67) and as an avant-garde artist, "free from everything artificial [. . . and] all sorts of conventions" (57), much as he presents the equally insidious Mr. Vladimir as a kind of artist in the text: "His wit consisted in discovering droll connections between incongruous ideas" (20). Vladimir descends socially and, in Conrad's terms, aesthetically to the level of the avant-garde by planning a "series of outrages" calculated to "influenc[e] the public opinion" (28), beginning with the Greenwich bombing, a quintes-

sential avant-gardist manifestation: "an act of destructive ferocity so absurd
as to be incomprehensible, inexplicable, almost unthinkable; in fact, mad"
(30). Conrad doubles the Professor and Vladimir with the idiot boy Stevie,
who is both a walking bomb and an artist of social protest whose abstract
designs of "circles, circles, circles [. . .] innumerable circles [. . . .] suggested
a rendering of cosmic chaos, the symbolism of a mad art attempting the in-
conceivable" (40), and juxtaposes them all to the only admirable character
in *The Secret Agent*, the Assistant Commissioner, the protector of England's
social and political institutions (read: the institution of autonomous art),
who by virtue of his "miraculous cleverness" (171) thwarts any attempt to
make "art productive for social change" (Huyssen 8).

The obvious artist figure in *Ulysses*, of course, is Stephen Dedalus, whose
ambition to "forge [. . .] the uncreated conscience of [his] race" (*P* 253),
though hardly yet realized, suggests as much his affinity for the avant-gardist attempt to reintegrate art and the praxis of life as his aesthetics in both *A
Portrait of the Artist as a Young Man* (e.g., the ideal of "esthetic stasis" [*P* 206])
and his discussion of Shakespeare, the artist as androgynous "only begetter"
(*U* 9.838–39), in the Scylla and Charybdis episode of *Ulysses* would suggest
his attraction toward the autonomy aesthetic of modernism. The most important point to stress, here, is that Joyce's similarly equivocal relationship
to the pas de deux between the autonomy aesthetic of modernism and the
activism of the avant-garde not only strongly distinguishes his receptiveness
to the avant-gardist critique of the bourgeois institutionalization of art from
Conrad's endorsement of institutional suppression in *The Secret Agent*, but
also acts a major, insufficiently acknowledged, governing tension in *Ulysses*.
And this tension, most apparent in the contradiction between the paradigms
of prophylaxis and fecundation in Oxen of the Sun, bears its ultimate fruit
in *Finnegans Wake*: a novel that sustains, as Norris has brilliantly argued, a
"dialectical relation" between avant-gardism and Joyce's "earlier aestheticism" (*Joyce's Web* 93).[18] The *Wake*, in its sheer complexity, would seem the
limit case of modernist textual condomization. Conversely, in its hypercom-
municativity—its superabundance of discourse, rather than thwarted intercourse—*Finnegans Wake* disseminates the seeds of the conclusion of Oxen
of the Sun, there held in reserve, to generate a work that stands equally as
a monument of literary modernism and of the avant-garde: a socially, politically, and aesthetically revolutionary attempt to make art possible for the
modern world.[19]

Although the historical origins of the condom are shrouded in mystery—Norman Himes finds apparent prototypes among "many primitive peoples, as well as the early Egyptians" (186)—interest in this means of protection from contamination seems clearly to have intensified by the sixteenth century when, as I mentioned at the opening of this chapter, "The first known published description of the condom" appears in a work by Fallopius, "one of the early authorities on syphilis," published in 1564 (Himes 188). Without question, the early modern knowledge, development, and use of the condom result from the sudden outbreak of syphilis in Naples in 1495 and its eventual mutation, by the middle of the sixteenth century, into the venereal disease that infected millions over the succeeding four centuries.[20] While the origins of this disease are as obscure as those of the condom, the chief protection against syphilis, the coincidence between the emergence of this infection in the 1490s and the contemporaneous return of the first voyagers of discovery and exploration in the New World led some early observers to conclude that sailors had contracted syphilis in the Americas and then brought it with them back to Europe. (Though controversial, many epidemiologists continue to accept this etiology.)

As a disease that literally eats away at human flesh, syphilis obviously lent itself to those metaphors of consumption and cannibalism that I discussed in my first chapter. What is less obvious is that some of the many early commentators on syphilis, such as Francis Bacon in his *Sylva Sylvarum* (1627), made the association between the disease and cannibalism direct by speculating that syphilis was "caused by anthropophagy" (Lestringant 161; see chapter 1, note 9). What is striking about this for our present context is that the historic anxiety about this disease and its origins precisely parallels modernism's "anxiety of contamination by its other: an increasingly consuming and engulfing mass culture" (Huyssen vii). The modernist writer fears a contagion—like the venereal disease that manifests itself as a form of consumption—contracted from those who are themselves consumers. The condom, in other words, is both literally and metaphorically a prophylactic against cannibalism.

If this is so, how can I maintain that James Joyce employs a technique of textual prophylaxis while simultaneously engaging an art of creative cannibalism? The answer to this question lies in the distinction between Joseph Conrad and Joyce that I have drawn in this chapter. Whereas Conrad illustrates the modernist's fear of contamination by mass culture, Joyce, through his juxtaposition of the motifs of prophylaxis and fecundation in *Ulysses* and *Finnegans Wake*, both enacts the modernist's reaction against, and celebrates his avant gardist conversation with, the masses. These two apparently irreconcilable responses generate the dialectical tension between blockage and assimilation characteristic of the act of cultural transfer, and they directly parallel the situation of the "spitting cannibal": he who has defensively fed off of others will now generously invite others to feed off of him.

7

His Master's Voice and Joyce

This history of every art form shows critical epochs in which a
certain art form aspires to effects which could be fully obtained only
with a changed technical standard, that is to say, a new art form.
—Benjamin 237

What writers astonished by gramophones, films, and typewriters—
the first technological media—committed to paper between 1880
and 1920 amounts [. . .] to a ghostly image of our present as future.
—Winthrop-Young and Wutz xl

Rare is the essay on the intersections of modern art and technology that
doesn't begin by invoking "The Work of Art in the Age of Mechanical Reproduction" (1936), as I have in my first epigraph, but rarer yet is the critic who,
while adducing Walter Benjamin, does full justice to the equivocal nature
of Benjamin's response to the technology of reproduction or to the limitations in his analysis introduced by his nearly exclusive focus on visual media.
Ostensibly hailing the mass mechanical reproduction of art as the cultural
equivalent and harbinger of the Marxist political evolution toward a classless
society—through the erasure of "outmoded" individualist and elitist conceptions "such as creativity and genius, eternal value and mystery"—Benjamin
nonetheless mourns that which is lost through this leveling process. His word
choice makes this sense of loss clear: "Even the most perfect reproduction
is *lacking*" in uniqueness and "authenticity," the original "is always *depreci-
ated*," and the "'aura'" of the work of art "*withers*" (emphases mine). Twice
echoing the contemporaneous Stalinist euphemism, Benjamin observes "the
liquidation of the traditional value of the cultural heritage" in its mechanical reproduction, "a far-reaching *liquidation*" (Benjamin 218, 220–21, 221–22;
emphases mine). Thus Benjamin's subsequent progressivist claims that mechanical reproduction has emancipated "the work of art from its parasitical
dependence on ritual" are tinged with a melancholia that Max Pensky locates

at "the heart of Benjamin's critical vision," an expression of loss unclearly specified in his essay but suggested by the observed loss of "presence" in the reproduction (Benjamin 224, 221; Pensky 16). If melancholia, unlike mourning, involves a "shift[ing] away" of the sense of loss from a beloved object to another site, according to Freud's distinction of these terms, I would argue that Benjamin's virtual exclusion of the technology of sound reproduction from his argument betrays the displaced origin of his melancholy (Freud 586). As Friedrich A. Kittler observes in *Gramophone, Film, Typewriter*, "lithography and photography [. . .] (according to Benjamin's thesis) in the first third of the nineteenth century merely propelled the work of art into the age of its technical reproducibility," whereas Edison's inventions of the phonograph (1877) and the kinetoscope (1892), "storage technologies that can record and reproduce the very time flow of acoustic and optical data," had by far the greater impact on twentieth-century culture: these new media "changed the state of reality" (3). These two technologies, Kittler maintains, subverted the cultural hegemony of "Gutenbergiana" and ultimately superseded the written/printed text and image; the gramophone, specifically, provoked in modern writers a compensatory response—"the transformation of literature into sound"—lest "Record grooves dig the grave of the author" (9, 59, 83). Joyce's *Ulysses*, though but once cited by Kittler (*Gramophone* 12), provides a striking illustration for his argument. More than this, *Ulysses* evokes in its readers something analogous to the source of Benjamin's melancholy, for the loss they experience in this book is generated by the sound of the master's *voice*, or what Jacques Derrida describes, with an echo of a recording industry slogan, as the "so-called living presence" that "is represented" in "the work of mourning" ("By Force" 178, 172).[1]

In his essay "The Storyteller" (1936), published in the same year as "The Work of Art in the Age of Mechanical Reproduction," Benjamin more directly confronts the losses of immediacy and authenticity, what he calls the "decay of the aura" in the latter essay, in the work of literature per se, attributing this deterioration once again to the technology of reproduction. "The art of storytelling is reaching its end," he claims, locating the "earliest symptom" of this process in "the rise of the novel at the beginning of modern times," another new art form that arose from technological change: "The dissemination of the novel became possible only with the invention of printing" (87). Here Benjamin explicitly mourns the loss of the storyteller's "living presence" in terms of voice, of sound no longer heard, in the silent reading of the printed text: "Familiar though his name may be to us, the storyteller in his living immediacy is by no means a present force" (83). This decay of storytelling, "a process that has been going on for a long time," Benjamin sees as "a concomitant symptom of the secular productive forces of history, a concomitant that has quite gradually removed narrative from the realm of living speech and at the same time is making it possible to see a new beauty in what is vanishing" (87). What Benjamin elides in this argument is the fact that his recognition of the new beauty in the purportedly dying oral tradition is itself a concomitant symptom of the technological development of sound recording. As Kittler remarks, "since it has become possible to record the epics of the last Homeric bards, who until recently were wandering through Serbia and Croatia, oral mnemotechnics or cultures have become reconstructible in a completely different way. [. . .] 'Primary orality' and 'oral history' came into existence only after the end of the writing monopoly, as the technological shadows of the apparatuses that document them" (*Gramophone* 7). What I want to argue, through the example of Joyce's response to the technology of sound recording in *Ulysses*, is that Benjamin's saturnine temperament, his conviction of "the impossibility of recovering what was lost" (Pensky 19), prevents him from recognizing that the age of mechanical reproduction brought to artists like Joyce a new awareness of the beauty that had vanished in the silent reading of the printed text; rather than disappearing, the voice of the storyteller becomes immediate in the "talking machine" of the new modernist novel.[2]

But more than just a recovery of voice is involved in the transformation of literature into sound. The phonograph is not only a machine for recording "talk," but also a *sound* machine, a technology capable of storing and reproducing the full range of auditory information, all ordered and disordered sounds, from speech or music to *noise*, which "neither the mirror of the imaginary [film] nor the grid of the symbolic [typewriter] can catch: the physiological accidents and stochastic disorder of bodies" that Kittler equates with the Lacanian *réel* (*Gramophone* 16). As Geoffrey Winthrop-Young and Michael Wutz observe, Kittler identifies the real with the phonograph because, "regardless of meaning or intent, [it] records all the voices and utterances produced by bodies, thus separating the signifying function of words (the domain of the imaginary in the discourse network of 1800 [i.e., prior to photography or film]) as well as their materiality (the graphic traces corresponding to the symbolic) from unseeable and unwritable noises" (xxviii).

In *Ulysses,* Joyce's thorough assimilation of these manifold consequences of sound reproduction that move him to represent the full range of auditory stimuli from voice to noise and, as I shall argue, his recognition of the commercial impact of the contemporary recording industry as well, combine to realize the prophecy of Paul Valéry, which Benjamin quotes in his epigraph for "The Work of Art in the Age of Mechanical Reproduction": "*We must expect great innovations to transform the entire technique of the arts, thereby affecting artistic invention itself and perhaps even bringing about an amazing change in our very notion of art*" (qtd. Benjamin 217). It would be possible to argue *Ulysses'*s appropriateness to Valéry's thesis, or to Kittler's contention that modern literature, under the influence of phonography, turns toward the reproduction of sound, strictly in terms of Joyce's strategies for incorporating "unseeable and unwritable noises" into his book. For economy's sake, however, I want to concentrate my argument on his strategy of approximating the heretofore unrepresentable sound of animals, nonhuman voices, in *Ulysses.* My narrowing of focus allows me to make the collateral argument that Joyce was alive to both the aesthetic and the commercial challenges offered by the contemporary technology of sound reproduction in the first quarter of the twentieth century, epitomized in the multinational industry of His Master's Voice and its trademark symbol of the attentive fox terrier, Little Nipper. To make these arguments, however, I must begin with the last of the many voices Joyce ventriloquizes in *Ulysses,* the mistress's voice, Molly Bloom's.

Through the course of the Penelope chapter of *Ulysses,* Molly enumerates her husband Leopold's many eccentricities and flaws, but she also fairly estimates his numerous virtues, admitting, for instance, that "he knows a lot of mixedup things" (*U* 18.179–80). Better yet, "Poldy anyhow whatever he does always wipes his feet on the mat when he comes in wet or shine and always blacks his own boots too and he always takes off his hat when he comes up the street" (*U* 18.225–27). And Leopold, we learn from his wife, has a "splendid set of teeth" (*U* 18.307). She is proud, too, that her husband is more financially responsible than the average Dubliner: "he has sense enough not to squander every penny piece he earns down their gullets and looks after his wife and family" (*U* 18.1277–79). Of course, she's grateful for his gift of a name, Bloom, that's "better than Breen or Briggs [. . .] or those awful names with bottom in them" (*U* 18.843–44). First of her monologue's list of his virtues, however, is his kindness to old women—"still I like that in him polite to old women" (*U* 18.16)—even if it be an old crone like Dante Riordan with her irritating "Skye terrier" (*U* 8.848). In Lestrygonians Bloom remembers Molly "fondling" Mrs. Riordan's dog "in her lap" when they all lived in "the City Arms hotel" and her attempt to converse with the terrier in its own language: "O, the big doggybowwowsywowsy" (*U* 8.848–49). Molly's memory of Dante's "dog smelling my fur" when she was pregnant with Rudy is less fond; evidently like most males in her life, the terrier was "always edging to get up under my petticoats especially then" (*U* 18.14–16), not that she's averse to males, like Mulvey, attempting to "touch me inside my petticoat" (*U* 18.811). Thinking later of a different kind of dog in another kind of hotel, she recalls from her Gibraltar days that "I tormented the life out of [Mulvey] first tickling him I loved rousing that dog in the hotel," and she and Joyce once again attempt a kind of doggy transliteration—"rrrssstt awokwokawok his eyes shut" (*U* 18.812–13)—to approximate Mulvey's animal response when Molly "pulled him off into [her] handkerchief" (*U* 18.809–10).

So far as I know, no one has put a name to Joyce's representation of such sounds in written text, whether it be Molly's attempt at animal language, such as "doggybowwowsywowsy," verbalized animalistic human sound like her rendering of Mulvey's "rrrssstt awokwokawok," nonverbal animal sound like Bloom's fart in Sirens—"Prrprr […] Fff! […] Rrpr. […] Pprrpffrrppffff" (*U* 11.1286–93)—not to mention actual animal speech, like the cat's meows in Calypso, or, ranging even further, such mechanical noises as the tram that muffles Bloom's fart—"Tram kran kran kran . […] Krandlkrankran. […] Kraaaaaa" (*U* 11.1290–91)—or the "door of Rutledge's office whisper[ing]: ee: cree" and the "Sllt . […] sllt […] Sllt . […] sllt […] sllt […] Sllt" of the printing press in Aeolus (*U* 7.50, 174–77): "Sllt. Almost human the way it sllt to call attention. Doing its level best to speak" (*U* 7.175–76). We should probably call Joyce's orthographical strategy "phonography" or "gramophony," could we free these two terms from their immediate association with the mechanical reproduction of sound, misnomers that were already in general misuse by the beginning of the twentieth century. Thomas A. Edison and Emile Berliner coined the neologisms *phonograph* and *gramophone*, respectively, for their competing inventions that could capture and reproduce sound, despite the fact that each word actually signifies the *written* representation of sound.[3] Derrida touches on this same recognition in his 1984 Frankfurt symposium address "*Ulysses* Gramophone," referring to Joyce's "dream of a reproduction which *preserves*" writing "in the liveliest voice" as his "gramophone effect," but he turns from this to attend to the ways he hears Joyce's submerged voice in

Figure 7.1. Photograph of Thomas Alva Edison proudly displaying his newly invented cylindrical phonograph, 1878. For an example of his perfected phonograph of 1888, see figure 7.5. Courtesy of U.S. Department of the Interior, National Park Service, Edison National Park Service.

the text (43–44). Another implication of Joyce's phonography, however, is its reflection of the enormous impact of Edison's sound-recording machine, "the most important" invention of his career, not only on popular culture early in the twentieth century, but also on a literary culture moved to "an aesthetics of terror" by its reasonable fear that mechanical sound reproduction could rival the novel's textual representation of narrative (Israel 142; Winthrop-Young and Wutz xl).

Edison's phonograph was born less than five years before Joyce, in the autumn of 1877, commercially developed in the late 1880s, and reached maturity, like Joyce, at the turn of the century, commonly to be found in places of public entertainment like the brothels of Dublin's nighttown, also like Joyce, in 1904. By the early 1920s, about the same time that James Joyce's name and his novel *Ulysses* became household words, the gramophone was the popular domestic form of entertainment that it remains, in its various current incarnations, today. As the invention of photography, for example, led visual artists to compensatory forms of response—this is one explanation for the development of impressionism and later movements in painting—so also did the invention of mechanical sound reproduction lead a writer like Joyce to develop a kind of compensatory or competitive narrative strategy for the representation of sound in the written text, much as he contends with and assimilates the new audio and visual technologies of radio and television in *Finnegans Wake*. On a number of occasions in *Ulysses* Joyce alludes to the nascent technology of sound reproduction, as it would be found in Dublin in 1904, as well as to the contemporary fascination with the possibilities for this invention that might rival traditional forms of narrative entertainment. Moreover, although this association may seem arbitrary, in *Ulysses* Joyce connects the idea of gramophony with the representation of, specifically, the animal's voice. And finally, Joyce cannibalizes the most famous trademark of the gramophone, the little dog Nipper and the slogan "His Master's Voice," for his own uses in *Ulysses*.

One of Leopold Bloom's virtues that Molly fails to list or appreciate in Penelope is his kindness to animals, perhaps because it has led him in the past to bring home wounded creatures, "like the night he walked home with a dog if you please" (*U* 18.1086–87), a "dog (breed unknown) with a lame paw" (*U* 16.1607–08), or like the evening of *Ulysses* when he brings home the "poor dogsbody" Stephen Dedalus (*U* 1.112) who has "hurt his hand too" (*U* 16.1609). Among Bloom's first actions in the book is his morning feeding of the family cat. The cat responds to Bloom's "kindly" attentions (*U* 4.21) not with a simple meow, "m-e-o-w," but with a rich vocabulary that announces Joyce's intention to expand the range of representable voice in fiction: "Mkgnao!" "Prr. [. . .] Prr," "Mrkgnao!" "Mrkrgnao!" and "Gurrhr!" (*U* 4.16, 19–20, 25, 32, 38). At lunchtime, in Lestrygonians Bloom feeds "two Banbury cakes" to the gulls, "those poor birds" on the Liffey, strangely receiving, as he notes, not a sound of thanks: "Lot of thanks I get. Not even a caw" (*U* 8.74–75, 73, 84). In Circe, however, the gulls compensate for their in-

Figure 7.2. The world-famous HMV trademark, from a mid-1920s recording by the organist and notoriously eccentric author Cecil Whitaker-Wilson. "Little Nipper" and the gramophone first began to appear on British record labels in February 1909. Courtesy of EMI Archives.

gratitude by testifying to Bloom's generosity in "doing good to others": "Kaw kave kankury kake" (*U* 15.682, 686). In Cyclops Bloom's normal kindness to animals is tested by the Citizen's hostile dog Garryowen, the most famous talking animal in *Ulysses*, who seems to be the same dog as Gerty MacDowell's "grandpapa Giltrap's lovely dog Garryowen that almost talked" (*U* 13.232–33; also see *U* 12.753). Joyce's delightfully parodic account of "the famous old Irish red setter wolfdog['s]" recitation of "canine" verse, however, a "really marvellous exhibition" (*U* 12.714–15, 734, 714), might make us overlook the cameo appearance of an even more famous dog, the Victor Talking Machine Company's "distinctive symbol," the "quaint little fox terrier" Little Nipper, who shows up in the Circe chapter of *Ulysses* (Wile 225n). Expanding upon

Figure 7.3. Francis Barraud's *His Master's Voice* (1899), his revised version of *Dog Looking at and Listening to a Phonograph* (see figure 7.5 below). The dog listening to a Berliner gramophone was adopted as the trademark of the British Gramophone Company (1899–), later HMV, of the Victor Talking Machine Company in America (1901–), and subsequently of numerous continental affiliates of HMV. Courtesy Thomson (RCA) and EMI Archives.

his usual role of listening to "His Master's Voice," in *Ulysses* Little Nipper also speaks.

Pursuing Stephen and Lynch as Circe opens, Leopold Bloom enters night-town via Mabbot Street, briefly stopping into *"Olhausen's, the porkbutcher's"* to purchase *"a lukewarm pig's crubeen"* and *"a cold sheep's trotter"* (*U* 15.155, 158–59). *"A liver and white spaniel,"* who moments before has growled at a passing Stephen (*U* 15.100), *"approaches"* Bloom, *"sniffing"* out the crubeen and trotter (*U* 15.247). Over several pages of the text, the same dog literally *hounds* Bloom into giving him the crubeen and trotter with a series of plead-ing sounds and gestures: *"whining piteously, wagging his tail,"* *"his tongue out-lolling, panting,"* *"driv*[ing] *a cold snivelling muzzle against* [Bloom's] *hand,"* and finally *"sprawl*[ing] *on his back, wriggling obscenely with begging paws, his long black tongue lolling out"* (*U* 15.532, 633, 659, 663–64). "Strange how they take to me," Bloom muses (*U* 15.660), tentatively calling the dog "Garryowen" (*U* 15.663). At least Joyce's scene directions make clear that this is one and the same hound that hounds Bloom through these pages, although either because, like the dog he once took home, its "breed [is] unknown" (*U* 16.1607), or because the episode is dominated by magical Circean transformations, the dog metamorphoses in the episode's scene directions from "*spaniel*" (*U* 15.100), to "*retriever*" (*U* 15.247), to "*terrier*" (*U* 15.357), to "*retriever*" again (*U* 15.659), to "*wolfdog*" (*U* 15.663), to "*setter*" (*U* 15.667), to "*mastiff*" (*U* 15.673), to "*spaniel*" once again (*U* 15.690), to "*bulldog*" (*U* 15.692), to "*boarhound*" (*U* 15.706), to "*greyhound*" (*U* 15.708), to "*beagle*" (*U* 15.1204), and then to "*dachshund*" (*U* 15.1206), before reaching his final incarnation as the "little fox terrier" Nipper (Wile 225n). Toward the end of these canine transformations, the night watch accost Bloom as he feeds the dog and arrest him for committing a public "nuisance" (*U* 15.680); once the trial sequence begins, the dog more or less disappears until he closes the trial, reentering as both Paddy Dignam and Little Nipper, five-hundred lines later. For the last dogspeech in *Ulysses*, then, Joyce sets up a reenactment of one of the "Top 10" marketing symbols of the twentieth century: a dog listening to his master's voice accurately reproduced by the gramophone horn, the trademark of the Victor Talking Machine Company in the United States (which merged with the Radio Corporation of America in the late 1920s to become RCA Victor), the symbol too of the affiliated British Gramophone Company (later renamed "HMV," and now EMI), of the German Gramophone Company ("Die Stimme Seines Herrn"—ultimately Deutsche Grammophon Gesellschaft, DGG), of the Italian firm "La Voce Del Padrone," and, among still others, of the Compagnie Française du Gramophone ("La Voix de Son Maitre"—ultimately Pathé-Marconi).[4] Although Joyce has already placed "a battered brazen trunk" of a "gramophone" in the window of a nearby brothel (*U* 15.605–06)—the same gramophone that will shortly play a recording of "The Holy City" heard "*Outside*" Bella Cohen's (*U* 15.2115)—the dog, as "Paddy Dignam," more immediately listens to a "*megaphone*" (*U* 15.1244) brandished subterraneously by the cemetery caretaker John O'Connell. "[W]*ith pricked up ears*," the dog "*winces* [...] *wriggles forward and places an ear to the ground*," and with recognition, announces "My master's voice!" (*U* 15.1246–47).

Joyce's cannibalization of the Victor trademark is by no means unique. Apparently staging dogs listening to gramophone horns was an international vogue during the first decades of the century, in vaudeville, in the films, on postcards, and in arranged photographs, reaching even to Antarctica where,

Figure 7.4. One of countless reenactments, visual adaptations, or parodies of the His Master's Voice trademark, here with a sled dog performing the role of "Little Nipper" in a January 1911 photograph taken during Robert Scott's ill-fated second Antarctic expedition (1910–12). Courtesy of EMI Archives.

during the 1910–12 South Pole expedition, some of Captain Scott's men recreated the scene, substituting a sled dog for the fox terrier Nipper. But Joyce does more than simply cannibalize the HMV trademark in Circe; he also alludes to one of the commonly understood but now largely forgotten messages coded into the Liverpool artist Francis Barraud's original 1898 painting entitled *Dog Looking at and Listening to a Phonograph*.[5] Little Nipper's master is dead. Barraud's *His Master's Voice*, then, is a representative work of the Victorian subgenre of the art of animal mourning, akin to Sir Edwin Landseer's *The Old Shepherd's Chief Mourner* or W. Archer's *The Empty Cradle*, for example.[6]

Barraud's model for his painting, Nipper, was born in Bristol in 1884, and his first master was the painter's brother Mark Barraud, who had died in 1887. (Nipper was so named, apparently, because of his habit of nipping the back of visitors' legs.) Francis Barraud inherited the bereaved Nipper and, remembering the dog's fascination with his Edison talking machine, immortalized him on canvas some three years after Nipper himself died in 1895. Renaming

Figure 7.5. Francis Barraud's original painting *Dog Looking at and Listening to a Phonograph* (1899). Barraud succeeded in selling the painting to the English Gramophone Company, in October 1899, only after replacing the Edison cylinder phonograph with a Berliner gramophone. Courtesy of EMI Archives.

his painting *His Master's Voice* and failing both to exhibit it at the Royal Academy and to convince the British Edison Bell Company to purchase it—"Dogs don't listen to phonographs" the company told him—Barraud eventually sold the picture to Edison's chief competition, the British Gramophone Company, in late 1899. Barraud completed the sale only after he agreed to paint over his original Edison cylinder phonograph and replace it with Berliner's rival disk machine, the gramophone. Although the British Gramophone Company waited until 1910 to register Little Nipper as its trademark, Emile Berliner purchased the American copyright in 1900, recognizing the symbolic value of the painting as a trademark for faithful sound reproduction. Berliner also understood the painting's implied representation of mourning. Like Edison, Berliner believed one of the chief marketing appeals of gramophone recording, as he remarked in his speech before the members of Philadelphia's Franklin Institute in 1888, was that it could preserve "the voices of dear relatives and friends long departed, the utterances of the great men and women who lived centuries before," and thus allow us to hold "communion even with immortality!" (Wile 173–74).

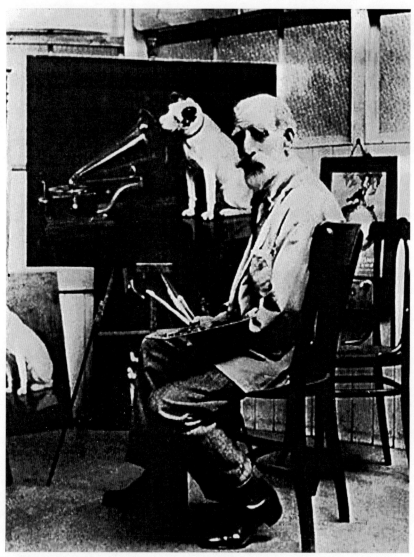

Figure 7.6. The artist Francis Barraud (1856–1924) late in life, in his studio, painting one of approximately twenty-four copies of *His Master's Voice* that were commissioned by the English Gramophone and American Victor companies. According to several accounts, each time Barraud copied his most famous work, he did so exactly: initially painting "Little Nipper" listening to a cylinder phonograph and then superimposing the Berliner gramophone. Courtesy of EMI Archives.

By reversing the message encoded in Barraud's painting, then, by merging and cannibalizing Little Nipper with the dead Paddy Dignam to become mournee as well as mourner, and by having the dog speak as well as listen, Joyce efficiently refers both to the well-known trademark for faithful sound reproduction and to one of the chief early notions of the value of the gramophone. Earlier in *Ulysses* Joyce has Bloom arrive at a similar realization of the preservation function of the gramophone. In Hades Bloom thinks, "Have a gramophone in every grave or keep it in the house. After dinner on a Sunday. Put on poor old greatgrandfather. Kraahraark! Hellohellohello amawfullyglad kraark awfullygladaseeagain hellohello amawf krpthsth. Remind you of the voice like the photograph reminds you of the face" (*U* 6.963–67). What strikes the readers perhaps as an extravagant flight of fancy by Bloom here, one more example of his fascination with the possible applications for modern technology like a municipal cattle tram or "funeral trams like they have in Milan" that he proposes earlier in Hades (*U* 6.406), is actually a commonplace contemporary enthusiasm, a version of what Edison, already a quarter-century earlier, had promoted as one of the practical applications of his new invention. In his 1878 *North American Review* article "The Phonograph and Its Future," published only a few months after his celebrated first demonstration of the talking machine in the offices of the *Scientific American* magazine in December 1877, Edison suggests thirteen uses for the phonograph.[7] Two of these applications bear directly on Bloom's thought:

> *Family Record.*—For the purpose of preserving the sayings, the voices, and *the last words* of the dying member of the family—as of great men—the phonograph will unquestionably outrank the photograph. [. . .]
> *Speech and other Utterances.*—It will henceforth be possible to preserve for future generations the voices as well as the words of our Washingtons, our Lincolns, our Gladstones, etc., and to have them give us their "greatest effort" in every town and hamlet in the country, upon our holidays. (533–34)

Edison's other predictions for his phonograph's future are extraordinarily accurate, embracing dictation machines and recorded correspondence, books for the blind, pedagogical applications to teach correct pronunciation, recorded music, talking toys and clocks, and advertising. One of his anticipated

Figure 7.7. Photography, sound recording, and film (see chapter 8), storage technologies for recording and preserving the living presence of individuals, were all initially wedded to the contemplation of death, as this Victor advertisement from about 1904 illustrates. Nellie Melba (1861–1931), aka "Madame Delba" in *Finnegans Wake* (200.09), was the greatest prima donna of the first quarter of the twentieth century and recorded extensively for HMV between 1904 and 1926. The world-renowned soprano Jenny Lind (1820–87), the "Swedish Nightingale" (*viz.* "Jinnyland [. . . the] sweetishad lightandgayle" [*FW* 359.35–360.02]), died six months before Edison introduced his improved phonograph in May 1888. Courtesy of EMI Archives.

uses for the phonograph might, however, have struck any writer of fiction as ominous. Edison foresees

> *Phonographic Books.*—A book of 40,000 words upon a single metal plate ten inches square thus becomes a strong possibility. The advantages of such books over those printed are too readily seen to need mention. Such books would be listened to where now none are read. They would preserve more than the mental emanations of the brain of the author; and, as a bequest to future generations, they would be unequaled. For the preservation of languages they would be invaluable. (534)

In this light, we might consider Joyce's gramophony in *Ulysses* to be his competitive attempt to realize the audio potential of the heretofore silent text of writing, to create a book that can be listened to, in a sense, as well as read, and thus to preserve more than the "mental emanations of [his] brain."[8] In other words, Joyce realizes that, if his attempts to create the socially, politically, and aesthetically revolutionary works of literary modernism and of the avant-garde that, as I argued in my previous chapter, both *Ulysses* and *Finnegans Wake* represent, are to succeed, these books must be *heard*.

But this does not explain why Joyce extends his audio experiment to focus not just on nonverbal sound, but particularly to include previously unrepresented animal speech. Early in the book Joyce exploits onomatopoeia traditionally for literary sound effects and has Stephen gramophonically approximate to himself the "squealing" of his "trailing [. . .] ashplant," "My familiar, after me, calling, Steeeeeeeeeeeephen!" (12 e's) in Telemachus (*U* 1.627–29), and the "fourworded wavespeech" of the sea in Proteus: "seesoo, hrss, rsseeiss, ooos" (*U* 3.456–57). Nevertheless, not until the cat's first meow in Calypso do the readers of *Ulysses* begin to notice Joyce's strategic representation of sound in text, his new technology of gramophonic sound reproduction. The cat's initial "Mkgnao" (*U* 4.16) has the same impact on the readers as the baffling word "Chrysostomos" on the novel's first page (*U* 1.26), by which Joyce announces his interior monologue technique. Joyce's representation of the cat's variegated speech, I suggest, is related to one of the applications for the phonograph that Edison did not foresee, a use that stimulated early twentieth-century speculation that this new technology might make it possible for humans finally to capture and decipher the language of animals, or for masters to hear their animals' voices, as had, for example, another memorable literary character of the early 1920s, Doctor Dolittle. Although I have never seen the name of the popular children's author Hugh Lofting (1886–1947) linked with Joyce's, they were near contemporaries; Lofting's first novel, *The Story of Doctor Dolittle* was published in 1920, and both his award-winning sequel, *The Voyages of Doctor Dolittle*, and Lotte Reiniger's animated film *Dr. Dolittle*, with music by Paul Hindemith, among others, followed in the year of *Ulysses*'s publication, 1922 ("Doctor Dolittle"). Lofting's good Doctor did not use the gramophone to learn nearly 500 animal languages, since these novels are set in the mid-nineteenth century—"Once upon a time, many years ago—when our grandfathers were still children" (*Story* 3)—yet Lofting's fantasies clearly capitalize on the popular fascination with the possibility of decoding animal communication. If animals did in fact have languages, it was clear that the technology of the gramophone would now make their study feasible. Since there was no practicable method for representing animal sounds orthographically, recordings could capture and facilitate the search for pattern, for meaning, in the "speech" of animals. "The phonograph permitted for the first time," as Friedrich Kittler observes, "the recording of vibrations that human ears could not count, human eyes could not see, and writing hands could not catch up with. Edison's simple metal needle, however, could keep up" (*Gramophone* 118). Geoffrey Winthrop-Young and Michael Wutz similarly remark that "Without phonography and its new ability to faithfully manipulate the spoken word in ways that no longer require that speech be translated into writing, there would be no academic enterprises aimed at understanding the communicative household of cultures with few or no symbol-based external storage capacities" (xii).

Francis Arthur Jones, in his early biography of Edison, published in 1908, provides a half-serious, extended account of one enterprising animal linguist's efforts to decipher, significantly for our present concern, the speech of cats:

> The phonograph has been employed for many queer purposes, perhaps the queerest being to assist a certain American professor in his study of the language of cats. This gentleman interested himself many years ago—together with one or two others—in the Simian language, but ultimately abandoned the problem of interpreting "monkey talk" in order to find out what a cat means when it stands on the back fence at night and emits those blood-curdling cries that make householders so reckless regarding their personal property.

" 'He talks English!' "

Figure 7.8. The good doctor has a communications breakthrough. From *The Voyages of Doctor Dolittle* (New York: Stokes, 1922), 201. Courtesy of Rare Books and Special Collections, University of South Carolina.

"It is not easy," said this gentleman to the writer, "to secure good records of cat language, and, in fact, I have waited night after night in my backyard for the purpose only to be disappointed." (159)

After summarizing the professor's solution to this difficulty, a primitive re-mote-control mechanism for starting the phonograph from a distance, Jones continues to quote his source:

"When they were fairly started [caterwauling] I pressed the button and set the machinery in motion. The yowling became awful after a bit, and I was very much afraid that the missiles which began to fly would strike my machine, but fortunately they didn't, and when I thought I had secured a sufficient quantity of the cats' vocal powers I put on some clothes and brought in the phonograph. When I tested the record I found it an excellent one. I was exceptionally lucky in this, for a few nights later the cats completely and mysteriously disappeared. [. . .] we shall never hear their voices again, save in the phonograph." (Jones 160–61)

Thus the professor, I would note, accomplishes one of Edison's foreseen applications for the phonograph: immortalizing historic voices for posterity. But Jones's correspondent continues:

"I have, by the aid of Mr. Edison's invention, secured records of cats purring, cats in pain [. . .] , cats spitting, and so forth. It is not difficult to secure the record of an angry cat's voice, for all you have to do is to hold the animal near the mouth of the phonograph and give its tail a twist. [. . .] All together I have secured twenty-five cat records, which repeat twenty-five different cries. [. . .] I am convinced there is a cat language just as there is a Simian language, and if I live long enough I am going to find out what it means. I feel I have a difficult task before me, but with the aid of the 'talking machine' I think I shall succeed." (Jones 161)

To support his conviction that there is a communicative function in feline sounds, the professor tests the response of his own household pet to the recordings:

"Sometimes I place the phonograph near my own cat (a quiet respectable parlor animal that doesn't go out at night) and turn on a few nocturnal yowls for her especial benefit. When she hears the sounds of the other cats having a good time she races round the room in a remarkable manner and does her best to perform a feline harlequin act through the window. It is perfectly evident that she knows what is being said, and if she'd only respond in some intelligible way I should begin to understand. However, I am not without hope." (Jones 161–62)

I would suggest that the professor has missed here a veritable "Rosetta Stone" for the decipherment of cat language, since it seems "perfectly evident" to me what these cats are saying and why his own cat so wants to join in the fun. The American professor concludes, however, by not quite unexpectedly promising to give a paper on his research:

> "In a short time I intend to give a serious lecture on the Feline Language illustrated with cat cries on the phonograph. People will laugh, of course, but I hope in the end that they will come to believe with me that even cats have a language of their own, and one which, if we study sufficiently, we shall some day understand." (Jones 162)

Joyce's Garryowen parody in Cyclops, thus, is less an outlandish exaggeration than a satire at the expense of "All those who are interested in the spread of human culture among the lower animals (and their name is legion)" (*U* 12.712–13), in the early part of the twentieth century. If we laugh, too, at this American professor, we should also credit him for being a forerunner in the now respectable field of animal communication, or bioacoustics, a research discipline that grew out of the new opportunity for recording sound afforded by the invention of the phonograph.[9]

Rather than simply reproducing the relations in Barraud's *His Master's Voice*, then, Joyce also reverses them, poising the readers of *Ulysses* in the position of listening to the sound of the animal's voice, among the multiple voices and noises that resound in his book. It is now a commonplace to remark Joyce's mastery of many stylistic voices in his composition of *Ulysses*, to which we now add his representation of animal voice.[10] This multi-vocality of the text, I want to suggest, owes something to the library of voices that the new storage technology of a gramophone and a collection of recordings could readily provide to a consumer of the early 1920s. T. S. Eliot, in another work of many voices published in 1922, *The Waste Land*, seems equally aware of the gramophone as a competitive form of artistic experience, although he is clearly more hostile to popular culture than Joyce. Eliot associates the typist's playing of her gramophone with debased, mechanistic sexual life in the modern waste land: she gains as little pleasure "put[ting]a record on the gramophone['s]" spindle as she has had from her sex with the "young man carbuncular" (ll. 256, 231; *Complete Poems* 44). Joyce, on the other hand, was fascinated by the materials of contemporary popular culture—from condoms and phonographs to film, radio, and television, as we will see in the next chapter—preferring to appropriate and assimilate them into his literary design, in his art of creative cannibalism, consistent with his rejection of the apolitical autonomy aesthetic of "high" modernism discussed in the previous chapter. In retrospect, it is clear that neither Joyce nor Eliot had much to fear from the development of the gramophone—both, in fact, would eventually record readings of their own works for posterity—because another, even more popular sound medium would shortly usurp the gramophone's place in contemporary culture. In 1922, the same year as the publication of *Ulysses* and *The Waste Land*, the British "Postmaster-General permitted the formation of a broadcasting company," the BBC, "which would give regular programs of entertainment from several stations," and by "1923 the wireless began to enjoy a boom" in Britain and on the continent (Graves and Hodge 89, 91). Characteristically, Joyce would find a place and use for radio in *Finnegans Wake*.

Derrida seems to miss an irony in his search for Joyce's subterraneous voice in "*Ulysses* Gramophone," for what he seeks, and what all readers seek in the welter of voices in *Ulysses*, is "a regaining of presence, [. . .] the presence that is represented, the so-called living presence" ("By Force" 178); in other words, what he and we seek in *Ulysses*, like Little Nipper in Circe, is to hear the "Master's Voice." As is so often the case with *Ulysses*, moreover, we can see that Joyce intends us to do just this, to hear the master's voice, by positioning the "poor dogsbody" Stephen Dedalus (*U* 1.112) in the role of Little Nipper earlier in the book, in its most self-reflexive episode, Proteus. Near the beginning of this chapter which ultimately and self-reflexively asks, "Who ever anywhere will read these written words" (*U* 3.414–15), Stephen considers visiting his aunt Sara and uncle Richie Goulding. What follows is Stephen's rendition of an imagined visit, in Simon Dedalus's voice. Stephen prefaces his rendering by self-consciously alluding to the gramophone's trademark slogan, remarking that he can hear, as he puts it, "My consubstantial father's voice" (*U* 3.61–62). Or as we might put it, Stephen may indeed hear "His Master's Voice" at this moment, the voice of Simon, but Joyce's readers hear a consubstantial trinity of voices in this scene: Stephen's, Simon's, and that of the progenitor of both, "his manjester's voice" (*FW* 73.15).

8

The Cultural Transfer of Film, Radio, and Television

In my beginning is my end.
—T. S. Eliot, "East Coker"

a long the [. . .] riverrun
—*FW* 628.15–16, 03.01

The advent of commercial radio broadcasting in the 1920s initiated a fundamental change in the consumers' relation to communication technology, a change that effectively reduced the users' autonomy in the communicative relationship, thus heightening the phenomenon of passive consumption in contemporary culture. Eliot's typist may behave like a machine, placing the record on her gramophone with an "automatic hand" (l. 255; *Complete Poems* 44), yet both her action and whatever music she plays remain matters of her choice, susceptible to social and cultural influences, but not necessarily or entirely determined by these. With the arrival of radio, however, individual agency suffers a shrinkage, and the active listener becomes a passive audience, disengaged from and incapable of interacting with the speaker(s) or performer(s), with little choice remaining but to turn the receiver on or off. These listeners become subjects, with consequent reduction of their subjectivity. This clearly is why the radio rapidly developed into the 1930s as the preferred medium for political propaganda, whether as perfected by Goebbels and Hitler in Nazi Germany or more subtly via Roosevelt's "Fireside Chats" that, at least, preserved the semblance of a conversational relationship. It follows that the ultimate dream of the authoritarian leader—witness Orwell's *1984* (1949)—is the radio that must be heard, the omnipresent loudspeaker that cannot be turned off.

Of course, the older communication technology of the telephone, well established at the time of broadcast radio's arrival, had preserved the users' autonomy in the exchange of information, the conversation, between its users. In the 1920s, no one knew whether the developing technology of television would find its primary application by following the example of radio, with broadcast television, or that of the telephone, with the video-phone. (Despite its potential value for a totalitarian regime, I can find no evidence that any researcher seriously proposed the two-way telescreen of Orwell's *1984*, a sinister extrapolation from the video-telephone.) And although today the technology for video-conferencing or one-to-one video telecommunication via the internet is generally available and inexpensive, it is unlikely ever to supplant the "blind" telephone. In the words of one recent commentator, the "Picturephone remains one of technology's most prominent examples of an elaborate solution in search of a problem" because, in fact, "[m]ost people simply don't want to see or be seen by the person they're talking to" in telephone conversations (Schwarz 56). Nonetheless, although these same people will jealously guard their sense of privacy when engaged in a direct communication via the telephone, it seems they have no reservations about sacrificing their personal autonomy and allowing their subjectivity and critical intelligence to be controlled by an entertainment medium—secure in their anonymity as a passive audience—as evidenced by the enormous popularity of broadcast radio and, eventually, television.

The arrival of the radio not only intensified the tendency of the audience to willingly suspend its critical subjectivity but also increased the alarm of cultural commentators through the 1920s at what they perceived, in Wyndham Lewis's terms, as a kind of hypnotic passivity in the general public. In a book that broadly surveys the state of modern subjection, *The Art of Being Ruled* (1926), which Joyce transposes into "the art of being rude" (*FW* 167.03), Lewis attributes this "hypnotism" not just to radio, but to three primary information sources drawing mass audiences: the "cinema, wireless, and press" (164–65). As we shall see in the following pages, Lewis was not alone in including the film in his indictment, although as a form of communication the motion pictures represent a different case from the radio for, because film is a storage medium, it lacks the impact of presence found in radio and television.

This is not the place to consider Lewis's reasons—chiefly political—for attacking the press for its cooptation of the readers' subjectivity, but rather the place to emphasize that his charges testify to a broader concern during this era for the public's passive consumption of the printed word, as well as of aural and visual information, that he shares with James Joyce. (Both Lewis, the bête noire "windy Nous" of *Finnegans Wake* [*FW* 56.29], and Joyce would be mortified to learn they have this much in common.) As we have already seen, Joyce betrays an anxiety response toward sound recording as a potential threat to the power of literature to engage its audience and thus seeks to pre-empt its appeal by incorporating a kind of sound technology into *Ulysses*. As we shall see in this chapter, he seems to have sustained a similarly ambivalent response to both motion pictures and radio—technologies he could likewise cannibalize to his advantage in *Ulysses* and *Finnegans Wake*—seeing both as forms of communication inferior to literature in terms of their abilities to actively engage the critical consciousness of their consumers and not as the fully hypnotic media that Lewis decries. This was clearly not the case, how-ever, with Joyce's response to the emergent medium of television, for reasons I will elucidate in the second part of this chapter.

Ulysses and the Kingdom of Shadows

Let us return to Mr. Garrett Deasy's letter that I discussed in the opening of my fourth chapter. Toward the end of the Nestor episode of *Ulysses*, Deasy has given Stephen Dedalus his letter concerning the hoof and mouth disease, telling him that he "want[s it . . .] to be printed and read" as soon as possible (*U* 2.338). At this moment in the text, Stephen's eyes evidently glance down the page of Deasy's pompous and cliché-ridden letter, and a string of frag-ments follows: "May I trespass on your valuable space. That doctrine of *laissez faire* which so often in our history. Our cattle trade. The way of all our old industries [. . . .]" (*U* 2.324–26). And so on. In one of the wittier moments in this chapter, Joyce allows Deasy to interrupt Stephen's skimming to remark: "I don't mince words, do I?" Through the next paragraph Stephen continues to skim, continues in fact to mince Deasy's words through the balance of the letter. I will return the favor by further mincing Joyce's minced text: "Foot and mouth disease. Known as Koch's preparation. Serum and virus. Percent-age of salted horses. Rinderpest. [. . . .] In every sense of the word take the bull by the horns. Thanking you for the hospitality of your columns" (*U* 2.332–37). Several things are happening here. Most readers will probably conclude that Deasy's language is so bloated that he should have considered mincing some of it himself. Many will deduce that Joyce fragments Deasy's letter to suggest that it is so tediously predictable, for Stephen if not for them, that it doesn't need to be read in the same completeness and detail as, say, Milly Bloom's letter to her father in Calypso, which Bloom reads and rereads for every possible nuance, or Martha Clifford's letter in Lotus Eaters, refrains from which will echo in Bloom's mind throughout the day. Joyce gives us the full texts for Milly's and Martha's letters, yet leaves us only the minced version of Deasy's. But the fact remains that this hoof-and-mouth letter is *not* predictable or readable for the readers of *Ulysses*. In its minced text, it contains a number of non sequiturs that will send most of them to Don Gifford's Ulysses *Annotated*, or some other guide, to puzzle out the references to the "Galway harbour scheme" (*U* 2.326), perhaps to "Cassandra" (*U* 2.329), and certainly to the Emperor of Austria (*U* 2.333–34). As I stressed in chapter four, Joyce's technique here emphasizes the gaps in the text, or what Wolfgang Iser calls the "blanks" (167–70 and passim), rather than promoting in his readers any sense of their easy fill-ability. Joyce leaves them searching, as the book will later have it, for "The Man in the Gap" (*U* 12.186). Accordingly, Deasy's "I don't mince words, do I?" becomes one of those many self-reflexive moments in *Ulysses* when Joyce calls attention to the textuality of his text, more or less announcing "But I *do* mince words, don't I?"

One could argue that Joyce's technique in this passage furthers the theme of "disappointed" bridges in the Nestor episode (*U* 2.39), or in other words, that the textual non sequiturs correspond with and emphasize the failure of culturally constructed systems of meaning such as history to tell a coherent story or to connect with observed reality. This demand that the readers of *Ulysses* read between the lines and connect them for meaning thus establishes Nestor's otherwise curious technical parallel to Ithaca in Joyce's schema, as a "*Catechism (personal)*" to the later episode's "*Catechism (impersonal)*" (Gilbert 108, 369), just as its theme of the social construction of meaning culminates in Ithaca's undermining of all logical orders, including the novel's own matrices of symbols, as "ineluctably constructed upon the incertitude of the void" (*U* 17.1014–15). Here, however, I want to argue that Joyce owes his inspiration for this mincing of the text, not exclusively to this theme or to the literary tradition that his book both incorporates and resists—symptomatic of the cannibalistic art of cultural transfer—but particularly to the technological influence of the cinema, an art composed "in principle," as Friedrich Kittler notes, of "nothing but cutting and splicing" (*Gramophone* 117). And ultimately I will contend that this debt is one more of many signs that *Ulysses* is a *liber in tempore belli*, reflecting the contemporary World War, for it demands that its readers will life into being in its gaps, animating meaning in the no man's land between the lines of his text.

Of course, Joyce has practiced his mincing technique from the beginning of his career, drawing his readers' attention to Old Cotter's "unfinished sentences" (*D* 11) in the first story of *Dubliners*, for instance, and elsewhere in this text creating similar gaps for his readers to bridge, "*gnomon*[s]" for them to complete (*D* 9), as I attempted to do in terms of the absent quotation from Browning in "The Dead," in chapter 4. Furthermore, logical and syntactical gaps become a primary feature of his interior monologue technique as it matures and gains complexity from *A Portrait of the Artist as a Young Man* into *Ulysses*. There is no reason, however, to believe that Joyce cannibalistically severs the ligaments of discourse to promote the reality or psychological depth of his representation of his characters' inner lives; Henry James had done as much with no violations of standard English diction and syntax. If anything, Joyce's strategy calls attention to his characters' status as textual representations rather than intensifying the illusion of their reality. Joyce's principal motivation for his mincing of text is to draw his readers even more actively into the making of meaning, animating the inanimate symbols on the page in their imaginations, and thus investing these readers with the task of willfully constructing a reality out of the fragments of his partial text, giving life to partial bodies littering the field.

What do I mean by asserting that Joyce's mincing of language is indebted to the battlefield of the World War and, further, that this debt is implicated with the emergent technology of film, both developments exactly contemporaneous with his composition of Nestor between 1915 and 1917? Simply this: first, that the art of cinema and the art of war developed concurrently, mutually supporting one another and supported by the same technological advances, and second, that Joyce's fragmentation of his text places his readers in exactly the same relationship to his book as that of the audience in the cinema. As I noted in my preface, in 1861 Colonel Gatling, inspired by a steamer's paddle wheel, developed his prototype of the machine gun, the ancestor of the weapon that both redefined warfare on the Western Front and inspired Étienne-Jules Marey's invention of the prototype of modern motion-picture camera (Virilio 11; see Kittler, *Gramophone* 124). Is it any surprise that today we refer to photographs as "shots" and make films by "shooting"? Friedrich Kittler has well-described the symbiosis of these two arts:

This history of the movie camera thus coincides with the history of automatic weapons. The transport of pictures only repeats the transport of bullets. In order to focus on and fix objects moving through space, such as people, there are two procedures: to shoot and to film. In the principle of cinema resides mechanized death as it was invented in the nineteenth century [. . . .] With the chronophotographic gun, mechanized death was perfected: its transmission coincided with its storage. (*Gramophone* 124)

All that remained was to solve the problems of projecting these stored sequential photographs in a manner that an audience of many could view—unlike with Edison's single-viewer kinetoscope—problems that were solved by some of the same technological advances that allowed a pilot, for example, to fire his machine gun without cutting off his propeller blades.

It seems counterintuitive to connect the cinema with death, "mechanized" or otherwise, as Kittler does, because of all art forms it would seem that film has the greatest capacity to generate the illusion of life. But this is precisely the point: the cinema, also oxymoronically called "motion pictures," is an illusion, creating both an impression of life in *motion* and its negation in the frozen frames of the individual *pictures*. The film thus shares this curious initial association with death with two other late-nineteenth century technologies whose preservation of the living was inevitably wedded to the contemplation of death. I refer to the now familiar, and macabre, vogue of memorial photography and to Edison's ambitious plan to preserve historic voices for posterity, with his phonograph, cited in the previous chapter. And Joyce was not alone in understanding this association between "Cinema and the Kingdom of Death," as Peter Donaldson nicely puts it in a recent essay. Donaldson quotes, for example, Maxim Gorky's initial reaction to the motion pictures in an 1896 review of a Lumière program:

Last night I was in the Kingdom of Shadows. [. . .] If you only knew how strange it is to be there. It is a world without sound, without colour. Everything there—the earth, the trees, the people, the water and the air—is dipped in monotonous grey. Grey rays of sun across the grey sky, grey eyes in grey faces, and the leaves of the trees are ashen grey. It is no life but its shadow, it is not motion but its soundless spectre. [. . .] And all this is in a strange silence where no rumble of wheels is heard, no sound of footsteps or of speech. Nothing. Not a single note of the intricate symphony that always accompanies the movements of people. (qtd. 241)

Antonia Lant has extensively explored connections "between cinema and the cult of the dead" similar to Gorky's, to demonstrate "that related ideas of living death, spectral life, and mummification were already a pervasive presence in the discursive world into which the film was introduced" (Donaldson 243, 242; viz. Lant 87–112).

This association between the cinema and death was not simply a result of the technological limitations of early films, their lack of color and sound that Gorky seems most affected by, although it is clearly true that the advances in film technology have made it less likely that an audience would draw this association today. Other viewers of the early cinema, however, and I would contend that Joyce was among them, were equally affected by their awareness of the "psychotechnological" trick—a term coined by Hugo Münsterberg in his *Grundzüge der Psychotechnik* (1914)—by which the mind of the viewer, rather than the medium of the film, creates the perception of movement in the act of viewing and so gives life to inanimate images (Kittler, *Gramophone* 159–60). Münsterberg, whom William James invited from the University of Freiburg to Harvard in 1892 on the strength of his world-famous studies of the relations between "psychology and media technology" (Griffith vii; Kittler, *Gramophone* 160), makes this case in his book *The Photoplay: A Psychological Study*, probably the first essay in film theory, published in the Nestor-year of 1916. I can find no evidence that Joyce knew of Münsterberg or his work, yet the central thesis of *The Photoplay* that "film presents its spectators with their own processes of perception" (Kittler, *Gramophone* 161) is an insight that Joyce could have arrived at, as easily as Münsterberg, while he was writing a book that constantly draws its readers to a consciousness of their act of reading, focusing their attention on the processes of literary perception. But there is literally a *vital* difference between what Münsterberg and Joyce make of their similar recognitions.

In *The Photoplay* Münsterberg surveys the evolution of the motion pictures—noting along the way one stroboscopic device intriguingly called the daedaleum (*The Film* 3)—and ultimately discounts the prevailing assumption among psychologists that an audience perceives motion in the rapid succession of photographic stills through a combination of two optical phenomena: the eye's retention of afterimages and the stroboscopic effect (*The Film* 25–26). "What objectively reaches our eye," Münsterberg writes, "is one motionless picture after another, but the replacing of one by another through a forward movement of the film cannot reach our eye at all. Why do we, nevertheless, see a continuous movement?" (*The Film* 24). From a review of research into optical phenomena, he concludes

> that the apparent movement is in no way the mere result of an afterimage and that the impression of motion is surely more than the mere perception of successive phases of movement. The movement is in these cases not really seen from without, but is superadded, by the action of the mind, to motionless pictures. [. . . In] the film world, *the motion which* [the viewer] *sees appears to be a true motion, and yet is created by his own mind.* The afterimages of the successive pictures are not sufficient to produce a substitute for the continuous outer stimulation; the essential condition is rather the inner mental activity which unites the separate phases in the idea of connected action. [. . . .] It is only a suggestion of movement, and the idea of motion is to a high degree the product of our own reaction. *Depth and movement alike come to us in the moving picture world, not as hard facts but as a mixture of fact and symbol. They are present and yet they are not in the things. We invest the impressions with them.* (*The Film* 29–30; emphases in original)

Although Münsterberg's insistence on the audience's mental engagement with the cinema would explain his lofty expectations for this art form—he signed-on as a contributing editor to one of the earliest screen magazines, Hodkinson and Zukor's *Paramount Pictograph* in 1915 (Griffith viii–ix)— nevertheless, his analysis of audience response has a double-edge. His fourfold discussion in *The Photoplay* of the various cinematic devices that direct attention, represent memory, and evoke imagination and emotion in the viewers unintentionally suggests the degree to which the film both enacts *and* usurps the audience's "processes of perception." A close-up may replicate the viewers' act of attention, for instance, but they also have no choice but to attend; when a cut-flashback simulates the mind's memory operation, the viewers cannot choose but to share the act of remembrance. Thus, in a brilliant analysis of Paul Wegener's film *The Golem* (1914; remade 1920), Kittler argues that "the transformation of a psychic apparatus into film-trick transformations," such as Münsterberg describes, "is lethal for the mind [*Geist*] as such," and that "film theories based on experimental psychology are at the same time theories of the psyche (soul) based on media technologies" (*Gramophone* 166). Hence, the "deceased soul" of the Golem becomes a "doppelgänger" for both the protagonist Pernath who confronts him and for the inert audience that perceives him in the film (*Gramophone* 166). "All the historical attributes of a subject who around 1800 celebrated his or her authenticity under the title literature," Kittler concludes, "can around 1900 be replaced or bypassed by Golems, these programmed subjects" (*Gramophone* 166).

If Hugo Münsterberg's affirmation of audience engagement and response in the cinema was a losing battle, it was not his only one. Over the years from 1892 to 1914 Münsterberg had "rationalized his long stay in the United States," Richard Griffith writes, "on the then-common premise that the future of civilization lay in an increasing *rapport* between Germany and the 'Anglo-Saxons'—the United States and Britain. He saw himself as a missionary of that *rapport*, cementing bonds, forging links" (ix). Accordingly, Münsterberg published books about America in Germany and acted as "the friend and councilor of both Theodore Roosevelt and Woodrow Wilson" in the United States (viii). When the European war broke out in 1914, he saw it as an "unimaginable catastrophe, nearly the wreck of everything" he had stood for. In the two remaining years of his life, Münsterberg "tried to use all his influence to stop the war, or [. . .] to ensure that the United States did not enter it on the British side" (ix), ultimately failing on both counts and along the way earning for himself public ridicule, the loss of his political friendships, suspicion of being a secret agent, and academic ostracism. Münsterberg died, appropriately of heart failure, in December 1916. "Even twenty years after his death," Griffith remarks, "American intellectuals felt toward Hugo Münsterberg and his fate and the fate of his work, a kind of guilt" (vi). *The Photoplay* languished out of print until its reissue by Dover Publications in 1970 and recovery of importance under its new title *The Film: A Psychological Study*.

Joyce's conviction that a work of literature can present "its spectators [or readers] with their own processes of perception" (Kittler, *Gramophone* 161), not only resembles Münsterberg's analysis of cinematic effects, but also shares with him the medium of film for its inspiration by fostering this recognition through the textual strategy of "cutting and splicing"—mincing words (Kittler, *Gramophone* 117). I would further argue, to paraphrase *The Photoplay*, that *Ulysses*'s demand that its readers unite the "separate phases" of its text in "the idea of connected" meaning, through their "inner mental activity" (30), is likewise an essential, though unnoted, element in this book's frequently discussed debt to the contemporary cinema. There is at least one book-length study of this topic, Craig Barrow's *Montage in James Joyce's* Ulysses, and numerous Joyceans have described his avid interest in motion pictures, in Trieste and after, as well as his abortive Cinema Volta project in Dublin. I myself have discussed the end of the final story in *Dubliners*, "The Dead," in terms of Joyce's understanding of the motion-picture projection technology called *gnomonic* projection (Rice 49–50). What I want to stress here, however, is that in Joyce's cultural transfer of film technology to the literary text, he took from the cinema only what he could *use* for his art, as he always did when he cannibalized from both popular and "high" culture, and ignored—or in this case, rejected—the rest. In other words, by actively engaging his readers' inner mental activity and promoting their consciousness of their own processes of perception, Joyce makes them the creative participants in the making of the art that Münsterberg envisions in the moviegoers, animating the meaning between its lines, rather than turning them into the revenants, automata, or Golems that Münsterberg's analysis of the cinema portends. This has everything to do with the cultural status of literature though the nineteenth and into the twentieth centuries, and particularly the status of the novel, as the bright book of life, as the art of the mind, the soul, the *Geist*—as Kittler observes (*Gramophone* 166)—a role that liberates literature from cinema's "Kingdom of Shadows" (qtd. Donaldson 241).

The novelist thus becomes a "resurrection man"—in the better sense of the term—and so also do his readers, as they bring to life that which lies dismembered and inert between the lines. The affirmative vision that Hugo Münsterberg sought and failed to realize for cinematic art, Joyce achieves in fiction, while both men share in a common political desire that deeply motivates their ideas, in the time of trench warfare, to affirm the value of life over death between the lines.

From Radio to Television in *Finnegans Wake*: *"the charge of a light barricade"*

Following the publication of *Ulysses* on his fortieth birthday, 2 February 1922, James Joyce rested his pen for slightly more than a year. Wherever he rested it, he seems to have had some difficulty either finding his pen again, or employing it, as he remarks in an 11 March 1923 letter to Harriet Shaw Weaver:

"Yesterday I wrote two pages—the first I have written since the final *Yes* of *Ulysses*. Having found a pen, with some difficulty I copied them out in a large handwriting on a double sheet of foolscap so that I could read them" (*Letters*, I 202). In 1938 Joyce would return to these two pages, the King Roderick O'Connor sketch, and elaborate them into the final pages of the Pub chapter (II, 3) of *Finnegans Wake* (*FW* 380.07–382.30), late in the final stages of completing his "Work in Progress" for publication (Hayman, "Preface" xiii).

Also dating from early 1922, in fact from less than two weeks after the appearance of *Ulysses*, on 14 February 1922 the Marconi Company inaugurated regular radio broadcasting in England (Briggs 20), introducing the "technological development" that, in the words of James Connor, was to exert the greatest "influence on cultural change" in the "early part of the twentieth century" (826).[1] Thus Joyce's composition of *Finnegans Wake*, from early 1923 through late 1938, not only closely coincides with the introduction and worldwide growth of radio broadcasting, but as Connor and others have argued, his experience of the wireless deeply influences his experiment with "a new way of communicating" via "a kind of language that imitate[s] so many of [the] audial characteristics" of radio: "The language of the *Wake* flows and shifts, is noisy and hard to grasp, much like competing radio signals. The reader is enticed to read, to *listen*, with the same intensity as a radio hound in 1933" (Connor 830). In *Ulysses* Joyce's fascination with contemporary technology, such as the phonograph and film—as we have just seen—clearly influenced both his linguistic and formal experimentation, so it is hardly surprising that the new medium of radio would similarly inform his conception of *Finnegans Wake*. And, as with *Ulysses*, Joyce's embrace of modern technology and information media in the *Wake* is both a cultural transfer and cannibalization of popular culture and a kind of anxiety response to rival appeals to the audience for literature. As Valentine Cunningham observes, the "mass media obsessed the mass-conscious writer" during the era of Joyce's composition of the *Wake* (280).

Facetiousness aside, the difficulty Joyce remarks in his letter to Weaver has little to do with locating his pen and everything to do with his deteriorating vision, starting with a recurrence of his iritis in the spring of 1922, followed by other complications (Ellmann, *James Joyce* 535–38), that initially made it a challenge for him to read anything, including his own handwriting, and gradually reduced him to virtual blindness as he labored on "Work in Progress." The story of Joyce's "Miltonic Affliction" recounted in contemporary profiles and early biographical accounts, and eventually with medical expertise by

J. B. Lyons (*James Joyce* 185–210), as much as the rhythms and resonances of the language in its text, has led to one of the most entrenched commonplaces in *Wake* criticism: "the art of dim-sighted Joyce is, like that of Milton, mainly auditory" (Burgess, "What It's All About" xxvii). Connor, for instance, is quite typical when he remarks that Joyce entices his readers "to *listen*" (830). One of the book's earliest critics, Edmund Wilson, is also one of the most representative spokespersons for this tradition in commentaries on the *Wake*:

> Joyce through a large part of his adult life has been almost as blind as Milton; and he has ended, just as Milton did, by dealing principally in auditory sensations. There is as little visualization in *Finnegans Wake* as in *Samson Agonistes*. Our first criticism, therefore, is likely to be that nothing is *seen* in Earwicker's dream. [. . .] we must assume with *Finnegans Wake* that Earwicker's imagination, like Joyce's, is almost entirely auditory and verbal. ("The Dream of H. C. Earwicker" 207–8)

Like the experience of radio, then, it would seem that Joyce's book appeals essentially to the ear. Nevertheless, although it is inarguable that the *Wake* will frustrate any reader's attempt to visualize scene and action in the manner of the conventional novel, the fact remains that reading is first and foremost a visual activity, a caveat that some of these same critics have acknowledged. After asserting that the "strangest feature of this dream vision is that it lacks visual imagery," another influential early commentator on Joyce, Harry Levin, concedes that "If ever he appeals to the eye, it is to the eye of a reader. A full reading must be simultaneously oral and literary, [. . .] dividing our attention between vocal and verbal images. Joyce is interested in both the sound of a word and the figure it cuts on the page" (148–49). Yet the visual dimension of *Finnegans Wake* extends beyond the fact that its linguistic "richness and complexity [are] only revealed to the eye" (Burgess, *Re Joyce* 343).[2] For a book that constantly thwarts its readers' attempts at "seeing" the story as they habitually do with a conventionally realistic narrative, the *Wake* is notably preoccupied with the act of vision, principally in the interplay between voyeurism and exhibitionism, from the scopophilia of HCE, the observation of his indiscretions, and the exhibitionistic narcissism of Issy, through the repeated voyeurism of Mamalujo (e.g., in II, 4 and III, 4), or that of Private Buckley, who shoots the Russian General, and about whom I will have much to say in this chapter. So, although the primary compulsion of the *Wake* is to "tell," a recurring command that is voiced and enacted throughout the text, what the readers are told seems to be a "dream vision" of *vision*, over a variety of distances (time, space, experience); all this suggests that an alternate title for *Finnegans Wake* could have been *Television*.

In this chapter, therefore, I want to shift our attention to the role of television in *Finnegans Wake*, yet another influential communication technology that becomes a presence in the text, for apparently HCE's pub is equipped with both a twelve-tube radio—a "tolvtubular high fidelity dialdialler" (*FW* 309.14)—and a "*verbivocovisual*" TV set (*FW* 341.19). The visual medium of television complements the sound medium of the radio as part of the patterned juxtaposition of the eye and ear throughout the *Wake*, yet by the correlative association of the spatiality of the visible with Shaun and the temporality of the audible with Shem, the television carries with it a variety of negative associations that not only derive from Shaun's status as an authoritarian figure in the book, but extend Joyce's implied critique of film in *Ulysses* for similar aesthetic and political reasons. If radio represents a subversive, pluralistic, and libratory medium for Joyce, providing, like his language, "a broad enough bandwidth to permit a vast multitude of conflicting ideas" (Connor 835), television functions to subject the viewers' eyes, ears, and imaginations to its totalizing representation of the real: "Television's illusion was of seamless, simultaneous, coordinated access to global reality" (K. Williams 37). As such, television, even in its infancy, threatened to make the work of literature "culturally anachronistic in the near future" (K. Williams 13), but it was also becoming clear that television, far more completely than radio, had the potential to realize Max Horkheimer and Theodor Adorno's worst fears of "the culture industry": the suppression of the "need which might resist central control" through its "control of the individual consciousness" (121). Whereas radio is a monopolistic form of mass culture for Horkheimer and Adorno, if not for Joyce, turning "all participants into listeners and authoritatively [subjecting] them to broadcast programs which are all exactly the same" (122), television could even more thoroughly and seductively reduce its audience to subjects by co-opting the viewers' control of the visual field.

While Joyce's first response to new contemporary technologies, as evidenced by both *Ulysses* and *Finnegans Wake*, was to embrace and cannibalize them, selectively appropriating them for his own artistic purposes, he responded atypically to television, withholding the tacit and qualified endorsement that usually accompanies his embrace. In his act of cultural transfer, Joyce's assimilation of the new technology of television reveals a degree of resistance, of the kind of "blockage" Lüsebrink and Reichardt describe, not evident in his previous cannibalization of contemporary culture. Joyce's incorporation of television into the *Wake* betrays a powerfully negative response to this medium, a response that resembles the more characteristic modernist rejections of modernity. He seems to have found television indigestible because he recognized in this new communication technology a potentially totalitarian medium in Horkheimer and Adorno's sense, a visual medium that excluded him personally, and a competitive form of storytelling that threatened to exclude him as a literary artist. Joyce creatively appropriates radio throughout the *Wake*, yet he limits television's role to its appearance in the central section of the Pub chapter—the Butt and Taff episode—and thus juxtaposes the TV's performances to an account of resistance to totalitarianism: the tale of "Buckley shooting the Russian General."[3] More than this, he locates the Butt and Taff episode at the center of the Pub chapter and near the physical center of the book, in the darkest part of the *Wake* both conceptually, because the dialogue of Butt and Taff is tortuously difficult to read, and emotionally, because it is interlaced with references to war—primarily the Crimean War and World War I—allusions he was embedding in his text contemporaneously with a civil war in Spain and rising international tensions that shortly led to the Second World War. Ultimately, Joyce situates the television within a narrative of voyeurism and violence because he understood the technology of this new visual broadcast medium well enough to find in it an analogue to the butchery of war itself.

Frank Budgen claimed that "Joyce never saw any television at all" (Hart 158), yet the references to television in the *Wake*—particularly in the five broadcast sequences that punctuate the Butt and Taff episode (*FW* 341.19–342.31, 345.35–346.13, 349.07–350.09, 353.23–32, and 355.01–07)—demonstrate that he was familiar with the basic features of this emergent technology. In fact, it would be difficult for anyone, especially someone as interested in contemporary popular culture as Joyce, not to be aware of this potential new medium long before it became an ever-present reality. The concurrent development of visual media such as photography and film, and aural media, such as the telephone, the phonograph, and wireless radio, from the last quarter of the nineteenth century into the first quarter of the twentieth, as well as very recent evidence of their potential for combination (wirephoto services started in the early 1920s and the "talking" motion picture arrived in 1927), had encouraged many scientists and equally many commentators in the mass media to predict the eventual development of a technology for the electronic transmission of live picture and sound, either as a video-telephone like Tom Swift's "Photo Telephone" of 1914 (see chapter 5 and figure 5.2), or as a "*verbivocovisual*" broadcast medium (*FW* 341.19). The first use of the term "television"—which supplanted older names such as "telephot" and "telectroscope"—dates from a paper read by Constantin Perskyi on 25 August 1900, before the International Electricity Congress during the 1900 Paris Exhibition (Abramson, *History* 23), perhaps at the very same time Maximilian Berlitz was winning gold medals for his new language method elsewhere at the Exhibition (see chapter 3). There appears to have been only modest interest in the future of television in the popular media between 1900 and 1920—although international patent offices were dealing with a steady flow of applications for elements of the emergent technology and various prototypes (Abramson, *History* 23–50)—yet after broadcast radio arrived in the early 1920s and research into television accelerated, the mass media took notice. The American *Readers' Guide to Periodical Literature*, for example, identifies 8 articles on television between 1900 and 1920, yet 102 articles between 1921 and 1930, and 285 articles between 1931 and 1940. The television historian Albert Abramson notes several hundred articles that appeared from 1900 to 1939 in American and European technical journals and, even more important for our present discussion, in general audience magazines and the daily newspapers, either prophesying developments (e.g, "Distant Electric Vision," *London Times*, 15 November 1911), or later, describing some new demonstration of the medium (e.g., "Television Broadcast with Sound," *London Times*, 1 April 1930) (*History* 38, 300, n 3; see 277–326 passim). With the arrival of the "talkies" came the novel information medium of newsreels, several of which featured discussions and demonstrations of television research.[4] The British magazine *Television* began publication in July 1928, the same year American boy-wonder "Tom Swift" invented color TV—as I noted at the beginning of chapter 5—followed by his inventions of X-ray TV (1933) and three-dimensional TV (1934); the latter two devices have yet to make the successful transition from boys' books to our daily reality.

Given the extensive awareness in the general public of the imminence of television broadcasting through the 1920s and 1930s, in America, Europe, and the Far East—beginning in 1924, Professor Kenjiro Takayanagi made significant contributions to the developing technology in Japan (Abramson,

Figure 8.1. A profile shot of RCA president David Sarnoff announcing the beginning of regularly scheduled electronic, monochrome television broadcasts in the United States at the New York World's Fair in Queens, New York, on 20 April 1939. By permission of the David Sarnoff Library.

History 71, 101–2, and passim)—we might smile at William York Tindall's crediting Joyce for "having invented television" in *Finnegans Wake*: "there was no TV at the time of Earwicker's dream or Joyce's writing" (*A Reader's Guide to* Finnegans Wake 199, 197). As an American and a child of the Cold War era, however, I must confess that I long shared Tindall's apparent assumption that television was essentially an American invention, introduced to the world by David Sarnoff when he inaugurated NBC's television service at the opening of the New York World's Fair, on 20 April 1939, nearly three months after the *Wake* appeared. Our shared misimpression owes much to the exceptionalism that flourished in American popular culture through the pre-Vietnam era and even more to "General" Sarnoff's genius for self-promotion (see Tom Lewis's *Empire of the Air*).[5] In fact, regular television broadcast services were already in operation in Europe as Joyce completed his composition of *Finnegans Wake*.

Rather than just demythologizing Joyce, this fact also provides a simple explanation for why television is so prominent in chapter II, 3 of *Finnegans Wake*, although Joyce does make a handful of television references elsewhere in the book.[6] The Pub chapter was, save the final Roderick O'Connor sketch, the penultimate section of the *Wake* to be composed, between 1935 and 1938 (the final chapter was, appropriately, the last he composed, in 1937–38), and thus its composition coincided with the arrival of broadcast television in Germany in March 1935, in England in November 1936, and irregularly in France in 1935–36 (Hayman, "Preface" vii–xiii; Crisel 72; Wheen 32). Sad to say, Joyce neither "invented" television, nor was he gifted with prophecy in *Finnegans Wake*. Although accessible to limited numbers of people who could afford receivers—most notably proprietors of public houses like HCE, for the entertainment of their customers[7]—and although broadcasting would shortly cease in England and the United States with their entries into World War II (but not in Germany and Vichy France until 1943), as Joyce was writing the Butt and Taff episode for chapter II, 3 of the *Wake*, television was a contemporary reality with an ominous potential to make the work of literature "culturally anachronistic in the near future" (K. Williams 13).

Joyce nests the Butt and Taff episode (*FW* 338.05–355.07), the account of how Buckley shot the Russian General, in the center of chapter 3 of Part II of *Finnegans Wake*, following the notoriously opaque tale of Kersse the tailor and the Norwegian Captain that, after a brief prologue, occupies the first third of the chapter. Although the anecdote of Private Buckley shooting a general—"I was a bare prive" (*FW* 351.20)—represents just one of many versions of the archetypal attack of the son(s) on the father in the *Wake*, here Joyce emphatically sets off this section from the rest of the Pub chapter by presenting the story through a dramatic dialogue, reminiscent of the Circe episode of *Ulysses*, complete with parenthetical descriptions heading each speech by Butt and Taff. These gestures toward visualization parallel Joyce's introduction of the television at this point in the chapter; earlier and later only the radio receiver intrudes into the text. Evidently the pub patrons gather to watch this television, which "immerges" as "a mirage in a merror" every evening "for one watthour"—the typical length of the earliest daily broadcasting schedules—before the "host of [the] bottlefilled" calls "time jings [gents] pleas" (*FW* 310.24–26).[8] While Joyce supports both the battle between Kersse and the Norwegian Captain and the attacks on HCE in the last third of the chapter with copious military references, the pub-battlefield parallel—as well as the television—becomes central for the tale of Buckley in the chapter's midsection. It is far less clear, however, whether the pub patrons are watching a kind of slapstick routine on the TV (*"swapstick"* [*FW* 342.31]) performed by Butt and Taff, who seem to be fading from the *"screen"* at one point (*FW* 349.09). Equally likely, Butt and Taff are just two pub-crawlers—ordering their drinks, filling their pipes—whom the other patrons urge to retell the story of Buckley and the Russian General, even though they've "heard it sinse sung thousandtimes" (*FW* 338.01–02).

As the Butt and Taff section begins, introduced by the patrons' applause, a scene emerges: we are in a public house, and there are two characters, a soldier and a citizen: "A public plouse. Citizen soldiers" (*FW* 338.04). In their dialogue, Butt assumes the role of the military veteran Buckley—reminiscing about the battlefield and his fallen companions—while Taff becomes the citizen urging him to tell the tale (or tell-his-vision): "What see, buttywalch? Tell ever so often?" (*FW* 338.09–10). Similar to the radio transmissions that surface elsewhere in the chapter, television sequences periodically interrupt their dialogue, either interruptions *in* the broadcast itself, or interruptions *by* the broadcast during the pub dialogue. Whichever is the case, Joyce sets off these sequences, or televised intervals (*"swishingsight teilweisioned"* [*FW* 345.36; German *zwischenzeit*]), by placing them within brackets, indented, and italicized in the text, challenging his readers to find some connection between these paragraphs and the main dialogue, or the relation of these parts (*teilen*) to the whole. One discernible pattern, paralleling the Butt and Taff speeches, is the escalation of violence and increase of military references—"paramilintary langdwage" (*FW* 338.20)—through the five sequences; moreover, as the atmosphere of brutality and warfare increases, so also does the televisual dimension of these intervals.

The first section of the Butt and Taff dialogue (*FW* 338.04–341.17), leading up to the initial television sequence, establishes the imposing dress and features of the Russian General, an HCE figure, and culminates in Butt/Buckley's vision of the "aged monad" (*FW* 341.13)—the General is now a monarch—driven by necessity to relieve himself. Such human frailty and vulnerability in the General may reduce Butt and Taff to ridicule, but they do so only after Joyce has established his enormity as a "Bog carsse" (*FW* 339.06). That is, the General/HCE is a big arse, a big carcass, and/or a God-Tsar (Russian *бог-Царь*). His monstrousness inspires terror akin to the fear of thunder and lightning, not only in Butt, who shares his creator's dread of

Figure 8.2. The 1937 British HMV-900 entertainment console that contains both radio and television receivers and has a large mirror in its lid to reflect the television screen for the viewers. Joyce, who describes the television picture in HCE's pub "immerg[ing as] a mirage in a merror" (*FW* 310.24), presumably had just this kind of television receiver in mind. By permission of the Early Television Museum.

"Tenter and likelings" (*FW* 339.16–17), but also in Taff who, trembling and stuttering in response to Butt's narration, "shookatnaratatattar" (*FW* 339.18) and exclaims "Grozarktic!" (*FW* 339.21; i.e., "magnificent" [German *großartig*] and/or "thunderstorm" [Russian *гроза*]). The first television sequence that follows is a telecast of a day at the races (*FW* 341.19–342.32), featuring a contest rather than combat, although the winner of the race, "*Emancipator*" (*FW* 342.19), anticipates the Russian General by rudely exhibiting his "*Barass*" to the also-rans (*FW* 342.10), before mutating into the figure of the immense and terrifying patriarch "*Immensipater*" (*FW* 342.26).[9] Besides being a "*verbivocovisual presentment*" (*FW* 341.19–20), the passage contains no other references to television, and the violence in the dialogue, too, up to this point, resides mostly at the verbivoco-level of Joyce's allusions to warfare. Since the story of Buckley and the Russian General takes place during the "Crimealian wall" (*FW* 347.10), in this first part of the episode Joyce works in several allusions to the Crimea itself ("Chromean" [*FW* 339.09–10]), to campaign locales like Sevastopol and the Black Sea ("Sea vast a pool!" [*FW* 338.14]; "*a blackseer*" [*FW* 340.13]), to military figures from the conflict like Lords Raglan and Cardigan, General Scarlett, and Prince Menshikov (all clustered into one sentence, *FW* 339.10–13), as well as to both the title and memorable lines from the most famous British literary work to come out of the Crimean War, Tennyson's poem "The Charge of the Light Brigade," to which we shall return. Of course, one war is all wars in *Finnegans Wake*, or perhaps all wars devolve into the book's archetypical Battle of Waterloo, so here as elsewhere in the text we also find references to General Blücher ("blutcherudd" [*FW* 338.09]), the Duke of Wellington ("jupes of Wymmingtown" [*FW* 339.26]), and Napoleon ("boney" [*FW* 340.03]). Waterloo appears, merged with Austerlitz ("*awstooloo*" [*FW* 343.16]), and several times by itself later in the section, along with recurrent references to the three generals.[10] At the linguistic level—and as one would expect—here and throughout the Butt and Taff episode Joyce plays with Russian, Ukrainian, and a little Turkish, among several other languages, including Malay, for (to me) no obvious reason, and Armenian, for a very good reason: as the level of violence escalates through this section, Joyce will allude to other nightmares of history, such as the Easter Rising (*FW* 338.20), the assassination of General Bobrikoff (*FW* 338.32)—that other Russian General, murdered on 16 June 1904—the Boxer Rising (*FW* 347.29), the massacres of Huguenots and Albigensians (*FW* 350.30, 32), and ultimately, through language, to the genocidal slaughter of the Armenian people during the First World War: the "*Armenian Atrocity*" (*FW* 72.11).

In the second part of the dialogue (*FW* 342.34–345.33), Taff, scorning Butt for showing mercy to the General in his state of vulnerability, urges him both to return to his tale and to turn his weapon again toward the patriarchal figure: "Tell the coldspell's terroth! [. . .] Think some ingain think [. . .] and despatch! [. . . the] Papaist!" (*FW* 343.08–09,12; 344.06). Butt, however, again describes his terror at the sight, as well as the scent (Latin *aura*), of the now spectral figure of the General: "I no sooner seen aghist of his frighteousness then I was bibbering with vear," especially "when I seeing him [. . .] exposing his old skinful self tailbottom by manurevring in open ordure [. . . .] and caught the pfierce tsmell of his aurals" (*FW* 343.34–35, 344.12–13, 16–17, 24–25). Butt/Buckley "adn't the arts to" shoot the General (*FW* 345.02–03). The story pauses as Taff orders another round of drinks and a fill of tobacco for their pipes, while Butt reflects that drink is one of the few delights, or "dilates for the improvement of our foerses of nature," in this cruel world, a true "boesen fiennd" (*FW* 345.31–32, 33; i.e., both his "bosom friend" and, via German, his "evil enemy"). The second, brief television sequence that follows (*FW* 345.35–346.13) ostensibly suggests that the other pub patrons in the Mulingar Inn, forgotten in the interim, or perhaps just the "four" (mamalujo), have become increasingly drunk and/or abused, and distracted by the television, or possibly are themselves on TV: "*The other foregotthened abbosed in the Mullingaria are during this swishingsight teilweisioned*" (*FW* 345.35–36). What follows are NEWS reports from the four compass points, NSEW: Nizhniy-Novgorod, Spain, Arabia, and New Haven ("*Yales boys*" [*FW* 346.07]), yet as the television itself has become more prominent, the word-play has become increasingly paramilitary: fuses/forces ("*furses*"), tattoo ("*tatoovatted*"), the deviltry of the Ku Klux Klan ("*Knives Riders axecutes devilances*"), and revolutions ("*rebolutions*") (*FW* 346.01, 03, 06, 08). The escalating violence of the preceding section of the Butt and Taff dialogue similarly resides at the level of language, especially in Butt's speech on 344–45 that begins by echoing Christy's brogue in Synge's *Playboy of the Western World*—a play about this son's attempted murder of his father (McHugh 344)—and intensifies the pattern of references to the First World War that have begun to appear in this section of the dialogue. Butt, for example, suffers a kind of shell shock when Taff urges him to shoot the General (World War references and slang underlined): "BUTT (*giving his scimmianised twinge*

[Siamese twin] *in acknuckledownedgment of this cumulikick* [communiqué], *strafe from the firetrench, studenly drobs ledi* [drop lead; drops dead], *satoniseels ouchyotchy* [i.e., father's ears; Russian *уши отцы*], *he changecors induniforms as he is lefting the gat out of the big* [machine gun (Gatling gun); cat out of the bag]: *his face glows green, his hair greys white, his bleyes bcome broon to suite his cultic twalette* [the symptoms of terror, the distortions of colors caused by flares or by a Yeatsean 'celtic twilight'])" (*FW* 344.08–12). Elsewhere in this section Joyce weaves in references, among other Great War allusions, to Mons ("armeemonds" [*FW* 343.05]), Tommy-lad (*FW* 343.08), the misfortunes of Siegfried Sassoon ("*unglucksarsoon*" [*FW* 344.01]), the flares over the battle-action ("sheenflare of the battleaxes" [*FW* 344.24]), and saphead (*FW* 344.26), and continues to conflate allusions to both the First World War and the Crimean War in the balance of the Butt and Taff episode, "Siamese twinning" the Great War veteran Butt, it would seem, with the Crimean War veteran Buckley.[11]

The third section of the Butt and Taff dialogue (*FW* 346.15–349.05) begins with Taff passing another drink—the black-stuff, Guinness stout, "*buckthurnstock*" (*FW* 346.15)—to Butt, offering him more of his "bosom friend," but also perhaps playing the role of his "evil enemy" by encouraging Butt both to "say your piece! How Buccleuch shocked the rosing girnirilles" (*FW* 346.20–21)—that is, tell the story!—and to commit the patr-, reg-, tsar-, HCE-icide himself. Butt drinks a toast to his fallen comrades in battles past—"bycorn spirits fuselaiding" (*FW* 348.11)—and follows this with rallying cries, as he moves to attack, urged on by Taff: "if you piggots, marsh! Do the nut, dingbut! [If you please, march! Do the nothing-but!]" (*FW* 349.03–04). As Butt charges (we presume), the text breaks off for the third, "*heliotropical noughttime*" television passage (*FW* 349.07), paralleling the rising violence in the dialogue with the most explicit and extensive treatment of this technology in the *Wake* and firmly establishing the connection between the creation of the television picture and the destruction of warfare: the television screen becomes Tennyson's "valley of Death" (ll. 7, 16) of Balaclava—"balaceivka" and "bullyclaver" (*FW* 341.09, 352.23)—and the Western Front as well. Preparing his readers for his translation of the double-envelopment and apparent annihilation of the British cavalry—"enmivallupped. Chromean fastion" (*FW* 339.09–10) in the Battle of Balaclava (25 October 1854) and promptly memorialized by Tennyson in "The Charge of the Light Brigade" (1854)— into television's "*charge of a light barricade*" (*FW* 349.11), Joyce alludes to the poem several times leading up to this central video interlude (e.g., also see *FW* 339.07, 347.14, 348.25) and specifically transforms Marshall Pierre Bosquet's famous response to the charge, "*C'est magnifique, mais ce n'est pas la guerre*," to allude to the anticipatory visual technologies of film and photography: "Say mangraphique [cinematographic], may say nay por daguerre!" (*FW* 339.23).[12]

The third, "*heliotropical noughttime*" sequence (*FW* 349.07–350.09) leaves little doubt that we are watching television as, on the immediate level, images of Butt and Taff "*fade*" into a purplish darkness and nonexistence on a "*screen*" (*FW* 349.07–09), and another figure, a spectral HCE—combining the father, the Pope, and Popeye ("*Popey*"), with the Father General of the Jesuits and the Russian General ("*the jesuneral of the russuates*") (*FW* 349.20–21)—emerges on screen to take control of the medium. Ever the exhibitionist, this "*idolon*" (*FW* 349.21), or specter, transported to the viewers through space, displays his several decorations and conducts a religious service, actions appropriate to a military and ecclesiastical leader, but he also blinks his eyes, blows his nose, holds up his fingers, and wipes his mouth, typical activities telecast in early demonstrations of television technology.[13] Naturally, Joyce has HCE extend the voyeuristic possibilities of the medium, for the General also confesses all his vices, discusses his sex life, and exhibits himself—"*he touched upon this* [his] *tree of livings*" (*FW* 350.01–02)—more or less anticipating current "reality TV," and then concludes his demonstration/service by taking a collection. Coins rattle on the plate—"*Dtin, dtin, dtin, dtin!*" (*FW* 350.09)—to close the passage.

Within this "*heliotropical noughttime*" passage Joyce alludes to several elements of electronic television technology, but not to the exclusion of references to the pioneering work of John Logie Baird, of "*the bairdboard bombardment screen*" (*FW* 349.09), who through much of his career employed the "flying spot" of light generated by a Nipkow disk (Abramson, *History* 83–84)—"*the scanning firespot*" (*FW* 349.15)—to develop mechanical devices for telecasting that ultimately proved inferior to electronic systems.[14] The Nipkow disk, patented by Paul Nipkow in 1884 as the "*elektrisches Telescop*," was a disk perforated by a series of holes, spiraling inward from its circumference; when rotating in front of and perpendicular to a source of light, one rotation of the disk would generate a spot of light that would completely scan an object before it, which in turn could be converted into electronic data for transmission. Into the early 1930s, most experimental television apparatuses used this bulky and temperamental mechanical device "for both

J. L. BAIRD WITH ONE OF HIS EARLIEST EXPERIMENTAL MACHINES.

Figure 8.3. John Logie Baird standing beside his 1925 apparatus for mechanically generating a television image. Baird is gesturing toward the Nipkow disk that directed the "flying spot" of light upon the image to be televised. Alfred Dinsdale, *Television* (London: Television Press, 1928), 48.

the transmitter and receiver" (Fisher and Fisher 17). The future of television, however, lay in the discovery of an all-electronic means of scanning an object (camera) and reproducing the object (receiver). This was the challenge met by the RCA engineer Vladimir Zworykin who adapted an electronic device called the Image Dissector, developed by Philo Farnsworth in 1926, which, as its name suggests, broke "down a visual image into a stream of electrons" (Fisher and Fisher 139). Zworykin developed and refined his "Iconoscope" between 1931 and 1935 (Abramson, *History* 195–225, and *Zworykin* 87–113 and passim). Until the arrival of digital technology at the end of the twentieth century, the "basic process" for generating and receiving television signals employed "almost exactly the same principles as [systems] designed by Farnsworth and Zworykin in the 1930s [. . .]: scan an image with a beam of electrons to create an electrical signal [via an iconoscope], and then recreate the image at the receiver by turning that signal back into an electron beam and bombarding a fluorescent screen" via a reciprocal device called a kinescope (Fisher and Fisher 341). (In 1928 Ricardo Bruni in Italy invented a device similar to Zworykin's Iconoscope, which he called a "Photoscope" [Abramson, *History* 111–12].) The essential component of the iconoscope/kinescope system is an "Electron gun" that generates an "Electron scanning beam" which, in the camera—and on the same principle as the machinegun of World War I—strafes a complete field upon which it is directed to detect a picture and dissects it into several hundred lines. In the receiver another electron gun—again replicating the strafing of a machine-gunner—bombards a screen, coated with cesium, with a beam of electrons, regenerating a picture in several hundred lines (Fisher and Fisher 204–5). One complete and nearly instantaneous sweep of the field, left to right and bottom to top, generates a single teleframe. In the first thirteen lines of the "*heliotropical noughttime*" paragraph (*FW* 349.07–19), Joyce alludes to these basic elements of television technology: "*a metenergic reglow of beaming Batt, the bairdboard bombardment screen*" (8–9), "*teleframe*" (10), "*the charge of a light barricade*"(11), "*photoslope*" (11), "*Spraygun rakes and splits them*" (13–14), "*alextronite* [electrons]" (15), "*scanning firespot*" (15), "*sgunners traverses* [. . .] *lines*" (16), "*caeseine coatings*" (17), "*Amid a fluorescence*" (18), "*through the inconoscope*" (19). To these, Joyce adds references to transformers ("*transformed Tuff*" [7–8]), "*step up*" amplifiers (10), electronic sync pulses that synchronize the transmitting and receiving electron guns ("*syncopanc pulses*" [11–12]), carrier waves that bear the broadcast signal ("*carnier walve*" [13]), and the "*double focus*" (14) that controls the horizontal and vertical paths of the scanning electron beam.

Although electron guns sound ominous, there would seem to be nothing inherently violent in this description of television technology; a second look, however, reveals that Joyce reimagines the television, like the pub generally, as a battlefield, and this battlefield fuses the Battle of Balaclava and the Western Front. Bruni's photoscope becomes a "*photoslope*," down which descend "*missledhropes*," that is, the misled troops in "*the charge of a light barricade*," with their misled hopes, but also missiled-troops under the "*bombardment*" of Russian ordnance, "*glitterglatteraglutt*" (*FW* 349.09–13). This scene matches Lord Cardigan's report of the charge:

> We advanced down a gradual descent of more than three-quarters of a mile, with the batteries vomiting forth upon us shells and shot, round and grape, with one battery on our right flank and another on

Fig.1.

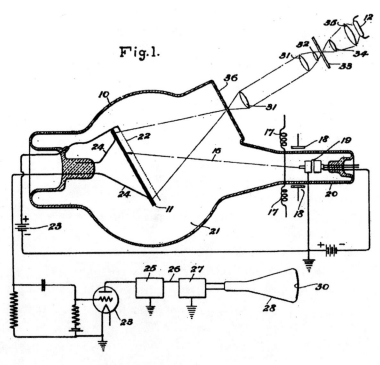

Fig.2.

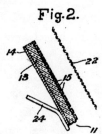

INVENTOR.

Vladimir K. Zworykin,

BY

HIS ATTORNEY.

Figure 8.4. Zworykin's schematic in his patent application for the Iconoscope, a high-vacuum, cathode-ray tube, the technological development that made electronic television possible. "Fig. 1." illustrates, in detail, the Iconoscope tube itself (10), from the lens admitting the televised image into the tube (12) to the circuit for transmitting the image to a receiver (25–30); "Fig. 2." enlarges the design of the photosensitive screen (11) in the Iconoscope. According to Zworykin's description of the operation of the Iconoscope in his patent application (here condensed), a "light image of [an] object" (12) is "projected on the photosensitive surface" (15, in Fig. 2), by a series of lenses (31–35). An "electron gun 19" "scan[s] the photosensitive surface" with a "cathode ray 16," creating "current pulses or picture signals to be developed in the grid circuit of a suitable amplifier tube 23." "The amplified picture signals are supplied to a suitable transmitting system 25 and over a connection 26 to a suitable receiving system 27, to which a cathode ray receiving tube 28 is connected." "In operation, a moving image of the object is reproduced on the usual fluorescent screen 30 on the large end of the tube 28." Although developed before the Iconoscope but not patented until 1938 (No. 2,109,245), this receiving tube, called the Kinescope, reciprocates the Iconoscope by containing another *electron gun* that scans the photosensitive inner lining of the picture tube with yet another beam of electrons. United States Patent Office.

the left, and all the intermediate ground covered with the Russian riflemen; so that when we came to within a distance of fifty yards from the mouths of the artillery which had been hurling destruction upon us, we were, in fact, surrounded and encircled by a blaze of fire, in addition to the fire of the riflemen upon our flanks. As we ascended the hill the oblique fire of the artillery poured upon our rear, so that we had thus a strong fire upon our front, our flank, and our rear. (*Hansard's* col. 1310)[15]

But the scene immediately mutates into a typical advance on the Western Front where the "six hundred" of Tennyson's refrain in "The Charge of the Light Brigade" are both the "*sunksundered lines*" of a 600-line teleframe[16] and the attacking soldiers, slaughtered by the enemy machine gunners in double enfilade—"*Spraygun rakes and splits them from a double focus* [. . .] *and the scanning firespot of the sgunners traverses the rutilanced* [glowing and pierced] *illustred* [lighted and bloodied] *sunksundered* [fallen and dispersed] *lines*" (*FW* 349.13–16). These too are "*missledhropes*" bombarded by grenades ("*grenadite*"), dynamite ("*damnymite*"), electrons ("*alextronite*"), and something Joyce calls "*nichilite*," carrying a suggestion of annihilation and, paired with "*alextronite*," alluding to the Tsars that led Russia in the Crimean and First World Wars, Alexander II and Nicholas II, respectively.[17]

The violence continues to escalate in the fourth section of the Butt and Taff dialogue (*FW* 350.11–353.21), and this escalation carries over into the fourth television sequence as well. Preparatory to his final assault, Butt/ Buckley whips himself into a fury against "His Heriness" (*FW* 351.31; i.e., Highness, Holiness, and Hairyness), the bearish Russian General—"his urssian gemenal" (*FW* 352.01)—by remembering his wartime sufferings and the General's infuriating philandering. Here again Joyce conflates the two wars in his narrative, now through the motif of tobacco, chiefly cigarettes, which were introduced to English soldiers during the Crimean campaigns and achieved general acceptance during the First World War (Meyer 72–80). Butt cadges cigarettes at the front, "we preying players and pinching peacesmokes, troupkers tomiatskyns all" (*FW* 350.26–28; Players cigarettes, pipes [Russian трубки], Tommies), and later accepts the "zyngarettes" distributed by "Woodbine Willie, so popiular with the poppyrossies" (*FW* 351.12–13; referring to a clergyman who distributed cigarettes to the troops in the First War [McHugh 351], plus Russian echoes of Crimea: "gypsies" [цыганы] and "cigarettes" [*папиросы*]). Butt recalls sleeping through nights when the only light was the enemy shelling the lines ("shellalite on the darkumen" [*FW* 350.29]), and reading his Bible in the trenches: "every warson wearier kaddies a komnate in his schnapsack" (*FW* 350.34; "komnate" combines the Soviet "comrade" and the Russian "room" (*комната*), while "schnapsack" blends "knapsack" and "schnapps," Butt's "boesen fiennd" [*FW* 345.33]). Mixing nostalgia with horror, Butt recalls "Then were the hellscyown [halcyon, hell's own] days for our fellows" (*FW* 351.05–06), and he is tempted to rationalize his sufferings as simply the nature of warfare, "Baghus the whatwar [Because that was war]" (*FW* 351.24), until Taff "*asbestos can, wiz the healps of gosh* [God] *and his bluzzid maikar*," whips him again into a fury (*FW* 352.35–36). So, Butt recounts and/or reenacts his assassination of the General because "He," the General himself or perhaps Taff, "deared me to it and he dared me do it" (*FW* 353.10–11). When the General by a single gesture insults Ireland and all the lads of Russia—"that instullt to Igorladns"—by raising a "sob of tunf [sod of turf] for to claimhis [clean his]" arse, "for to wollpimsolff," Butt/Buckley shoots, "Sparro [Italian, 'I fire']" (*FW* 353.16–19, 21).

The following brief television sequence (*FW* 353.23–32) depicts a worldwide cataclysm caused by this gunshot, this release of energy, which like the electron gun of the iconoscope—"*moletons skaping with mulicules* [electrons escaping from molecules]"—creates "*uttermosts confussion*" in Picadilly ("*Pinkandindy*"), with repercussions telecast back from various points on the globe (and through history): "*Similar scenatas are projectilised from Hullulullu, Bawlawayo, empyreal Raum* [Rome] *and mordern Atems* [Athens]" (*FW* 353.26–27, 29–30). More ominously yet, Joyce here transforms the electron gun of the television into a device for splitting the atom, a possibility widely under discussion among physicists during the 1930s—building on Baron Rutherford's orbital model of the atom ("*the grunder* [German 'founder'] *of the first lord of Hurtreford*" [*FW* 353.24])—and, ironically, ultimately accomplished in 1938 by Otto Hahn and Lise Meitner, although not publicized until January 1939, the month before the publication of *Finnegans Wake* (Pais 158; also see Graetzer and Anderson). Joyce would have known the possible consequence of nuclear fission is a thermonuclear "*explododetonat*[ion]" (*FW* 353.24–25), although he makes a common mistake by "confussing" fission with fusion. In short, Joyce's correlation of television with the increasing violence of warfare now moves from the technological achievement of the automatic weapon—the machinegun that revolutionized military tactics in the First World War—to an anticipation of the ultimate violence of atomic war, on the near horizon in 1939. More than this, the television's *"abnihilation of the etym"* (*FW* 353.23) signifies not only the destruction of the atom but the annihilation of the *word*, the eradication of literature.

The final section of the Butt and Taff episode (*FW* 353.34–354.36) is, properly speaking, a brief epilogue, for the tale has already concluded: the General is dead, the war is over, and the violence is past, although the rite will have to be repeated, much as the tale needs to be told "thousandtimes" over (*FW* 338.02). Just as nature recycles every spring ("germinal"), Buckley again will shoot the Russian General: "So till butagain budly [boldly] shoots thon rising germinal let bodley [Buckley/Taff] chow the fatt [—> ttaf] of his anger and badly [Buckley/Butt] bide the toil of his tubb [—> bbut; bite the tail of his butt]" (*FW* 354.34–36). In the meantime, the pub patrons join in celebrating the overthrow and destruction *"of Old Erssia's* [Russia/Eire] *magisquammythical mulattomilitiaman,"* the autocrat *"whose sway craven minions had caused to revile, as, too foul for hell"* (*FW* 354.10–12), while the two speakers, Butt and Taff, *"now"* resolve into *"one and the same person"* (*FW* 354.08). In effect, Joyce is emphasizing one feature of the Butt and Taff dialogue that might otherwise pass unnoted. Most of the other dialogic relations in the *Wake*, like "The Mookse and The Gripes" (*FW* 152.15 ff), "Burrus and Caseous" (*FW* 161.12 ff), or even the dialogue of the washerwomen in the "Anna Livia Plurabelle" chapter (I, 8; *FW* 196–216), all variations on the war between antithetical principles represented by Shaun and Shem—eye and ear, space and time, philistine and artist, authoritarianism and freedom, death (stone) and life (tree/stem), and so on—are unresolved. The Butt and Taff episode, however, is less another "tale told of Shaun [and] Shem" (*FW* 215.35), than a triumph of Shaun over Shem that will continue with Shaun's ascendancy in Book III of *Finnegans Wake*. By resolving Butt and Taff into a single Shaun-figure, Joyce finally protects his verbal artist from any association with the medium of television.

The following, final television sequence (*FW* 355.01–07) is similarly placid and brief. The thumb and five fingers of the typical broadcast demonstration return—last seen in the third sequence (*FW* 349.30–31)—and/or the tap and pipes and patrons of the pub reappear: *"The pump and pipe pingers are ideally reconstituted"* from their previous *"abnihilisation"* (*FW* 355.01, 353.23). *"All th[os]e presents"* return to fully sensory existence, having survived both war and televisualization, as Joyce emphasizes by weaving all five senses into the remainder of the central sentence (*FW* 355.02–05). Most important, the powder and shot of warfare have been put away—"*The putther and bowls are peterpacked up*" (*FW* 355.01–02)—this living world has returned, and the violence has ended because . . . the screen is now a "*Blunk*," the television has been turned off and is now closed, "Shutmup" (*FW* 355.07–08).

What did Joyce have against television? The mere word, a fusion of Latin (-vision) and Greek (tele-) roots, that is, a portmanteau word from "the lapins [rabbits] and the grigs [hens]" (*FW* 113.02), should have appealed to him, and—as we have seen elsewhere—he seemed generally to welcome contemporary mass cultural phenomena and technological developments as more raw material for his consumption and transformation into art, for his cannibalistic re-creation. His profoundly negative response to this visual medium, then, otherwise little different from the sound medium of radio that he embraced, seems contradictory. Of course, his distaste for television does not prevent him from dismembering its parts and reemploying them for his art of cultural transfer; but here, I think, is also the explanation for Joyce's association of this new technology with violence and warfare, for he seems to have suspected—indeed, feared—that television represented a powerful antithesis to creative art, that television, using a "gun" for both the production and reproduction of its signals, portended destruction of both creator and audience. Or, to put it simply, the loss of an audience for literature would be sufficient to put an end to authorship, and this audience can be lost both in the marketplace and, less directly, by the expropriation of its ability to engage intelligently with the work of literature. Joyce was not alone in seeing television as threatening both kinds of loss.

In *Revolution in Writing* (1935), C. Day Lewis expresses the anxiety felt by many British writers during the 1930s at the endangered literary market: "When television is perfected [. . . it] will provide us with an unreality far more unreal or a realism a hundred times more devastating than the most frenzied ambitions of the entertainment writers can rise to" (15; qtd. K. Williams 13). In the first part of this chapter I argued that Joyce felt that film offered little competition to the primacy of works of literature that could engage the readers' inner mental activity and promote their consciousness of "their own processes of perception" (Kittler, *Gramophone* 161), based on a conviction that the readers' desire and ability to animate a text remained literature's enduring appeal and source of power. This conviction was easier for Joyce to maintain, so long as competing attractions for this audience's attention remained limited in their power to usurp their processes of perception: the silent film, for example, appealed exclusively to the audience's vision, and was further limited by its lack of color, and the radio appealed exclusively to their hearing. Film, moreover, was a storage technology like the phonograph recording, so what it might gain by the, perhaps, greater immediacy of the visual was lost by its reproducibility; radio, on the other hand, had the power of presence, but lacked the immediacy of the seen. Such generalizations, however, were becoming less tenable as the 1920s moved into the 1930s—sound films had arrived and color was imminent—and television offered to introduce the most seductive appeal of all: sound, sight, and *presence.* The miracle that television promised was the possibility of distant-seeing, of viewing instantaneously something that was happening at the very same moment in another place. (There appears to have been no anticipation of the video-recording revolution—or even the seven-second delay—that has turned television, today, largely into a storage technology.) Television's lack of color was widely understood to be only a temporary limitation. The technology for color television developed together with television itself, but the industry initially withheld color from production to keep down the cost of receivers and, after World War II, delayed its introduction for a decade because of the costs of conversion for both broadcasters and consumers (Fisher and Fisher 299–332). This is why Day Lewis sees in television a medium that could produce a "realism a hundred times more devastating" than the printed word because of its power to fully co-opt the audience's processes of perception. And this, too, is Joyce's point in turning off the television at the conclusion of the Butt and Taff episode in chapter II, 3 of the *Wake.* Doing so returns the viewers to life, restoring the patrons of the pub to their individual *presence* and *sensory* completeness in their reality: "*All the presents are determining as regards for the future the howabouts of their past absences which they might see on at hearing could they once smell of tastes from touch*" (*FW* 355.02–05). The patrons have not been absent somewhere, while viewing the television; they have been absent *somehow,* and this is why they are recovering their "*howabouts.*" They have returned to life from the "valley of Death" that is television (Tennyson, ll. 7, 16), for the perceived threat of this medium was not simply its competition in the market, but also its capacity to usurp the viewers' individual reality and their subjectivity, their independent powers of thought.

T. S. Eliot, for example, although writing of film, laments the reduction of the audience to the state of automata: "what happens to the minds of the thousands of people who feast their eyes every night, when in a peculiarly passive state under the hypnotic influence" of the cinema? ("The Cinema Quota" 290; qtd. Cunningham 282). Eliot's question expresses a characteristic refrain that echoes in critiques of radio, as in Horkheimer and Adorno's observations on the subject's loss of subjectivity (122), and migrates into the cultural analyses of television.[18] Among the ways "television has altered our world," Raymond Williams claims, is that "its character and uses exploited and emphasised elements of a passivity, a cultural and psychological inadequacy, which had always been latent in people, but which television now organized and came to represent" (12). But James Joyce was far from the first to express this conviction that television could reduce its viewers to the living-death of a state of "mindless passivity" (Cunningham 282), as he does by associating this medium with individual and global annihilation in *Finnegans Wake*; Aldous Huxley anticipated him by seven years in his dystopia *Brave New World* (1932).

Huxley and Joyce would seem to have little in common, except their eye troubles that seem to have been the subject of a few "lugubrious discussions" between the two in a handful of visits they exchanged in Paris, in 1929–30 (Ellmann, *James Joyce* 621). Their works have less in common. Yet Huxley—responding even sooner than Joyce to a medium that, in 1932, was still a few years away from becoming a reality—foresees television as a dominant media technology in the future. Television functions throughout *Brave New World*, together with the "Feelies" and the narcotic "*soma*," to support a totalitarian system that maintains social stability by perpetually sedating the masses and thus preventing independent thought. As Mustapha Mond explains to John Savage, the greatest threat to the system is an individual capable of exercising critical intelligence, and for this reason science and literature—even "*Othello*"—have been suppressed in this future society: "But that's the price we have to pay for stability. You've got to choose between happiness and what people used to call high art. We've sacrificed the high art" (220). That Joyce similarly sees television's potential for "central control" and sedation of the masses by its totalizing and illusory representation of the real seems clear in his sustained association between the General and totalitarianism in the Butt and Taff episode (Horkheimer and Adorno 121); and while he offers a side-glance at Nazi storm troopers in this part of the *Wake* ("stormtrooping" [*FW* 344.23]), for Joyce totalitarianism seems to be synonymous with Russia, past and present. As we have already noticed, the General frequently mutates into the Tsar of all the Russias—"the sur of all Russers" (*FW* 340.35) or "the Saur of all the Haurousians" (*FW* 344.33)—but Joyce also alludes to the contemporary Soviet Union in several places (e.g., "*the sickle*" [*FW* 341.10], "*commonturn* [Comintern]" [*FW* 354.19], and paraphrases Soviet political and economic slogans in the final paragraph of the episode [*FW* 354.07–36]).[19]

Late in life, Frank Budgen told Clive Hart that Joyce hoped "readers of *Finnegans Wake* would be better able to appreciate the book if its material were presented partly in terms of the new medium [of television] in which the world was growing so interested" (158), and Hart speculates that the *Wake* might be considered a televisual book in the sense that when its thematic and linguistic "units" are "projected on to the resolving screen of the interpreting mind, their true significance is revealed" (160). In making this suggestion, Hart assumes from Budgen's remark that Joyce must have seen television positively and as an analogue to "his own creative process" (159). Unfortunately, this assumption completely overlooks the "paramilintary" dimension of virtually every reference to television in the *Wake* (*FW* 338.20), as well as the possibility that Joyce intended his use of television not to be an endorsement of this new medium, but a warning to the world, for Hart reverses the most fundamental point of the Butt and Taff episode: to Joyce, television does not stimulate, but portends the death of the "interpreting mind."

Forging Consciousness

James Joyce's conception of his art as a cannibalistic incorporation and re-embodiment of language, literary tradition, and contemporary culture, for the subsequent consumption of his readership, was a fundamental consequence of his personal formation as a Roman Catholic and Irishman, coming of age at the turn of the twentieth century. Joyce internalized and transmuted and thus culturally transferred into a positive aesthetic the barbarism projected upon the Irish by British imperialist ideology, a pattern of "false projection" that recurs throughout the history of religious persecution and colonialism, wherein the barbaric impulses "which the subject will not admit as his own even though they are most assuredly so, are attributed to the object—the prospective victim" (Horkheimer and Adorno 187). As we have seen, Joyce's portrayals of Gabriel Conroy, Stephen Dedalus, and Leopold Bloom demonstrate his complete awareness of the power of such projections to colo-

Figure 8.5. A visual parable of active consumption, and as good an illustration of a *Finnegans Wake* reading group in action as any. The body of the "spitting cannibal"—first seen facing his immolation in figure 1—is now being divided, to be eaten and drunk. (The active observer will notice that the artist has put two severed heads in the picture.) One of the "most sensational" illustrations by Théodore de Bry (Alexander 8) for his reprinting of Staden's *True History of His Captivity, 1557*, in *Americae Tertia Pars* (Frankfurt am Main: Ioannem Wechelum, 1592), 127. Courtesy of Rare Books and Special Collections, University of South Carolina.

nize not only the person but also the *mind* of the colonized. Paralleling the transformation in his native Ireland, much of which was freed from Britain's political control with the establishment of the Irish Free State in 1922, contemporaneously with his completion and publication of *Ulysses*, Joyce's attention turns more directly toward such cultural forms of subjection to illustrate, by his own example in *Finnegans Wake*, that the individual's best chance of preserving his subjectivity lies in consuming this culture and transferring it into palatable forms, rather than in being the subject consumed by it.

Individuals possessed of "interpreting mind[s]," then, fully engaged with their acts of reading, fully invested in the labor of their production of meaning, and fully conscious of "their own processes of perception" (Kittler, *Gramophone* 161), as *active* consumers of the literary text, we may call intellectual *cannibals*, for cannibalism is no doubt the most aggressive and active form of consumption imaginable in our culture. Through his career, Joyce clearly developed technical strategies to generate precisely this kind of reading, the reciprocal to his own creative cannibalism: his ingestion, digestion, and incorporation of the bodies of traditional and contemporary literature and culture into the living body of his own work. Thus Montaigne's "spitting cannibal," as I remark in my opening chapter, is to my mind the most apt image for Joyce as a creative artist: rather than acting as the mere passive victim of cannibalization, Joyce, the cannibal himself facing consumption, exhorts those who feed on him to consume actively, to "all come boldly and gather to dine off him, for they will be eating at the same time their own fathers and grandfathers, who have served to feed and nourish his body" (158). And thus moving the metaphor of cannibalization toward the literal, for both author and reader, helps us understand the fundamentally oxymoronic nature of the concept of *passive* consumption, so central to the critiques of the modern audience for mass media by Wyndham Lewis, T. S. Eliot, Aldous Huxley, and C. Day Lewis in the 1920s and 1930s, as we have seen, and extended by the Frankfurt School through mid-century. For instance, in 1938, Theodor Adorno rejects Benjamin's optimistic assumption that mechanical reproduction has productively changed "the mode of [the consumers'] participation" in the work of art—"Quantity has been transmuted into quality" (239)—by contending, in "On the Fetish-Character in Music and the Regression of Listening," that the mass performance and reproduction of contemporary music has instead effected a "decline of the individual" (Arato and Gebhardt 270), a reduction of the audience to "the infantile stage" of a pre-intellectual existence: "Not only do the listening subjects lose, along with freedom of choice and responsibility, the capacity for conscious perception of music, which was from time immemorial confined to a narrow group, but they stubbornly reject the possibility of such perception" (286). Subsequently Adorno and Max Horkheimer expand this argument in their examination of "The Culture Industry['s]" subjugation of the masses in *Dialectic of Enlightenment* (1944, 1947), which I have also cited above, and it reaches both its fullest exposition and widest audience in Herbert Marcuse's counter-cultural classic and best seller *One-Dimensional Man* (1964), to be echoed later in the century by, among many other examples, Raymond Williams's critique of television and Friedrich Kittler's commentary on the Golem-ization of the motion picture audience. Indeed, a full genealogy of this critique would probably start with Plato's "Allegory of the Caves" and lead us through the Enlightenment project, from Descartes' ideal of the analytical intelligence, Kant's autonomous subject (viz. "Beantwortung der Frage: Was ist Aufklärung?" ["Answer to the Question: What Is Enlightenment?" 1784]), Hegel's developed self-consciousness (viz. the master vs. the slave in *Phenomenology of the Mind* [1807]), that is, the "*Geist*," whose passing "around 1900" with the emergence of "programmed subjects" Kittler laments (*Gramophone* 166), together, one presumes, with the death in 1900 of Friedrich Nietzsche, whose worldview seems to resonate with that of the commentator I began with, Wyndham Lewis. In a passage from *The Art of Being Ruled* that Joyce may well have read and, if he did, would have approved for its allusion to Jesuit rules of discipline, Lewis once again oddly coincides with Joyce in his vision of the heteronomous modern consumer:

> Absence of responsibility, an automatic and stereotyped rhythm, is what men most desire for themselves. All struggle has for its end relief or repose. A rhythmic movement is restful: but consciousness and possession of the self is not compatible with a set rhythm. All the libertarian cries of a century ago were based on unreal premises, and impulses that are not natural to, and cannot be sustained by, the majority of men. Luxury and repose are what most men undeniably desire. They would like to be as much at rest as if they were dead, and as active and 'alive' as passivity will allow. [. . .] The extreme expression of this desire is the jesuit ideal of self-annihilating obedience, so that the adept becomes a disinterested machine, ecstatically obedient, delighted to find himself entirely in the power of another person, his superior in will and vitality. (142–43)

Lewis's conviction that "power is the ubiquitous principle of human affairs" would shortly lead him in a political direction that Joyce would consider an abomination: toward an admiration for Hitler as "the man who exercised [power] openly" (Kenner, *Wyndham Lewis* 72). Over the near quarter-century between the composition of the Nestor episode of *Ulysses* and the Butt and Taff sequence in *Finnegans Wake* we can trace a far different political trajectory for Joyce, because he was a man who, unlike Lewis, had actually experienced the rigors of the Jesuit rules of discipline, a man who, again unlike Lewis, could see himself as a victim of colonial political oppression, and thus a man who reacted far differently from Lewis to the ubiquity of power in human affairs. Responding to the ultimate expression of European imperial politics, World War I, contemporaneous with the writing of *Ulysses*, and to the increasing power of totalitarian regimes in Italy, Germany, Spain, and particularly Russia through the 1920s and 1930s, contemporaneous with the writing of *Finnegans Wake*, Joyce created works that attempt, far more ambitiously than his earlier fiction, to reclaim and forge the alienated consciousness of the human race.

Notes

Preface: From Cannibalism to Cannibalization

1. Here and throughout this study I abbreviate my citations from the standard editions of Joyce's five principal works of fiction—fully identified in the bibliography—as follows: *D = Dubliners, FW = Finnegans Wake, P = A Portrait of the Artist as a Young Man, SH = Stephen Hero*, and *U = Ulysses*. References to Joyce's early fiction provide the page numbers in the Viking Critical Editions of *Dubliners* and *A Portrait of the Artist as a Young Man*, and the New Directions edition of *Stephen Hero*; references to *Ulysses* are to the episode and line number(s) in the Gabler edition; references to *Finnegans Wake* are to the page(s) and line number(s) in the Viking edition.

2. Personal correspondence between Prof. Dr. Ewald Mengel and the author. I am also indebted to Professor Mengel for the translation of Lüsebrink and Reichardt, quoted below.

3. Personal correspondence between Prof. Dr. Ewald Mengel and the author.

Chapter 1. "Consumption, was it?": Joyce and Cannibalism

1. *Anthropophagy* specifically denotes the consumption of humans, whereas *cannibalism* means like-eating-like within a species, human or nonhuman. Hitchcock's "The Specialty of the House" was an adaptation of a short story with the same title, by Stanley Ellin, that first appeared in *Ellery Queen's Mystery Magazine* no. 54 (May 1948). Fortunately, Sbirro's seems to have no connection to the international pizza chain Sbarro's.

2. For a review of several uses (and abuses) of the idea of cannibalism in contemporary cultural critique, see King 106–23.

3. H. L. Malchow devotes two extended chapters, half the content, of his *Gothic Images of Race in Nineteenth-Century Britain* (1996) to the century's popular fixation on anthropophagy: "Cannibalism and Popular Culture" (41–123) and "Vampire Gothic and Late-Victorian Identity" (124–66).

4. The "Great Hunger," the potato famine in Ireland (1846–47) that caused 1 to 1.5 million deaths (estimates vary), was only the most recent in a series of famines to strike Ireland during the centuries of English colonial occupation; an estimated 737,000 Irish also perished during an earlier nineteenth-century famine in 1816–17 (Askenasy 62).

Kevin Whelan notes the ironic coincidence that the "worst season" of the Irish Famine and the misfortunes of the Donner party both occurred in the winter of 1846–47; rather than pursuing the additional implication that both these events drove their victims to cannibalism, Whelan simply argues that this parallel accounts for Joyce's insistent emphasis on "food and hospitality" in "The Dead" (71–72), an emphasis that the Famine alone would sufficiently explain.

5. The deep connection between Western imperialism and cannibalism is a major theme of Arens's *The Man-Eating Myth*; also see Barker, Hulme, and Iversen's collection of essays, *Cannibalism and the Colonial World*.

6. I. M. Lewis, for example, describes the widespread conviction throughout Africa "that Europeans were cannibalistic witches" (94), often held among the very tribes that were themselves portrayed as cannibals by the European colonizers (89–98). Also see King 110–11.

7. Swift also associates the American with a taste for cannibalism in "A Modest Proposal": "I have been assured by a very knowing American of my acquaintance in London, that a young healthy child, well nursed, is at a year old a most delicious, nourishing, and wholesome food, whether *stewed, roasted, baked,* or *boiled,* and I make no doubt it will equally serve in a *fricassee,* or a *ragout*" (493–94).

8. Although not as directly concerned with imperialism as *The War of the Worlds,* in his *The Time Machine* Wells nonetheless models his Time Traveler on the imperial explorer, seating him early in his story on a kind of golden throne from which he "survey[s] the broad view of our old world" and imposes his naïve construction of a future society upon the world he seems to command (42); toward the end of his narrative, he returns "to the same seat of yellow metal" and laughs "bitterly" at his mistaken "confidence" (89).

9. Another conceivable response of the colonized is direct resistance and reprojection of those behaviors projected upon them, back upon the colonizer—in the manner of the charges and counter-charges of cannibalism between Catholics and Protestants during the Reformation—but the power differential at play in imperialism will usually frustrate or silence such resistance. The common lore about the role of disease in the history of Western imperialism offers a concrete illustration, however, of "successful" reprojection: whereas the Europeans themselves brought contagious diseases with them that decimated the "degenerate" native populations in the Americas, ironically syphilis, which reached epidemic proportions in Europe in the early 1500s, was widely understood to have been transmitted back to the Old World by Caribbean natives through Columbus's crew. (This etiology is now in dispute.) Francis Bacon, in fact, directly connects the flesh-eating disease of syphilis with cannibalism, creating a "profound analogy between alimentary and sexual taboos" by hypothesizing that syphilis was originally "caused by anthropophagy" in his *Sylva sylvarum* (1627) (Lestringant 161). Bacon's thesis is unprovable, for the original "sin" that brought syphilis to humanity and "patient zero" are both lost to history. Yet his thesis is not outlandish, for modern science has traced the origins of several diseases—like scrapie, kuru, and "Mad Cow" disease (BCE)—to animal and human cannibalism (Walton 85–104). Ultimately Bacon also establishes a

powerful figurative association between a flesh-consuming disease and cannibalism that continues to exert influence today. Thus, while the Europeans savaged and consumed an alien culture in the name of civilization, the colonized American savages—consumed by disease—returned the gesture by transmitting to the Europeans the flesh-devouring disease that manifested on their bodies the very crime that they had projected upon the Other. Evidently Joyce never read *Sylva sylvarum* and offered his own thesis that the disease originated in another violated taboo, deriving the word syphilis from the Greek word for bestiality in a 1920 letter to Frank Budgen: "σῦφιλίς=swinelove?" (*Letters*, I 147; Lyons, *Thrust Syphilis* 24).

10. Both Friedrich and Whelan contend that Joyce purchased *Gabriel Conroy* in Rome in September 1906 and read the novel shortly thereafter, "as he began to think about 'The Dead'" (Whelan 71). Also see note 4, above.

11. In associating capitalism with cannibalism Marx ironically recycles one of the more persistent themes of Christian anti-Semitism, most notoriously echoed by Shakespeare in Shylock's curious requirement of "an equal pound / Of your fair flesh" as collateral for his loan to Antonio in *The Merchant of Venice* (I, iii, 148–49). The extraordinary Frenchman Jean de Léry, who claims to have witnessed ritual cannibalism in the New World, in his *History of a Voyage to the Land of Brazil* (122–33), and who certainly witnessed survival cannibalism in the Old World during the siege of Sancerre in 1573 (Whatley *xviii*), actually finds the Tupinamba savages of Brazil more merciful in their anthopophagy than the Jewish money-lenders of his own society: "I could add similar examples of the cruelty of the savages toward their enemies, but it seems to me that what I have said is enough to horrify you, indeed, to make your hair stand on end. Nevertheless, so that those who read these horrible things, practiced daily among these barbarous nations of the land of Brazil, may also think more carefully about the things that go on every day over here, among us: In the first place, if you consider in all candor what our big usurers do, sucking blood and marrow, and eating everyone alive—widows, orphans, and other poor people, whose throats it would be better to cut once and for all, than to make them linger in misery—you will say that they are even more cruel than the savages I speak of. And that is why the prophet [Micah 3.3] says that such men flay the skin of God's people, eat their flesh, break their bones and chop them in pieces as for the pot, and as flesh within the cauldron" (131–32). For more on Léry, see note 15 below.

12. Sanday discusses the strong correlation between male sexual aggression toward women and cannibalism, "the ultimate act of domination" (12).

13. A notorious recent example of "unification" cannibalism received worldwide attention in the December 2003 trial of Armin Meiwes, in Kassel, Germany, who had solicited his victim, Bernd-Jurgen Brandes, via an internet ad "for a well-built male prepared to be slaughtered and then consumed" ("German Cannibal Tells of Fantasy").

14. In *The Golden Bough*, Frazer discusses the antecedents of the cannibalism of the Eucharist ("Eating the God" 556–72), in conjunction with other forms of homeopathic cannibalism ("Homeopathic Magic of a Flesh Diet" 572–78), yet there is little evidence that Joyce might have read Frazer. Nevertheless, John Vickery finds strong similarities between Joyce's and Frazer's recognitions of the primitive underpinnings

of the Christian Eucharist (383), among numerous correspondences between these two that he traces in his extended discussion of Joyce in *The Literary Impact of* The Golden Bough (326–423). It seems clear that Joyce's debt to Frazer, by Vickery's own admission, is general rather than direct, amounting to a resemblance between their "habits of thought and imaginative methods" (350).

15. Montaigne's most likely source for the figure of the spitting cannibal seems to be Jean de Léry's chapter on "How the Americans Treat Their Prisoners of War and the Ceremonies They Observe both in Killing and in Eating Them" in his *History of a Voyage to the Land of Brazil* (122–33), first published in 1578, shortly before Montaigne wrote "Of Cannibals" (see figure 1.2). Léry pictures the cannibal facing his own imminent consumption by the Tupinambas as both cheerful and defiant: on "the day of execution [. . . e]ven he who is not unaware that this gathering is on his account, and that in a short time he will be clubbed to death in all his feathered regalia, is by no means downcast; on the contrary, leaping about and drinking, he will be one of the merriest ones there. However, after he has sung and caroused for six or seven hours, two or three of the most respected in the throng will take hold of him, and bind him with ropes made of cotton or of the bark of a tree that they call *yvire*, which is like our linden; without his offering any resistance, even though both his arms are left free, he will be walked for a little while through the village, and displayed as a trophy. But for all that, do you think that he bows his head, as our criminals over here would do? By no means: on the contrary, with an incredible audacity and assurance, he will boast of his past feats of prowess, saying to those who hold him bound: 'I myself, who am valiant, first bound and tied your kinsmen.' Then, exalting himself more and more, with a demeanor to match, he will turn from side to side and say to one, 'I have eaten your father,' and to another, 'I have struck down and *boucané* [i.e., cook on a rotisserie (79)] your brothers.' He will add, 'Of you Tupinamba that I have taken in war, I have eaten so many men and women and even children that I could not tell the number [. . .]'" (122–23).

The vividness and detail of Léry's full account of the ritual cannibalism of the Tupinambas in this chapter of his *History*, as well as his claims of having directly witnessed these rites ("In fact, one day when I was in a village called *Sarigoy*, I saw a prisoner [. . .]" [123]), would seem to refute Arens's contention that there exists no "adequate documentation of cannibalism as a custom in any form for any society" (21). Arens persuasively argues, however, that it is precisely this figure of the spitting cannibal that erodes our confidence in Léry's eyewitness report, locating three nearly identical accounts of this scene, originally in Hans Staden's, perhaps ghostwritten (25), *Warhaftige Historia und Beschreibung eyner Landtschafft der Wilden* [*The True History and Description of a Country of Savages*](1557), immediately repeated in André Thevet's *Les Singularitez de la France Antarctique* (1558) (translated as *The New Found Worlde or Antarctike* [1568]), and then by Léry. Arens concludes that for "the case of the Tupinamba, this means that rather than dealing with an instance of serial documentation of cannibalism, we are more likely confronting only one source of dubious testimony which has been incorporated almost verbatim into the written reports of others claiming to be eyewitnesses. Thus, rather than the scientific procedure of independent verification, we have instead an instance of its scholarly antithesis being used to construct a case for an assumed well-established instance of customary cannibalism for a traditional South American Indian culture" (31).

In Staden's 1557 account of the spitting cannibal, the victim facing his immolation merely swears that his death will be avenged (161); within a year, André Thevet embellishes this narrative, describing the cannibal "singing [. . .] I haue killed and eaten his parentes and friends, to vvhome I am prisoner" (61), which in turn evolves into Léry's most dramatic version, followed by his graphic description of the natives' consumption of the spitting cannibal, published twenty years later. This progressive elaboration of the "most sensational" account of New World cannibalism (Alexander 8), matched by the increasing sophistication and detail of the woodcuts accompanying their works (see figures 1, 1.2, and 8.5), is a wonderful example not only of cultural transfer, but also of discourses that formally emulate the spitting cannibal by themselves *cannibalizing* discourses on, ironically, cannibalism.

16. St. John Chrysostom (d. 407), Bishop of Constantinople, "did not hesitate to tell his hearers that Christ 'gave us his body pierced with nails, that we might hold it in our hands and eat it, as a proof of his love; for those whom we love dearly we are often wont to bite'" (qtd. Tannahill 59); for the rumors concerning Chrysostom's "revolting" diet, see Voraigne 137.

17. "Lévi-Strauss called 'cannibalism an alimentary form of incest'" (Price 23); for the strong symbolic associations between cannibalism and incest, see Arens 146–47 and Price 23–24.

18. Spielberg nicely observes that the four-part sequence of breakfast, lunch, dinner, and supper in this line, paralleling the Viconian cycle of life, further associates eating with death in the *Wake*: "Therefore, whenever I smell food, I look for death and corpses" (297–98). I would add that, in an earlier passage also cited by Spielberg, Joyce parallels the consumption of corpse-flesh with both the daily meal-rota and the seven ages of man in "the gipsy mating of a grand stylish gravedigging with secondbest buns (an interpolation: these munchables occur only in the Bootherbrowth [German *butterbrot* (bread and butter); Russian бутерброд (sandwich)] family of MSS., Bb—Cod [zygote] IV, Pap [breast] II, Brek XI, Lun III, Dinn XVII, Sup XXX, Fullup [repletion-death] MDCXC [. . .])" (*FW* 121.31–35). Although the mock-bibliographical terminology in this passage may relate to the motif of bibliophagy in the *Wake*, discussed below, I am at a loss to explain Joyce's Roman numeral-code here, short of the final 1690 date for the catastrophic Battle of the Boyne, an appropriate suggestion of the end of life.

19. Patricia Morely, while tracing the archetypal associations of Joyce's fish symbolism to the Christian *ichthus*, to fertility cults, and to both Eastern and "Mystery religions" (269), also notes that "in *Finnegans Wake*, Earwicker is Finn MacCool," who in legend consumed the Salmon of Knowledge, "and the great salmon of the Liffey, but Shem is also identified with salmon" (268). In other words, father and son are somatophages, portrayed as both fish and eaters of fish. For an entertaining listing of the various foodstuffs in the *Wake*, arranged as a lengthy menu, see Benstock ("The Gastronome's *Finnegans Wake*" 188–94); the egg and fish courses are extensive.

Chapter 2. The Distant Music of the Spheres: Language as Axiomatic System

1. The likelihood that Joyce had Gabriel's "distant music" phrase in mind when he drafted the opening of chapter 3 of *A Portrait* increases when we realize that he completed writing "The Dead" in September 1907, immediately before turning his attention to his revision of *Stephen Hero*; he had completed the third chapter by 7 April 1908 (Ellmann, *James Joyce* 264). Gabler argues convincingly that the relations between Joyce's composition of "The Dead" and the early chapters of *A Portrait* are considerably more complex than Ellmann suggests, and that "Chapters I-III [. . . are], in the form in which we possess them, five or more years removed in time from *Dubliners*, and the consummation of its art in 'The Dead'" (*James Joyce* 37). It seems clear, nonetheless, from Gabler's study of the novel's chronology of composition, that Joyce's subsequent revisions were concentrated on the latter portions of the third chapter, rather than its opening, where the "distant music" phrase reappears (26–33).

2. In the words of Galileo, "we cannot understand" that "great book which ever lies before our eyes, I mean the universe, [. . .] if we do not first learn the language [. . .] in which it is written. The book is written in the mathematical language" (qtd. J. Barrow, *World* 238). For an extended discussion of the "language of mathematics" and the "intrinsically mathematical aspects" of "natural phenomena" (238), see J. Barrow, *World* 238–92.

3. Hollander's working assumption is that the music of the spheres ceased to function as a belief and had become, at best, only a poetic conception by the beginning of the eighteenth century; however, to accept this assumption we would have to ignore both distinguished scientific speculations about the musical nature of the cosmos (e.g., Newton) and important, representative artistic attempts to embody this idealization (Mozart's *Die Zauberflöte*) through the eighteenth century. See James's chapter "Newton and *The Magic Flute*," 159–79.

4. Joyce himself seems to anticipate this development in his schoolboy essay "The Study of Languages": "Now the study of languages is based on a mathematical foundation, and sure of its footing, and in consequence both in style and syntax there is always present a carefulness, a carefulness bred of the first implantings of precision" (27). Also see J. Barrow, *Artful* 207–9.

5. For useful overviews of the impact of Pythagorean ideas on Plato and of the influence of Platonism on the development of Western mathematics, see J. Barrow, *Pi* 251–76.

6. Dante, it would appear, is the only mortal who has claimed to have heard the music of the spheres, expressing wonderment at "l'armonia" [the harmony] and "La novità del suono" [The newness of the sound] that greet him upon his entry into Paradise in Canto I of the *Paradiso* (Sinclair, *Dante's Paradiso* 22). Dante continues to listen to, and marvel at, the music of the spheres (see conclusion of Canto X [Sinclair, *Dante's Paradiso* 152–55]), through the sixth sphere, Jupiter, beyond which he is not privileged to hear the transcendent harmonies of the highest heavens (see opening of Canto XX [Sinclair, *Dante's Paradiso* 286–87]).

7. Hollander discusses the "long history" of the images of the "World-Lyre" and "the stringed instrument of the human soul," from the Classical era through the Renaissance (44), and observes the survival of "the very notion of heart strings," still current today (49).

8. For valuable discussions of the development of mathematical formalism, the work of David Hilbert, and the axiomatic movement at the turn of the century, see Kline, *Certainty* 245–64; for an account of Henri Poincaré's popularization of these developments through his "conventionalist" philosophy in "such works as *Science and Hypothesis* (1902)," see Passmore 326–27 and passim.

9. There is a large literature on the musical elements and allusions in Joyce's work; see, particularly, Bauerle *Picking Up Airs*; Bowen "Libretto"; Bowen *Musical Allusions*; Hodgart and Bauerle; Hodgart and Worthington; Knowles (ed.), *Bronze by Gold*; and Martin.

10. For excellent studies of the mathematics of *Ulysses* and *Finnegans Wake*, see McCarthy and Solomon, respectively; Atherton considers the fact that "Numbers have a magical, not an arithmetical significance" one of the "main axioms of the *Wake*" (53, 52).

Chapter 3. "Mr. Berlicche and Mr. Joyce": Language as Comestible

1. As McHugh observes, reading *Finnegans Wake* is "like learning a language: one unconsciously inculcates background material while focussing upon odd nuclei of sense, which are due to aggregate at some future date" (1st ed., *v*). Lorraine Weir's *Writing Joyce* is the most explicit and extended correlation between the reading of Joyce's fiction and language acquisition, although not couched in precisely these terms, and develops a "semiotics" for the Joycean language: "Like any pedagogical system grounded in sequential processing of increasingly complex data and logical operations, the Joyce system initiates us [. . .] in *A Portrait of the Artist as a Young Man* into the practice of what Barthes refers to as the 'exercising of the *Exercises*' [*Sade/Fourier/Loyola* 42], an operation basic to the processing of the system as a whole, that is, to *Portrait, Ulysses*, and *Finnegans Wake* considered as one vast system" (L. Weir 6–7). As this quote indicates, Weir excludes *Dubliners* and *Exiles* from her analysis, but suggests that "anyone interested in this project" might "do an archeology of the system by exploring the relations of *Dubliners* and *Exiles*" (107, n 21).

According to Francini Bruni, to whom I owe this chapter's title ("Joyce" 26), Joyce was fond of playing with his employer's name by calling him "Mr. Berlicche," the "name of an Italian clown figure" (Potts 9, n 5).

2. Ellmann gives two versions of Joyce's famous and perhaps apocryphal claim that, in *Ulysses* and *Finnegans Wake* respectively, he had thus insured his immortality. In a 1956 interview with Ellmann, Jacques Benoît-Méchin recalled Joyce remarking "If I gave it all up immediately, I'd lose my immortality. I've put in so many enigmas and puzzles that [*Ulysses*] will keep the professors busy for centuries arguing over what I meant, and that's the only way of insuring one's immortality" (*James Joyce* 521). In an-

other interview, also in 1956, Jacob Schwartz recalled Joyce's claim that he wrote the *Wake* in a manner that would "keep the critics busy for three hundred years" (*James Joyce* 703). William Brockman, who has studied the career of Schwartz, the "original unreliable narrator" (personal correspondence with the author), reasonably questions the authenticity of both quotations; also see Brockman 174–90.

3. Anyone who has taken a university-level foreign language discussion class has directly benefited from the generally unacknowledged impact of the Berlitz Method on modern theories of language acquisition.

4. Kenner is quoting (inaccurately) Stephen's reflections on language during his conversation with the (English) dean of studies in chapter five of *A Portrait*: "The language in which we are speaking is his before it is mine. How different are the words *home, Christ, ale, master* on his lips and on mine! I cannot speak or write these words without unrest of spirit. His language, so familiar and so foreign, will always be for me an acquired speech. I have not made or accepted its words. My voice holds them at bay. My soul frets in the shadow of his language" (*P* 189).

Roy Gottfried examines "a copy of Berlitz's *First Book of English*, an edition more or less contemporary with Joyce's tenure" (223), in the best analysis of the possible impact of Joyce's teaching experience on his development as an artist, "Berlitz Schools Joyce." Gottfried observes parallels between the Berlitz text's catechetical approach and patterned language drills and Joyce's similar techniques and verbal patterns in *Ulysses*, and ultimately illustrates how the *First Book of English* could have functioned as a "source-book" for several domestic details in *Ulysses* (227), but only briefly notes the irony that the artist's "tormenting boss" might have intensified Joyce's inclination "to view language as a system" (225).

5. I have used the abbreviation "wbc" in this and the following paragraphs to acknowledge quotations and background information that I have drawn from the Berlitz corporation's Web page (www.berlitz.com). The Berlitz Corporation's official history gives the date of M. D. Berlitz's arrival in the United States as 1870, rather than 1872, and contends that the evidence in census records suggests an earlier date for his birth: "the year 1847 is probably more accurate" (*Berlitz* 2–3).

6. Although a tireless self-advertiser, Berlitz did acknowledge that his "innovative" technique was an adaptation of various "'direct' and 'natural' methods [that] were in fact being experimented with by several of Berlitz's contemporaries" (e.g., Gottlieb Heness, a former pupil of Johann Pestalozzi, and Lambert Saveur). "Berlitz's genius was to expand and elaborate upon the concept, to develop an array of materials that embodied it, and then to create an organization that could deliver this new language approach" (*Berlitz* 7; also see 66). Evidently Berlitz initially "formed an equal partnership with Nicholas Joly," but purchased his "interest in the U.S. schools and publishing business [...] for a lump sum of $23,000" on 31 August 1900 (*Berlitz* 12).

7. Among other signal achievements for the Berlitz corporation during World War II were the development of "intensive language training" for the U.S. armed forces and the short-order translation of "the 150,000 word engine manual for the [confiscated] French liner *Normandie*." Although its pertinence to the war effort escapes me,

"Another notable feat during this period was the translation of the entire Koran into twenty-seven languages in one year" (wbc).

8. Evidently the target clientele for the school in Pola, "a large naval station of Austria," was principally military, and Joyce was hired there specifically to teach "officers and imperial and royal employees," as advertised in the "magnificent notice" of his employment that he sent to Stanislaus in October 1904 (*Letters*, II 68 and 68, n 3). In November he wrote to his father that "nearly all my pupils are officers in the Austrian navy" (*Letters*, II 69).

9. Berlitz company policy prohibited independent tutoring (*Letters*, II 69). Recent biographical and background studies of Joyce's sojourn in Trieste do not substantially add to Ellmann's (*James Joyce*) and Gottfried's ("Berlitz Schools Joyce") discussions of his teaching career. See John McCourt's *Years of Bloom* (especially 20–22, 31–33)—McCourt nonetheless strongly emphasizes the importance of Joyce's exposure to the "linguistic wealth" of the Triestine community (51 and passim)—and his *James Joyce: A Passionate Exile* (43–45); also see Crivelli's *Itinerari Triestini* (passim); and the "Joyce and Trieste" special issue of the *James Joyce Quarterly* (38.3–4 [2001], guest edited by McCourt), particularly Bosinelli's contribution (395–409) on the "foreignizing" effect of Trieste on Joyce's conception of the English language.

10. See Kern 115–16, and passim, for a discussion of the influence of the theories of "scientific management" and the time-motion studies Frederick W. Taylor and his disciples (e.g., Frank B. Gilbreth) on the "technology of speed" in the early twentieth century. Antonio Gramsci echoes Francini Bruni and Joyce, quoted below, in seeing Taylorism as a quintessentially American phenomenon: "Taylor is in fact expressing with brutal cynicism the purpose of American society [. . .], breaking up the old psycho-physical nexus of qualified professional work, which demands a certain active participation of intelligence, fantasy and initiative on the part of the worker, and reducing productive operations exclusively to the mechanical, physical aspect" (290).

11. There are two reasons for the apparent contradiction in Francini Bruni's recollections of the Berlitz clientele, quoted here: the tone of his later memoir, written twenty-five years after the first, is considerably more reserved (see Potts 6), and his (and Joyce's) pupils in Trieste, whom he recalls in "Recollections," were clearly more "genteel" (*Letters*, II 94) than the naval officers and civil servants that enrolled in the Pola school, whom he describes in "Joyce."

12. For example, Lorraine Weir maintains that our "Felicity" as Joyce's readers "consists only in our readerly willingness to learn the [. . . .] Joyce system, [which] exists in a state of bounded implicature, knowing only itself, a feedback loop possessed of the materials necessary to its own invention. [. . . T]he system in itself produces a memory theater or teaching machine with its [own] lexicon" (3–4). More succinctly, Roy Gottfried comments that "*Ulysses* is a book, it is commonly held, that teaches how to read it" ("Reading the Text" 188).

13. "In the first sentence [of *Portrait* there are], three words we've never read before: we absorb them ['moocow,' 'nicens,' and 'Tuckoo'?]. Then for 'glass' we guess to read 'monacle,' a word Baby Tuckoo wouldn't know. And 'hairy face' says 'bearded,'

a decision we are put to the risk of making. We enjoy no position of privilege with a helpful author-cicerone at our side. We are Berlitz pupils, moving alert, inductively, substituting, comprehending. The English language is something this Irishman will have us *watch* as it's never been watched before. [...] For a page and a half we undergo a qualifying exam, until a row of asterisks inaugurates familiar narrative" (Kenner, *Colder Eye* 196).

Chapter 4. Consuming High Culture: Allusion and Structure in "The Dead"

1. For studies of the Ibsen influence, see Baker 19–32, Theoharis 791–810, and Tysdahl 55–59 and passim. For commentary on the parallels between the final cantos of Dante's *Inferno* and the conclusion in "The Dead," see Reynolds 156–57, 161–62.

2. The most obvious of many structural uses of allusion in *Ulysses* is Joyce's title for the novel, which establishes the parallel between the events of the *Odyssey* and the actions of Bloomsday. Similarly, Joyce's allusions to the Daedalus myth function structurally, accounting for the rising and falling rhythms in *A Portrait of the Artist as a Young Man*. Among the stories in *Dubliners*, besides "The Dead," only "Grace" would seem to be indebted to a literary allusion for its structure, also involving Dante; if Stanislaus's memory is to be trusted, Joyce modeled "Grace" upon the three-part structure of the *Commedia*: "the first instance of the use of a pattern in my brother's work" (*My Brother's Keeper* 228).

3. Two additional discussions of Browning's presence in the story accept Feeley's identification of *Asolando* as Joyce's source: see Torchiana 233–37, and Munich 126–34.

4. See Scharry 182–83; cited by Feeley (96, n 2). Torchiana also suggests two publications of selections of Browning's poetry, both of which appeared in 1903, as candidates for Gabriel's review (255, n 18).

5. This is the main point of Brook Thomas's *James Joyce's Ulysses: A Book of Many Happy Returns*. For the autobiographical basis of *Parleyings*, see DeVane, *Browning Handbook* 491–92. Also see DeVane's full study: *Browning's Parleyings: The Autobiography of a Mind*.

6. Anonymous reviewer, *Saturday Review*, 26 Feb. 1887; quoted by DeVane, *Browning Handbook* 493.

7. Browning's "Apollo and the Fates" concerns only Apollo's trickery of the Fates, to win the chance of Admetus's survival. As the prologue ends, the Fates grant Apollo's demand and impose their condition:

Such boon we accord in due measure. Life's term
We lengthen should any be moved for love's sake
To forego life's fulfillment [...] (ll. 251–53).

Apollo responds with the same optimism Admetus was to show, foreseeing the compliance of Admetus's subjects:

Importunate one with another they strive
For the glory to die that their king may survive. (ll. 259–60) (Browning 18)

Subsequent details of Admetus's story cited in this chapter are drawn from the account in Hamilton's *Mythology* (168–70), and, of course, Euripides' *Alcestis*.

8. Although Joyce, unlike Gabriel, might not have had a specific quotation from "Apollo and the Fates" in mind—the ghost of Browning's poem and its associations would have been satisfactory for his purposes—I will follow John Feeley's example and offer one possibility for the quote. The Fates describe Apollo's power to illuminate existence: "[. . .] from thee comes a glimmer / Transforming to beauty life blank at the best" (ll. 66–67; Browning 8). Gabriel could use these lines as an elegant compliment to his aunts, though his concern is justified that his audience would be disturbed by a view of life that would be "above the[ir] heads" (*D* 179). The sour view of a "blank" life underlying the Fates' remark chimes with Gabriel's mood, in his less confident moments, earlier in the evening; yet, it is highly likely that Gabriel's audience, whose "grade of culture differed from his [. . . would] not understand" his *fin-de-globe* worldview: "He had taken up a wrong tone" (*D* 179).

9. Joyce's stay in Rome also awakened his interest in Roman history, with equally substantial influence on his literary development; see Spoo 481–97.

10. Both Reynolds and Cope (362–64) note the symmetry of Joyce concluding *Dubliners* with an allusion to Dante, to balance his opening allusion to the inscription "Abandon all Hope ye who enter here" (III.9; Ciardi 42), over the gates of Dante's hell: "There was no hope" (*D* 9) (Reynolds 156–57). Torchiana has suggested that Joyce alludes to the Fates in both his opening and closing stories, "The Sisters" and "The Dead" (28–30, 228), although he does not notice that these allusions, which can be paired with the allusions to Dante via the legend of Apollo and the Fates, contribute to the symmetry of the opening and close of *Dubliners*. Also see Bierman 707–8.

11. Dante and Alberigo's conversation in the original Italian reads:

'Oh! diss' io lui 'or se' tu ancor morto?'
    Ed elli a me: 'Come 'l mio corpo stea
    nel mondo su, nulla scienza porto.
Cotal vantaggio ha questa Tolomea,
    che spesse volte l'anima ci cade
    innanzi ch'Atropos mossa le dea.' (Sinclair, *Dante's Inferno* 410)

12. For Friar Alberigo's story, see Ciardi (281, n 118). Reynolds explores the parallels between the stories of Gabriel and Ugolino, whom Dante encounters in Cocytus immediately before Alberigo (161–62; see figure 4.1), comparing them as "traitors to family, traitors to guests, traitors to benefactors, traitors to their country" (161). While these parallels are certainly valid, Alberigo's story, not Ugolino's, explicitly develops the fate of those who betray the law of hospitality. Sinclair comments: "Dante's singular device for the punishment of treachery to guests, that souls are plunged in Hell while their bodily life continues on earth, was probably suggested by the language of the fifty-fifth Psalm about treacherous friends: 'Let death seize upon them and let them go down quick into hell. Bloody and deceitful men shall not live out half their days,' with further reference to Judas from John xiii. 27: 'After the sop Satan entered into him.' 'These vio-

lators of hospitality who had broken a faith undertaken by their free choice had made themselves unfit for human fellowship. It was just, therefore, that they should be ipso facto excluded from it and that for the time of life remaining to them after their crime it would be human life only in appearance and in reality the life of devils' (V. Rossi)" (*Dante's Inferno* 417).

13. Despite the damning consequences of Gabriel's sin, I would not argue that the ending of "The Dead" is necessarily negative. Joyce's pattern of allusion, while associating Gabriel with Alberigo, through Dante, also associates him, through Browning, with Admetus's wife Alcestis, who has willingly accepted death for the sake of her spouse. If we read Gabriel's symbolic death in the conclusion as a death for Gretta's sake ("Generous tears filled Gabriel's eyes" [*D* 223], while the tears of those in Cocytus cannot flow; they are frozen and blind them), then Gabriel is still offered the possibility of resurrection. The oft-noted ambiguity of Gabriel's final position remains firm.

Chapter 5. A Taste for/of "inferior literary style": The (Tom) Swiftian Comedy of Scylla and Charybdis

1. For example, see the press coverage in *Time* ("Games: Season for Swifties"), *Life* ("I've Come Back, Cried Tom Swiftly"), *Newsweek* ("Swiftly, He Said Gamely"), and *Readers' Digest* ("Tom Swift Carries On—Gamely").

2. For discussions of Stratemeyer, see Billman and Watson.

3. Stratemeyer clearly sought to capitalize on the popular fascination with the heroes of modern technology at the turn of the century ("Tom" Edison, Marconi, the Wright brothers, et al.). He correctly judged that his young readers would be attracted to an inventor of their own generation; but adults could and did as readily fantasize about becoming successful inventors (witness Lee DeForest, or Leopold Bloom). See Earl Swift's article on Tom Swift, "The Perfect Inventor." Earl is evidently unrelated to Tom.

4. The original Tom Swift series concluded with its 40th title, *Tom Swift and His Magnetic Silencer* (1941); 33 titles appeared in the "Tom Swift Junior" series (1954–71). Two short-lived series starring Tom's grandson, Tom Swift III (nine titles, 1981–84), and just plain "Tom Swift" again (13 titles, 1991–93), both authored by "Victor Appleton," take the young man into outer-space and high-energy physics, respectively. Although "Appleton" remains the author, Tom Swift himself narrates the novels in the current "Tom Swift: Young Inventor Series" (2006–), to the evident impoverishment of our children's adverbial vocabulary.

5. E. B. White considers the persistent "use of adverbs after 'he said,' 'she replied,' and the like," as a prime characteristic of either inept writers or "Inexperienced writers" who have studied the inept: "They do this, apparently, in the belief that the word *said* is always in need of support, or because they have been told to do it by experts in the art of bad writing" (Strunk and White 68).

6. See the Buffalo typescripts of the episode (V.B.7), in volume twelve of *The James Joyce Archive*, edited by Michael Groden, et al. Once we recognize the presence of the narrator's voice in the episode, we have the answer to the puzzle of the "six heads of

Scylla": Stephen's audience of five (Lyster, Eglinton, A. E., Best, and Mulligan) expands to include a sixth auditor, a sixth "head," the teller of the tale.

7. Power identifies Joyce's original for Molly Bloom's latest reading, "*Ruby: the Pride of the Ring*" (*U* 4.346), as Amye Reade's *Ruby. A Novel. Founded on the Life of a Circus Girl*, published in 1889 (115), although Gryta's location of several similarly titled "circus dime novels that were popular around the turn of the century," suggests that Joyce has cannibalized "a composite of sources" (321) for his purposes.

8. Beaufoy's story is republished in the *James Joyce Quarterly*, with a commentary by Hugh Kenner ("Beaufoy's Masterplaster" 11–18).

Chapter 6. Condoms, Conrad, and Joyce

1. The first definition of "conversation" in the *Oxford English Dictionary* is "The action of living or having one's being *in* a place or *among* persons" (in use as early as 1340); the *OED*'s earliest citation for "conversation" to denote sexual intercourse is 1511 (third definition), and the earliest for our current primary usage, "Interchange of thoughts and words; familiar discourse or talk," the seventh definition in the *OED*, is dated 1580. "Intercourse" was similarly innocent of sexual denotation and connotation until even later, initially signifying trade and "Communication to and fro between countries" (circa 1494) and only acquiring its current meaning of sexual relations at the end of the eighteenth century (earliest citation, 1798).

2. See Himes 188, 190. As Janet Brodie observes, advertisers continued to recommend condoms primarily for protection against disease throughout the nineteenth century, much as they are again recommended in this era of AIDS (205–6). Norman E. Himes's chapter on the "History of the Condom or Sheath" from ancient times to their mass production into the 1930s, in his classic *Medical History of Contraception* (1936), remains the standard survey of the subject (186–206). Himes notes some early anticipations of the condom in the penis sheaths Egyptian males wore, either for decoration or for protection against insect bites and tropical diseases, in the myth of Minos and Pasiphae, and perhaps in imperial Rome, and considers Fallopius's claim to have perfected a linen sheath for protection against syphilis (1564), but he suspects the original inventor, long since lost to history, was "a medieval slaughter-house worker" who came up with the idea of using animal membranes to "protect against venereal infection" (191). The value of the sheath for contraception awaited the better understanding of the process of conception, but was well established by the eighteenth century. Casanova, in particular, appreciated this use of condoms, describing them as "preservatives that the English have invented [*sic*] to put the fair sex under shelter from all fear" (qtd. Himes 195). His contemporary Boswell was also a user of condoms, for self-protection rather than contraception, during his regular meetings with prostitutes. Referring to these encounters euphemistically as "engage[ments] in armour"—using one of many slang terms for the condom in the later eighteenth century—Boswell even recorded his first use of protection "in Saint James's Park" on "Friday 25 March," 1763, in his *London Journal: 1762–1763* (227; also see Kruck 7–8). As Himes notes, "[w]idespread, common use of the condom" followed the development of the vulcanization process for rubber

"by Goodyear" and the unfortunately named "Handcock in 1843–44" (201), while the twentieth century introduced the use of "liquid latex" and "automatic machinery" for their mass production (201). By the mid-1930s, just one American manufacturer, the Youngs Rubber Corporation, was producing 20 million condoms per year (201).

The etymology of the name "condom" has itself perplexed both historians and linguists. In his *Looking for Dr. Condom*, William E. Kruck identifies the first appearance of this term for the sheath, in the English language in 1705 (2), but his study thoroughly discredits the legend that the article was invented by a Restoration era physician in attendance on Charles II, named Condom or Condon: "The man and his act of invention [...] are a myth" (57).

The always circumspect *OED* first acknowledged the word "condom" in the initial volume of its *Supplement: A–G*, published in 1972 (Kruck 20).

3. Jane Ford has provided the only discussion, to date, on the relations between *Ulysses* and *The Secret Agent* in her "James Joyce and the Conrad Connection."

4. Most appropriately for my argument, Huyssen not only implies a metaphor of prophylaxis in describing the modernists' relations to mass culture as affected by an "anxiety of contamination," here and throughout his *After the Great Divide*, but also describes the persistent gendering of "Modernism's Other" as *female*; see "Mass Culture as Woman" (44–62).

5. Conrad equates the Professor in *The Secret Agent*, for instance, to a disease, probably venereal: he is a "moral agent" and "unwholesome-looking little agent of destruction" who "passe[s] on unsuspected and deadly, like a pest in the street full of men" (81, 83, 311); also see Haltresht 101–5. In a long list of euphemisms for the condom, Brodie mentions "membraneous [*sic*] envelopes," "apex envelopes," and "fibrous envelopes," but not *mortal* envelopes (207).

6. Joyce's anti-euphemism for the condom, "Killchild" (*U* 14.467), seems to be his own coinage.

7. Although Joyce left the Berlitz school in Trieste in the summer of 1907, he continued privately tutoring students in English (Ellmann, *James Joyce* 262–63, and "Introduction" *xii–xv*). For Joyce's probable use of *The Secret Agent* as an instructional text, see Gillespie 77, and for a description of his notations on his copies of Conrad's fiction, see Ford, "James Joyce's Trieste Library" 145–56. Although Joyce might have bought the book simply because of his interest in Conrad, or for the novel's treatment of anarchists, revolutionaries, and spies, he may also have known that Conrad modeled two of its characters, Michaelis and the Professor, on later nineteenth-century Fenians: Michael Davitt and Luke "Dynamite" Dillon; see Sherry 260–69, 283–85. In *The Secret Agent* Conrad also makes several references to cannibalism, and it is tempting to speculate about how attentive Joyce might have been to the possibilities of cannibalizing *The Secret Agent* for his own work: Conrad, for example, portrays a "mad" artist as a young man (40), a boy named *Stevie*, as both the cannibal and the cannibalized: Stevie initially "swallow[s ...] with an audible gulp" the terrorist *Karl* Yundt's Marxist attack on "cannibalistic" capitalism (44); after he accidentally blows himself to pieces for the cause of humanity, his body resembles "the by-products of a butcher's shop [...] an inexpensive

Sunday dinner"(71); late in the novel, Conrad describes the final meal of Verloc, the man responsible for Stevie's dismemberment, as a cannibal feast: "He partook ravenously, without restraint and decency [. . .]" (190).

8. Robert Scholes does not speculate about the date of the earliest surviving fragments of the holograph manuscript of "The Dead," which the printer used to set the aborted 1910 Maunsel edition of *Dubliners*, in his study of the story's textual history (192–94).

9. Raised when, where, and how he was, as Richard Brown observes, Joyce "could not but have had a strong awareness of the birth-control issue" (63). The standard study of Joyce's career-long preoccupation with the question of population control is Mary Lowe-Evans's *Crimes against Fecundity*. For Joyce's use of prophylactic imagery throughout *Dubliners*, also see Bowen, "Joyce's Prophylactic Paralysis" 257–73.

10. "Condoms had been associated only with the brothel, and many [at the end of the nineteenth century] saw their use within marriage as defiling the marriage bed. [. . .] As important as condoms were quickly to become in family limitation, they never quite lost their disreputability. They remained tainted by the old association with prostitution and venereal diseases and disreputable because they were often sold in shops that also carried pornography and erotica in the seamier areas of [. . .] cities" (Brodie 206). To counter the condom's ill-repute, in the 1920s in the United States Merrill Youngs, "an astute marketer," decided to capitalize on the "health aspect" of the sheath as a prophylactic against disease, selling his product "exclusively to druggists": "The natural outlet for their sale was the pharmacy." Consequently, Youngs' brand, "Trojans bec[ame] synonymous with condoms for many Americans" (Murphy 11). Himes describes the development of similar marketing strategies in England (326–29).

In the United States, the "Comstock Laws," "passed in 1873 at the insistence of Anthony Comstock, leader of the Society for the Prevention of Vice [, . . .] included sweeping prohibitions against mailing, interstate transporting, or importing 'obscene, lewd, or lascivious' articles. [. . .] The Comstock statutes did not forbid the manufacture or sale of contraceptives but did ban interstate commerce in these products" (Murphy 9). The situation in England was, apparently, comparable to that in the United States at the turn of the century. In Ireland, however, the sale of condoms, which "were banned in a papal bull of 1826" (Kruck 23), remained illegal until the 1980s (Duffy 211).

11. "Mildly erotic magazines like *Photo Bits* [. . .] were indeed among the most common popular sources for contraceptive information and for the purchase of contraceptives" (Brown 66). Despite Theodore Purefoy's charge, Bloom apparently does not use condoms for contraception with Molly and believes he has kept his possession of "rubber preservatives" a secret from her. That he and Molly have had sex, at least on occasion, over the past ten-plus years is clear; Joyce simply qualifies the nature of their relations: "carnal intercourse had been incomplete, without ejaculation of semen within the natural female organ" (*U* 17.2283–84). As David Hayman notes, this "statement does not preclude coitus interruptus, cunnilingus [. . .], or manual stimulation [. . .], to say nothing of the nightly buttock kiss" ("The Empirical Molly" 115); also see Brown 67.

12. Jane Ford, who finds several "parallels in character configuration and similarities in imagery and tone" between *Ulysses* and *The Secret Agent* ("James Joyce" 9), notes a number of late additions Joyce made to the text of *Ulysses* that suggest he was covertly acknowledging some debts his book owes to Conrad.

13. Although beyond the scope of the present chapter, Joyce's *Finnegans Wake* is obviously the limit case of textual prophylaxis in modern literature. As a narrative and linguistic experiment, moreover, the *Wake* seems to emerge, as many have noted, out of Joyce's composition of the Oxen of the Sun chapter of *Ulysses*, especially the tailpiece of the episode, discussed below. For discussions of the motifs of "immaculate contraceptives" (*FW* 45.14) and birth control in the *Wake*, see Lowe-Evans (75–99) and Brown 63–78 passim.

14. Although he, too, fails to find a contradiction in Joyce's intentions, Harry Levin, in another early response to Oxen of the Sun, registers both frustration with a "narrative [. . .] clotted with Shandyan digression and inflated with sheer linguistic exuberance" and exasperation with a structural "principle of embryonic growth," which "reduce[s] Joyce's cult of imitative form to a final absurdity" (95).

15. Richard Ellmann sees the conclusion of Oxen of the Sun as both "placental outpouring" and "ejaculative spray": "*coitus interruptus* becomes a verbal more than a genital matter in the episode's last pages, which are made up of a series of random ejaculations, a spray of words in all directions" (*Ulysses on the Liffey* 136, 135).

16. "The earliest teat-ended products which hold ejaculate appeared for sale in 1901" (Youssef 227).

17. Ellmann merely notes, in passing, Joyce's exposure to a "atmosphere of literary experimentation" in Zurich (*James Joyce* 409); as I observed in my preface, Norris considers Ellmann's biography, together with the common identification of Stephen's Thomistic aesthetic in *A Portrait of the Artist as a Young Man* as Joyce's, as the chief sources for "the powerful mythology of Joyce as modernist artist" in literary studies: "the Ellmann biography's blatant patronization of the way Joyce negotiated his material circumstances [. . .] serves to firmly demarcate and valorize the separation of his art from his material and domestic life. Perhaps more than other literary biographies, the Ellmann biography reinforces the ideology of artistic autonomy by trivializing and denigrating what falls outside Joyce's art, including [. . .] Joyce's socialist and other political tendencies" (*Joyce's Web* 8).

18. Differing with Peter Bürger, like Norris, Astradur Eysteinsson cogently argues that sharp distinctions between the avant-garde and modernism break down when dealing with many of the major works of the period. Although acknowledging that "one way to radicalize modernism fruitfully is to read 'modernist' works from the perspective of the avant-garde," Eysteinsson concludes that "rather than enforce a rigid separation, I find it a good deal more critically stimulating and historically challenging to work on the assumption that while texts such as *Ulysses*, *Der Prozeß*, *Nightwood*, and *The Cantos* are modernist works, they are also avant-garde in their nontraditional structure and their radicalized correlations of form and content, and that while the avant-garde movements are historical phenomena in their own right, they are also salient motors of modernism" (177–78).

19. Margot Norris makes a strong case for reading *Finnegans Wake* as an avant-garde work, particularly in her analysis of "Shem the Penman" (*FW* 169–95) as Joyce's unraveling of Stephen's privileging of aesthetic autonomy in *A Portrait of the Artist as a Young Man*, via the intermediary modifications of his Shakespeare commentary in *Ulysses*, in which Stephen emphasizes the artist's significant relation to the "material world" (*Joyce's Web* 77). Seeing Shem as the "*Bête Noire* of Modernism" (82), Norris persuasively "explor[es] 'Shem the Penman' as an avant-garde self-criticism of art" (*Joyce's Web* 73).

20. Jared Diamond writes that "when syphilis was first definitively recorded in Europe in 1495, its pustules often covered the body from the head to the knees, caused flesh to fall off people's faces, and led to death within a few months. By 1546, syphilis had evolved into the disease with the symptoms so well known to us today" (210). For the standard history of syphilis, see Oriel's *The Scars of Venus*. Lyons convincingly discredits claims that Joyce himself suffered from syphilis (*Thrust Syphilis Down to Hell* 21–39).

Chapter 7. His Master's Voice and Joyce

1. Although Derrida's use of this phrase may be coincidental, "Mercury Living Presence" 3-track recording technology was the state-of-the-art in the international high-fidelity recording industry in the 1950s.

2. Freidrich Kittler examines the impact of reading pedagogy on narrative voice, especially the ideal of silent reading and the concomitant development of the reader's "inner voice," in *Discourse Networks, 1800/1900* (32–33 and passim). For an excellent overview of (almost uniformly negative) responses to the gramophone among modernist writers, see Knowles, "Death by Gramophone" 1–13; for additional discussion of the influence of sound recording on modernist writers, see Johnston 88–96 and Pridmore-Brown 408–21; and, for the initially more positive responses of late-Victorian writers, see Picker 110–45.

3. Originally, the terms *phonograph* and *gramophone* distinguished between Edison's talking machine that recorded on "*vertical-cut cylinders*" and Berliner's later modification (1887), a machine that "employ[ed] *lateral-cut discs*" (Gelatt 60; emphases in the original). With time, the terms came to be used interchangeably for all record players, with phonograph becoming standard American usage and gramophone the standard British term. For recent histories of the development of recording technology, see Andre Millard's chapter "The Phonograph: A Case Study in Research and Development" in his *Edison and the Business of Invention* (63–87), and his book, *America on Record: A History of Recorded Sound*.

4. For a corporate history of the Victor Talking Machine Company, see Gelatt (130–40 and passim). Also see the internet Web site "Nipper and His Master's Voice." For discographies of the German, Italian, and French catalogs of the continental Victor affiliates, see the three volumes compiled by Alan Kelly.

5. For this and subsequent information about Barraud, see internet Web sites "Nipper and His Master's Voice" and "Nipper and the Story of 'His Master's Voice'"; also see Petts.

6. For Archer's *The Empty Cradle*, see Morley (plate 1). Morley observes that "Dogs were given a firm place in the Victorian language of grief: Landseer's *Faithful Hound* and *Shepherd's Last Mourner* [*sic*] had a large litter" (201).

7. For extracts from the account of this first demonstration by F. C. Beach (the editor of *Scientific American*), see Bryan 86–87; Edison's invention brought him immediate celebrity: "the papers had begun to call him 'the Wizard of Menlo Park'—a title that clung to him even after he had left Menlo forever" (Bryan 87).

8. Since musical recordings, by the 1920s especially, came to dominate the catalogs of the gramophone companies, the anxiety generated by this technology was even greater among professional musicians, many of whom "saw the gramophone as a modern usurper, eventually to kill live music" (Pearsall 102). Also see Knowles, "Death by Gramophone" 2–3.

9. For current scholarship in bioacoustics, consult the *Journal of the Acoustical Society of America* (*JASA*), which began publication in 1929, and *Bioacoustics*, which has appeared since 1988. For an expansive survey of linguistic research in animal communication, see the Roitblat, Herman, and Nachtigall essay collection *Language and Communication*.

10. See, for example, Kenner's *Joyce's Voices*.

Chapter 8. The Cultural Transfer of Film, Radio, and Television

1. There had been numerous earlier experimental and test radio transmissions in England, the United States, and elsewhere, so this date refers specifically to the initiation of a regular broadcasting schedule. The BBC was formed in the autumn of 1922 and "took over control of the air" on 14 November (Briggs 25), eight days after Radio Paris began regular broadcasting in France (*Wikipedia* "Radio France"). Regular radio broadcasting in the United States began considerably earlier, on 4 November 1920, with a broadcast of the results of the Harding-Cox election by station KDKA in Pittsburgh (T. Lewis 152–53). Radio Éireann inaugurated broadcasting on 1 January 1926 (Mink 459).

2. Anthony Burgess's *ReJoyce*, as here, offers a more nuanced discussion of the auditory and visual elements of the text (343–46) than his later introduction to *The Shorter Finnegans Wake*, "What It's All About," quoted above.

3. Joyce's "father's story of Buckley and the Russian General [...] wind[s] in and out of *Finnegans Wake*. Buckley [...] was an Irish soldier in the Crimean War who drew a bead on a Russian general, but when he observed his splendid epaulettes and decorations, he could not bring himself to shoot. After a moment, alive to his duty, he raised his rifle again, but just then the general let down his pants to defecate. The sight of his enemy in so helpless and human a plight was too much for Buckley, who again lowered his gun. But when the general prepared to finish the operation with a piece of grassy turf, Buckley lost all respect for him and fired. [...] Joyce told the story to [his] friends, convinced that it was in some way archetypal" (Ellmann, *James Joyce* 398).

4. The 5th Orphan Film Symposium at the University of South Carolina screened two such Fox Movietone Newsreel segments, on 22–23 March 2006, the first featuring

Dr. Herbert E. Ives of AT&T discussing the future of the videotelephone (1928) and the second presenting the first television images documented on sound film, produced by Ernst F. W. Alexanderson at G.E.'s "House of Magic," its laboratories in Schenectady, N.Y. (12 March 1931) (*The Schenectady Record*, 23 March 1931).

Walker, surveying the "reporting about mechanical television"—the precursor of the electronic television technology that would become standard in the mid-1930s—in the United States between 1927–33, has identified 477 stories that appeared in the *New York Times*: "over the seven year period, the *Times* wrote about mechanical television approximately once every 10 days" (24). I suspect we would find a comparable rate in the major newspapers of London and Paris, similar centers of research activity. Although the majority of *Times* reporting is positive or neutral concerning the feasibility and future of television, Walker also notes the occasional tendency toward negative reporting in the press, partly arising from a concern "about the impact of television on its own future" (22). Udelson, also quoted by Walker (22), claims that "rival media grew even more anxious and, in some instances, displayed overt hostility" toward this new technology in the 1930s (Udelson 49).

5. I will regretfully avoid the temptation to identify Sarnoff as the model for Joyce's Russian General, although he was, in fact, Russian by birth. Sarnoff, however, did not receive his promotion to General until 1944, after an impressive lobbying effort on his own behalf. See T. Lewis 295–97.

6. For example, while writing the latter portion of chapter I, 6 of *Finnegans Wake*—the 11th question, concerning Shaun—in the summer of 1927, Joyce introduces television into his book exactly contemporaneously with some of the most widely publicized demonstrations of new television technology. John Logie Baird, with his "mechanical" process (see below), transmitted television images from London to Glasgow (438 miles) on 24 May 1927. In June Baird announced his new device, the "phonoscope," for recording a television signal, and in July, in Paris, a new system developed by Georges Valensi was announced (Abramson, *History* 104). Correspondingly, Joyce has Shaun describe "Professor Loewy-Brueller" (*FW* 150.15) opining that the future "of Man is *temporarily* wrapped in obscenity [i.e., obscurity], looking through at these accidents with the faroscope [viz. 'phonoscope'] of television," yet unlike the electronic technology that he will later exploit for the Butt and Taff section of the *Wake* (II, 3), for Joyce television at the time of his writing is clearly a not-yet-perfected mechanical technology that he conceives as resembling an Edison phonograph with its tin-foil cylinder: "(this nightlife instrument needs still some subtractional betterment in the readjustment of the more refrangible angles to the squeals of his hypothesis [i.e., square of the hypotenuse] on the outer tin sides [i.e., insides])" (*FW* 150.31–35).

7. In England, for example, by "1938 about 5,000 sets had been bought, and it is estimated that by the time the [broadcast] service closed 18,000 to 20,000 sets had been sold during the three years it had been running" (Crisell 72).

8. Many early television receivers—see figure 8.2—used a large mirror to reflect a horizontally mounted picture tube and position the picture vertically. The television system that the Parisian researcher René Barthélemy demonstrated in April 1935 evi-

dently used such an arrangement; Abramson provides a photograph of Barthélemy and his receiver, dated 1935 (*History* 219).

9. The "emancipator" epithet also continues associations between the General and the Russian Tsar; Alexander II emancipated the serfs in 1861, partly in response to the loss of the Crimean War.

10. Benstock argues that the Crimean War, in fact, rather than the Battle of Waterloo, is the prototype for the theme of "the stupidity of war" in the *Wake* (*Joyce-Again's Wake* 172): "the opening battle is just a foreshadowing of the heroic struggles that take place throughout the *Wake*. Joyce is dealing with man's wars of expansion and colonization, and he utilizes the Crimean War of the mid-nineteenth century as the prototype of such conflicts. He seems to select this particular war for several interesting reasons: because it was typical of imperialistic England's 'necessary' conflagrations, because it was fought on the flimsiest of pretexts (England's concern for Turkey's rights violated by Russia's 'aiding' Christians persecuted in that country), because so many Irishmen were conscripted to fight for England, and because the word 'crime' is coincidentally incorporated into the name of the war" (*Joyce-Again's Wake* 171).

11. Notable among other references to the Great War in the Butt and Taff episode, in addition to several discussed below, are three allusions to the armistice (*Waffenstillstand*): "weeping stillstumms" (*FW* 347.11), "wapping stiltstunts" (*FW* 347.13), and "almistips" (*FW* 351.16); "*doughboys*" (*FW* 349.27); "redugout" (*FW* 351.06); "hand to hand" combat (*FW* 351.09); "preyers for rain" (*FW* 351.24); and Dead Man's Hill (Verdun)—"dead men's hills" (*FW* 352.32).

12. In fact, the Light Brigade was not annihilated, although it suffered substantial casualties in the Battle of Balaclava: "It is often stated that two-thirds of the brigade were killed or wounded. [...] The actual losses, out of 673 horsemen, were 113 killed and 134 wounded; 475 horses were killed" (Woodward 282, n 2).

13. For example, in the March 1931 Fox Movietone Newsreel documenting the demonstration of Alexanderson's television apparatus, his assistant, G.E. engineer Lowell J. Hartley, goes through a series of such actions—holding up his fingers, rolling his eyes clockwise and counterclockwise, moving his head from side to side, wiggling his ears, lighting a cigarette and blowing smoke rings—to illustrate the resolution of the television image.

14. Publicity hound and entrepreneur, Baird took every opportunity to demonstrate the various mechanical television devices he patented from the mid-1920s into the mid-1930s. By 1936 his role as a television pioneer ended when the corporation he founded, Baird Television Ltd., failed to persuade the BBC to adopt its belatedly developed electronic system (developed despite Baird's opposition). See Fisher and Fisher 23–36, 228–30, 246–50, and passim.

15. *Hansard's Parliamentary Debates* for 19 March 1855 contains this account, quoted from Lord Cardigan's "speech delivered at the Mansion-house on the 6th of February, and reported in *The Times*" (House of Commons, col. 1310).

16. A state of the art, high-definition picture in February 1937 had a teleframe of 405 lines, far from the 600 that would match Joyce's "*charge of the light barricade*" parallel

(Crisell 72). In 1941, the American National Television System Committee adopted a broadcast "standard of 525 lines, with thirty frames per second" (Fisher and Fisher 295).

17. As should be obvious from my analysis of the "*heliotropical noughttime*" passage, I find unconvincing Hart's directly contradictory assertion that Joyce here is "mak[ing] a direct and illuminating analogy between the electronic techniques of television and his own creative process." Hart, ignoring the violent imagery and associations in the passage, reads this paragraph as a description of "the act of copulation and the subsequent fusion of the two seeds into a single embryo" (159).

18. Ironically, T. S. Eliot was one of the first contemporary writers to appear on a television broadcast, joining with Rebecca West and Somerset Maugham to discuss books for an early, trial program on the BBC, on 26 August 1936, three months before regular broadcasting began (Wheen 25). Horkheimer and Adorno also discuss the viewer's loss of subjectivity as moviegoers: "The more intensely and flawlessly [the film producer's] techniques duplicate empirical objects, the easier it is today for the illusion to prevail that the outside world is the straightforward continuation of that presented on the screen. This purpose has been furthered by mechanical reproduction since the lightning takeover by the sound film. Real life is becoming indistinguishable from the movies. The sound film, far surpassing the theater of illusion, leaves no room for imagination or reflection on the part of the audience" (126).

19. Among other Tsarist references, beyond the already noted "Bog carsse" epithet (*FW* 339.06), "*Emancipator*" (*FW* 342.19), and the names of Alexander II and Nicholas II, are the Russian endearment "*little farther* [father]" (*FW* 339.36), two opera titles, Glinka's *A Life for the Tsar* ("my pife for his cgar" [*FW* 341.17]) and Lortzing's *Czar und Zimmermann* ("zahur and zimmerminnes" [*FW* 349.04]), and the names of two other Tsars, Peter the Great ("Peder the Greste" [*FW* 344.27]) and Ivan the Terrible ("*ivanmorinthorrorumble*" [*FW* 353.25]). Also, at the moment Butt/Buckley shoots the General, he somewhat incongruously proclaims himself Tsar: "Yastsar!" (*FW* 353.09), combining "Yes sir!" and the Russian "*Я Царь*!"

Bibliography

Abramson, Albert. *The History of Television, 1880 to 1941*. London: McFarland, 1987.

———. *Zworykin, Pioneer of Television*. Urbana: University of Illinois Press, 1995.

Adorno, Theodor. "On the Fetish Character in Music and the Regression of Listening." [1938.] *The Essential Frankfurt School Reader*. Ed. Andrew Arato and Eike Gebhardt. New York: Continuum, 1992, 270–99.

Alexander, Michael, ed. *Discovering the New World: Based on the Works of Theodore De Bry*. New York: Harper and Row, 1976.

Alfred Hitchcock Presents, Episode # 165. <www.tv.com/alfred-hitchcock-presents/specialty-of-the-house/episode/42872/recap.html>, accessed 2 February 2007.

Appleton, Victor. *Tom Swift and His Photo Telephone*. New York: Grosset & Dunlap, 1914.

———. *Tom Swift and His Wireless Message*. New York: Grosset & Dunlap, 1911.

Arata, Stephen. "The Occidental Tourist: Stoker and Reverse Colonization." *Fictions of Loss in the Victorian Fin de Siècle*. Cambridge: Cambridge University Press, 1996, 107–32.

Arato, Andrew, and Eike Gebhardt, eds. *The Essential Frankfurt School Reader*. New York: Continuum, 1992.

Arens, William. *The Man-Eating Myth: Anthropology and Anthropophagy*. New York: Oxford University Press, 1979.

Askenasy, Hans. *Cannibalism: From Sacrifice to Survival*. Amherst, N.Y.: Prometheus, 1994.

Atherton, James S. *The Books at the Wake: A Study of Literary Allusions in James Joyce's Finnegans Wake*. [1959.] New York: Viking Press, 1974.

Attridge, Derek. *Peculiar Language: Literature as Difference from the Renaissance to James Joyce*. Ithaca: Cornell University Press, 1988.

Baker, James R. "Ibsen, Joyce, and the Living-Dead." *James Joyce Miscellany*. 3rd series. Ed. Marvin Magalaner. Carbondale: Southern Illinois University Press, 1962, 19–32.

Bakhtin, M. M. *The Dialogic Imagination: Four Essays*. Ed. Michael Holquist, trans. Caryl Emerson and Michael Holquist. Austin: University of Texas Press, 1981.

Barker, Francis, Peter Hulme, and Margaret Iversen, eds. *Cannibalism and the Colonial World.* Cambridge: Cambridge University Press, 1998.

Barrow, Craig W. *Montage in James Joyce's Ulysses.* Potomac, Md.: Studia Humanitas, 1980.

Barrow, John D. *The Artful Universe.* Oxford: Clarendon, 1995.

———. *Pi in the Sky: Counting, Thinking, and Being.* Oxford: Clarendon, 1992.

———. *The World within the World.* Oxford: Oxford University Press, 1988.

Bauerle, Ruth. "Date Rape, Mate Rape: A Liturgical Interpretation of 'The Dead.'" *New Alliances in Joyce Studies.* Ed. Bonnie Kime Scott. Newark: University of Delaware Press, 1988, 113–25.

———. *Picking Up Airs: Hearing Music in Joyce's Texts.* Urbana: University of Illinois Press, 1993.

Beckett, Samuel. "Dante . . . Bruno . Vico . . Joyce." *Our Exagmination round His Factification for Incamination of Work in Progress.* Samuel Beckett, et al. New York: New Directions, 1972, 3–22.

Benco, Silvio. "James Joyce in Trieste." *Portraits of the Artist in Exile: Recollections of James Joyce by Europeans.* Ed. Willard Potts. Seattle: University of Washington Press, 1979, 49–58.

Benjamin, Walter. *Illuminations: Essays and Reflections.* Ed. Hannah Arendt, trans. Harry Zohn. New York: Schocken, 1969.

Benstock, Bernard. "The Gastronome's *Finnegans Wake.*" *James Joyce Quarterly* 2.3 (1965): 188–94.

———. *Joyce-Again's Wake: An Analysis of* Finnegans Wake. Seattle: University of Washington Press, 1965.

Berlitz, 1878–1998: One Hundred and Twenty Years of Excellence. Princeton, N.J.: Berlitz International, 1998.

Berlitz, Charles F. *Native Tongues.* New York: Grosset & Dunlap, 1982.

Bhabha, Homi K. *The Location of Culture.* London: Routledge, 1994.

Bierman, Robert. [Letter.] *James Joyce Quarterly* 27 (Spring 1990): 707–8.

Billman, Carol. *The Secret of the Stratemeyer Syndicate: Nancy Drew, The Hardy Boys, and the Million Dollar Fiction Factory.* New York: Ungar, 1986.

Bosinelli, Rosa Maria Bollettieri. "Joyce Slipping across the Borders of English: The Stranger in Language." *James Joyce Quarterly* 38.3–4 (2001): 395–409.

Boswell, James. *Boswell's London Journal, 1762–63.* Ed. Frederick A. Pottle. New Haven: Yale University Press, 1950.

Bowen, Zack. "Joyce's Prophylactic Paralysis: Exposure in *Dubliners.*" *James Joyce Quarterly* 19.3 (1982): 257–73.

———. "Libretto for Bloomusalem in Song: The Music of Joyce's *Ulysses.*" *New Light on Joyce from the Dublin Symposium.* Ed. Fritz Senn. Bloomington: Indiana University Press, 1972, 149–66.

———. *Musical Allusions in the Works of James Joyce: Early Poetry through* Ulysses. Albany: State University of New York Press, 1974.

———. Ulysses *as a Comic Novel.* Syracuse: Syracuse University Press, 1989.

Briggs, Asa. *The BBC: The First Fifty Years*. Oxford: Oxford University Press, 1985.

Brockman, William S. "Jacob Schwartz—'The Fly in the Honey.'" *Joyce Studies Annual 1998*. Ed. Thomas F. Staley. Austin: University of Texas Press, 1998, 174–90.

Brodie, Janet Farrell. *Contraception and Abortion in Nineteenth-Century America*. Ithaca: Cornell University Press, 1994.

Brown, Richard. *James Joyce and Sexuality*. Cambridge: Cambridge University Press, 1985.

Browning, Robert. *Parleyings with Certain People of Importance in Their Day*. Ed. Susan Crowl and Roma A. King, Jr. *The Complete Works of Robert Browning, Volume XVI*. Athens: Ohio University Press, 1998, 5–154.

Bry, Théodore de. *Americae Tertia Pars Memorabile Provinciae Brasiliae Historiam Contines, Germanico Primùm Sermone Scriptam à Ioane Stadio Hombergensi Hesso, Nunc Autem Latinitate Donatam à Teucrio Annaeo Privato Colchanthe Po: & Med: Addita est Narratio Profectionis Ioannis Lerij in Eamdem Provinciam, Qua Ille Initio Gallicè Conscripsit, Postea Verò Latinam Fecit. His Accessit Descriptio Morum & Ferocitatis Incolarum Illius Regionis, Atque Colloquium Ipsorum Idiomate Conscriptum*. Frankfurt am Main: Ioannem Wechelum, 1592.

Bryan, George S. *Edison: The Man and His Work*. New York: Knopf, 1926.

Budgen, Frank. *James Joyce and the Making of* Ulysses *and Other Writings*. London: Oxford University Press, 1972.

Bürger, Peter. *Theory of the Avant-Garde*. Trans. Michael Shaw. Minneapolis: University of Minnesota Press, 1984.

Burgess, Anthony. *Joysprick: An Introduction to the Language of James Joyce*. London: Deutsch, 1973.

———. *Re Joyce*. New York: Norton, 1965.

———. "What It's All About." *A Shorter* Finnegans Wake. Ed. Burgess. New York: Viking Press, 1967, xi–xxviii.

Campbell, Joseph, and Henry Morton Robinson. *A Skeleton Key to* Finnegans Wake. New York: Harcourt, 1944.

Carens, James F. "Some Points on Poyntz and Related Matters." *James Joyce Quarterly* 16.3 (1979): 344–46.

Casas, Bartolomé de las. *An Account of the First Voyages and Discoveries Made by the Spaniards in America. Containing the Most Exact Relation Hitherto Publish'd, of Their Unparallel'd Cruelties on the Indians, in the Destruction of Above Forty Millions of People. With the Propositions Offer'd to the King of Spain, to Prevent the Further Ruin of the West-Indies*. London: D. Brown, 1699.

Cheng, Vincent J. *Joyce, Race, and Empire*. Cambridge: Cambridge University Press, 1995.

Ciardi, John. *Dante Alighieri: The Inferno*. New York: New American Library, 1954.

Cixous, Hélène. *The Exile of James Joyce*. Trans. Sally A. J. Purcell. New York: Lewis, 1972.

Connor, James A., S.J. "Radio Free Joyce: *Wake* Language and the Experience of Radio." *James Joyce Quarterly* 30.4–31.1 (1993): 825–43.

Conrad, Joseph. *Youth, Heart of Darkness, The End of the Tether: Three Stories*. London: Dent, 1946.

———. *The Secret Agent*. Ed. Norman Sherry. London: Dent, 1974.

Cope, Jackson I. "An Epigraph for Dubliners." *James Joyce Quarterly* 7 (1970): 362–64.

Crisell, Andrew. *An Introductory History of British Broadcasting*. London: Routledge, 1997.

Crivelli, Renzo S. *Itinerari Triestini—James Joyce—Triestine Itineraries*. Trieste: Università Degli Studi Di Trieste, 1996.

Cunningham, Valentine. *British Writers of the Thirties*. Oxford: Oxford University Press, 1988.

Day Lewis, Cecil. *Revolution in Writing*. London: Hogarth, 1935.

Derrida, Jacques. "By Force of Mourning." *Critical Inquiry* 22:2 (Winter 1996): 171–92.

———. "*Ulysses* Gramophone: Hear say yes in Joyce." Trans. Tina Kendall, with Shari Benstock. *James Joyce: The Augmented Ninth: Proceedings of the Ninth James Joyce Symposium, Frankfurt 1984*. Ed. Bernard Benstock. Syracuse: Syracuse University Press, 1988, 43–44.

DeVane, William C. *A Browning Handbook*. 2nd ed. New York: Appleton-Century-Crofts, 1955.

———. *Browning's Parleyings: The Autobiography of a Mind*. New Haven: Yale University Press, 1927.

Devlin, Kimberly J. *Wandering and Return in* Finnegans Wake: *An Integrative Approach to Joyce's Fictions*. Princeton: Princeton University Press, 1991.

Diamond, Jared. *Guns, Germs, and Steel: The Fates of Human Societies*. New York: Norton, 1999.

Dinsdale, Alfred. *Television*. London: Television Press, 1928.

"Doctor Dolittle." <members.tripod.com/~Puddleby/author.html>, accessed 2 February 2007.

Donaldson, Peter S. "Cinema and the Kingdom of Death: Loncraine's *Richard III*." *Shakespeare Quarterly* 53.2 (2002): 241–59.

Duffy, Enda. "Interesting States: Birthing and the Nation in 'Oxen of the Sun.'" Ulysses—En-Gendered Perspectives. Ed. Kimberly J. Devlin and Marilyn Reizbaum. Columbia: University of South Carolina Press, 1999, 210–28.

Eckley, Grace. *Children's Lore in* Finnegans Wake. Syracuse: Syracuse University Press, 1985.

Edison, Thomas Alva. "The Phonograph and Its Future." *North American Review* 126 (May–June 1878): 527–36.

Eliade, Mircea. *The Sacred and the Profane: The Nature of Religion*. Trans. Willard R. Trask. San Diego: Harcourt Brace, 1959.

Eliot, T. S. "The Cinema Quota." *Criterion* 6.4 (October 1927): 290.

———. *The Complete Poems and Plays, 1909–1950*. New York: Harcourt, Brace, and World, 1962.

————. "The Metaphysical Poets (1921)." *Selected Prose of T. S. Eliot*. Ed. Frank Kermode. New York: Harcourt Brace Jovanovich, Farrar, Straus and Giroux, 1975, 59–67.

————. "*Ulysses*, Order, and Myth." *James Joyce: Two Decades of Criticism*. Ed. Seon Givens. 2nd ed. New York: Vanguard Press, 1963, 198–202.

Ellin, Stanley. "The Specialty of the House." *The Specialty of the House, and Other Stories 1948–1978*. New York: Mysterious Press, 1979, 1–24.

Ellmann, Richard. "Introduction." *Giacomo Joyce*, by James Joyce. New York: Viking Press, 1968, xi–xxvi.

————. *James Joyce*. Rev. ed. Oxford: Oxford University Press, 1982.

————. *Ulysses on the Liffey*. New York: Oxford University Press, 1972.

Eysteinssohn, Astradur. *The Concept of Modernism*. Ithaca: Cornell University Press, 1990.

Fargnoli, A. Nicholas, and Michael Patrick Gillespie. *James Joyce A to Z: The Essential Reference to His Life and Work*. New York: Oxford University Press, 1995.

Feeley, John. "Joyce's 'The Dead' and the Browning Quotation." *James Joyce Quarterly* 20 (Fall 1982): 87–96.

Fish, Stanley E. *Self-Consuming Artifacts: The Experience of Seventeenth-Century Literature*. Berkeley: University of California Press, 1973.

Fisher, David E., and Marshall Jon Fisher. *Tube: The Invention of Television*. Washington, D.C.: Counterpoint, 1996.

Ford, Jane M. "James Joyce and the Conrad Connection: The Anxiety of Influence." *Conradiana* 17.1 (1985): 3–18.

————. "James Joyce's Trieste Library: Some Notes on Its Use." *Joyce at Texas: Essays on the James Joyce Materials at the Humanities Research Center*. Ed. Dave Oliphant and Thomas Zigal. Austin: Humanities Research Center, 1983, 141–57.

Francini Bruni, Alessandro. "Joyce Stripped Naked in the Piazza." Trans. Camilla Rudolph et al. *Portraits of the Artist in Exile: Recollections of James Joyce by Europeans*. Ed. Willard Potts. Seattle: University of Washington Press, 1979, 7–39.

————. "Recollections of Joyce." Trans. Lido Botti. *Portraits of the Artist in Exile: Recollections of James Joyce by Europeans*. Ed. Willard Potts. Seattle: University of Washington Press, 1979, 39–46.

Frazer, James G. *The Golden Bough*. Abridged edition. New York: Macmillan, 1922.

French, Marilyn. *The Book as World: James Joyce's Ulysses*. Cambridge: Harvard University Press, 1976.

Freud, Sigmund. *The Freud Reader*. Ed. Peter Gay. New York: Norton, 1989.

Friedrich, Gerhard. "Bret Harte as a Source for James Joyce's 'The Dead.'" *Philological Quarterly* 33 (1954): 442–44.

Gabler, Hans Walter. "The Seven Lost Years of *A Portrait of the Artist as a Young Man*." *Approaches to Joyce's Portrait*. Ed. Thomas F. Staley and Bernard Benstock. Pittsburgh: University of Pittsburgh Press, 1976, 25–60.

"Games: Season for Swifties." *Time* 81 (31 May 1963): 36.

Gay, Peter, ed. *The Freud Reader*. New York: Norton, 1989.

Gelatt, Roland. *The Fabulous Phonograph: From Edison to Stereo*. Rev. ed. New York: Appleton-Century, 1965.

"German Cannibal Tells of Fantasy." <news.bbc.co.uk/1/hi/world/europe/3286721. stm>, accessed 2 February 2007.

Gifford, Don. *Joyce Annotated: Notes for* Dubliners *and* A Portrait of the Artist as a Young Man. 2nd ed. Berkeley: University of California Press, 1982.

———, with Robert J. Seidman. Ulysses *Annotated: Notes for James Joyce's* Ulysses. Rev. ed. Berkeley: University of California Press, 1988.

Gilbert, Stuart. *James Joyce's* Ulysses: *A Study*. New York: Random House, 1952.

Gillespie, Michael Patrick, ed. *James Joyce's Trieste Library: A Catalogue of Materials at the Harry Ransom Humanities Research Center, University of Texas at Austin*. Austin: Humanities Research Center, 1986.

Gorky, Maxim. "A Review of the Lumière Programme at the Nizhni-Novgorod Fair." *Nizhegorodski Listok*, 4 July 1896.

Gottfried, Roy K. *The Art of Joyce's Syntax in* Ulysses. Athens: University of Georgia Press, 1980.

———. "Berlitz Schools Joyce." *James Joyce Quarterly* 16.3 (1979): 223–38.

———. "Reading the Text of *Ulysses*, 'Reading' Other 'Texts': Representation and the Limits of Visual and Verbal Narratives." *Pedagogy, Praxis,* Ulysses: *Using Joyce's Text to Transform the Classroom*. Ed. Robert Newman. Ann Arbor: University of Michigan Press, 1996, 181–94.

Graetzer, Hans G., and David L. Anderson. *The Discovery of Nuclear Fission*. New York: Van Nostrand, 1971.

Gramsci, Antonio. *An Antonio Gramsci Reader: Selected Writings, 1916–1935*. Ed. David Forgacs. New York: Schocken, 1988.

Graves, Robert, and Alan Hodge. *The Long Week-End: A Social History of Great Britain, 1918–1939*. New York: Norton, 1963.

Greenblatt, Stephen J. *Marvelous Possessions: The Wonder of the New World*. Chicago: University of Chicago Press, 1991.

Griffith, Richard. "Foreword." *The Film: A Psychological Study*, by Hugo Münsterberg. New York: Dover, 1970, v–xv.

Groden, Michael, Gen. ed. *The James Joyce Archive*. 63 vols. New York: Garland, 1978.

Grose, Francis. *A Guide to Health, Beauty, Riches, and Honour*. London: S. Hooper, 1783.

Gryta, Caroline Nobile. "Who is Signor Maffei? and Has *Ruby: the Pride of the Ring* Really Been Located?" *James Joyce Quarterly* 21.4 (1984): 321–28.

Haltresht, Michael. "Disease Imagery in Conrad's *The Secret Agent*." *Literature and Psychology* 21 (1971): 101–5.

Hamilton, Edith. *Mythology*. New York: New American Library, 1942.

Hansard's Parliamentary Debates. London: Hansard, 1855.

Hart, Clive. *Structure and Motif in* Finnegans Wake. London: Faber, 1962.

Hayman, David. "The Empirical Molly." *Approaches to* Ulysses: *Ten Essays*. Ed.

Thomas F. Staley and Bernard Benstock. Pittsburgh: University of Pittsburgh Press, 1970, 103–35.

———. "Preface." Finnegans Wake, *Book II, Chapter 3: A Facsimile of Drafts, Typescripts, and Proofs.* 2 vols. *The James Joyce Archive.* Gen. ed. Michael Groden. New York: Garland, 1978, I, vii–xiv.

———. Ulysses: *The Mechanics of Meaning* [1970]. Rev. ed. Madison: University of Wisconsin Press, 1982.

Hegel, G. W. F. *Phenomenology of Spirit.* [1807.] Trans. A. V. Miller. New York: Oxford University Press, 1979.

Heims, Neil. "*Robinson Crusoe* and the Fear of Being Eaten." *Colby Library Quarterly* 19.4 (1983): 190–93.

Himes, Norman E. *Medical History of Contraception.* Baltimore: Williams & Wilkins, 1936.

Hirsch, Edward. "The Imaginary Irish Peasant." *PMLA* 106.4 (1991): 1116–33.

Hodgart, Matthew J. C., and Mabel P. Worthington. *Song in the Work of James Joyce.* New York: Columbia University Press, 1959.

Hodgart, Matthew J. C., and Ruth Bauerle. *Joyce's Grand Operoar: Opera in* Finnegans Wake. Urbana: University of Illinois Press, 1996.

Hollander, John. *The Untuning of the Sky: Ideas of Music in English Poetry, 1500–1700.* Princeton: Princeton University Press, 1961.

Horkheimer, Max, and Theodor W. Adorno. *Dialectic of Enlightenment.* [1947, 1969.] Trans. John Cumming. New York: Continuum, 1993.

Houston, John. *Joyce and Prose: An Exploration of the Language of* Ulysses. Lewisburg: Bucknell University Press, 1989.

Huxley, Aldous. *Brave New World.* [1932, 1946.] New York: Harper Collins, 1998.

Huyssen, Andreas. *After the Great Divide: Modernism, Mass Culture, Postmodernism.* Bloomington: Indiana University Press, 1986.

Iser, Wolfgang. *The Act of Reading: A Theory of Aesthetic Response.* Baltimore: Johns Hopkins University Press, 1978.

Israel, Paul. *Edison: A Life of Invention.* New York: Wiley, 1998.

"I've Come Back, Cried Tom Swiftly." *Life* 54 (31 May 1963): 19.

James, Jamie. *The Music of the Spheres: Music, Science, and the Natural Order of the Universe.* New York: Springer, 1993.

Janusko, Robert. *The Sources and Structures of James Joyce's "Oxen."* Ann Arbor: UMI Research, 1983.

Johnston, G. "After the Invention of the Gramophone: Hearing the Woman in Stein's *Autobiography* and Woolf's *Three Guineas.*" *Virginia Woolf Miscellanies,* ed. Mark Hussey and Vara Neverow-Turk. New York: Pace University Press, 1992, 88–96.

Jones, Francis Arthur. *Thomas Alva Edison: Sixty Years of an Inventor's Life.* New York: Crowell, 1908.

Joyce, James. *Dubliners: Text, Criticism, and Notes.* [1914.] Ed. Robert Scholes and A. Walton Litz. New York: Viking Press, 1969.

———. *Finnegans Wake.* [1939.] New York: Viking Press, 1959.

———. *Giacomo Joyce.* New York: Viking Press, 1968.

———. *The Letters of James Joyce.* 3 vols. Ed. Stuart Gilbert and Richard Ellmann. New York: Viking Press, 1957, 1966.

———. *A Portrait of the Artist as a Young Man: Text, Criticism, and Notes.* [1916.] Ed. Chester G. Anderson. New York: Viking Press, 1968.

———. *Selected Letters.* Ed. Richard Ellmann. New York: Viking Press, 1966.

———. *Stephen Hero.* [1944.] Ed. Theodore Spencer. New York: New Directions, 1959.

———. "The Study of Languages (1898/99?)." *The Critical Writings of James Joyce.* Ed. Ellsworth Mason and Richard Ellmann. New York: Viking Press, 1959, 25–30.

———. *Ulysses.* [1922.] Ed. Hans Walter Gabler. New York: Random House, 1984, 1986.

Joyce, Stanislaus. *My Brother's Keeper.* Ed. Richard Ellmann. New York: Viking Press, 1958.

Kellogg, Robert. "'Scylla and Charybdis.'" *James Joyce's* Ulysses: *Critical Essays.* Ed. Clive Hart and David Hayman. Berkeley: University of California Press, 1974.

Kelly, Alan, comp. *His Master's Voice/Die Stimme Seines Herrn: The German Catalogue; A Complete Numerical Catalogue of German Gramophone Recordings Made from 1898 to 1929 in Germany, Austria, and Elsewhere by The Gramophone Company, Ltd.* Westport, Conn.: Greenwood, 1994.

———. *His Master's Voice/La Voce Del Padrone: The Italian Catalogue; A Complete Numerical Catalogue of Italian Gramophone Recordings Made from 1898 to 1929 in Italy and Elsewhere by The Gramophone Company, Ltd.* Westport, Conn.: Greenwood, 1988.

———. *His Master's Voice/La Voix de Son Maitre: The French Catalogue; A Complete Numerical Catalogue of French Gramophone Recordings made from 1898 to 1929 in France and Elsewhere by The Gramophone Company, Ltd.* Westport, Conn.: Greenwood, 1990.

Kelly, Dermot. *Narrative Strategies in Joyce's* Ulysses. Ann Arbor: UMI Research Press, 1988.

Kenner, Hugh. "Beaufoy's Masterplaster." *James Joyce Quarterly* 24.1 (1986): 11–18.

———. *A Colder Eye: The Modern Irish Writers.* New York: Penguin, 1984.

———. *Joyce's Voices.* Berkeley: University of California Press, 1978.

———. Ulysses. [1980.] Rev. ed. Baltimore: Johns Hopkins University Press, 1987.

———. *Wyndham Lewis.* New York: New Directions, 1954.

Kermode, Frank. *The Genesis of Secrecy: On the Interpretation of Narrative.* Cambridge: Harvard University Press, 1979.

Kern, Stephen. *The Culture of Time and Space 1880–1918.* Cambridge: Harvard University Press, 1983.

Kershner, R. B. *Joyce, Bakhtin, and Popular Literature: Chronicles of Disorder.* Chapel Hill: University of North Carolina Press, 1989.

Kilgour, Maggie. *From Communion to Cannibalism: An Anatomy of Metaphors of Incorporation.* Princeton: Princeton University Press, 1990.

———. "The Function of Cannibalism at the Present Time." *Cannibalism and the Colonial World*. Ed. Francis Barker, Peter Hulme, and Margaret Iversen. Cambridge: Cambridge University Press, 1998, 238–59.

Kinealy, Christine. *The Great Irish Famine: Impact, Ideology and Rebellion*. New York: Palgrave, 2002.

King, C. Richard. "The (Mis)Uses of Cannibalism in Contemporary Cultural Critique." *diacritics* 30.1 (2000): 106–23.

Kittler, Friedrich A. *Discourse Networks, 1800/1900*. Trans. Michael Metteer and Chris Cullens. Stanford: Stanford University Press, 1990.

———. *Gramophone, Film, Typewriter*. Trans. Geoffrey Winthrop-Young and Michael Wutz. Stanford: Stanford University Press, 1999.

Kline, Morris. *Mathematics in Western Culture*. London: Oxford University Press, 1953.

———. *Mathematics: The Loss of Certainty*. New York: Oxford University Press, 1980.

Knowles, Sebastian D. G. "Death by Gramophone." *Journal of Modern Literature* 27.1–2 (2003): 1–13.

———. *The Dublin Helix: The Life of Language in Joyce's* Ulysses. Gainesville: University Press of Florida, 2001.

———, ed. *Bronze by Gold: The Music of Joyce*. New York: Garland, 1999.

Kruck, William E. *Looking for Dr. Condom*. Publication of the American Dialect Society. No. 66. University: University of Alabama Press, 1981.

Lant, Antonia. "The Curse of the Pharaoh, or How the Cinema Contracted Egyptomania." *October* 59 (1992): 87–112.

Larbaud, Valéry. "The *Ulysses* of James Joyce." [1922.] *James Joyce: The Critical Heritage*. Ed. Robert H. Deming. London: Routledge, 1970, 252–62.

Lawrence, D. H. *Lady Chatterley's Lover*. New York: Grove Press, 1957.

Lawrence, Karen. *The Odyssey of Style in* Ulysses. Princeton, N.J.: Princeton University Press, 1981.

Léry, Jean de. *History of a Voyage to the Land of Brazil*. [1578.] Trans. Janet Whatley. Berkeley: University of California Press, 1990.

Lestringant, Frank. *Cannibals: The Discovery and Representation of the Cannibal from Columbus to Jules Verne*. Trans. Rosemary Morris. Berkeley: University of California Press, 1997.

Levenson, Thomas. *Measure for Measure: A Musical History of Science*. New York: Simon & Schuster, 1994.

Levin, Harry. *James Joyce: A Critical Introduction*. 2nd ed. New York: New Directions, 1960.

Lewis, I. M. *Religion in Context: Cults and Charisma*. 2nd ed. Cambridge: Cambridge University Press, 1996.

Lewis, Tom. *Empire of the Air: The Men Who Made Radio*. New York: HarperCollins, 1991.

Lewis, Wyndham. *The Art of Being Ruled*. London: Chatto and Windus, 1926.

Lofting, Hugh A. *The Story of Doctor Dolittle.* New York: Lippincott, 1920.

———. *The Voyages of Doctor Dolittle.* New York: Stokes, 1922.

Lowe-Evans, Mary. *Crimes against Fecundity: Joyce and Population Control.* Syracuse: Syracuse University Press, 1989.

Lüsebrink, Hans-Jürgen, and Rolf Reichardt. "Kulturtransfer im Epochenumbruch. Fragestellungen, methodische Konzepte, Forschungsperspektiven. Einführung." *Kulturtransfer im Epochenumbruch Frankreich Deutschland 1770 bis 1815.* Ed. Lüsebrink and Reichardt, et al. Leipzig: Leipziger Universitätsverlag, 1997, 9–26.

Lyons, J. B. *James Joyce and Medicine.* Dublin: Dolmen, 1973.

———. *Thrust Syphilis Down to Hell and Other Rejoyceana: Studies in the Border-Lands of Literature and Medicine.* Dublin: Glendale, 1988.

Lysaght, Patricia. "Women and the Great Famine: Vignettes from the Irish Oral Tradition." *The Great Famine and the Irish Diaspora in America.* Ed. Arthur Gribben. Amherst: University of Massachusetts Press, 1999, 21–48.

MacCabe, Colin. *James Joyce and the Revolution of the Word.* [1978.] 2nd ed. New York: Palgrave Macmillan, 2003.

Macey, David. *The Penguin Dictionary of Critical Theory.* New York: Penguin, 2000.

Malchow, H. L. *Gothic Images of Race in Nineteenth-Century Britain.* Stanford: Stanford University Press, 1996.

Marcuse, Herbert. *One-Dimensional Man.* [1964.] 2nd ed. Boston: Beacon Press, 1991.

Martin, Timothy. *Joyce and Wagner: A Study of Influence.* Cambridge: Cambridge University Press, 1991.

McCarthy, Patrick A. "Joyce's Unreliable Catechist: Mathematics and the Narration of 'Ithaca.'" *ELH* 51 (1984): 605–18.

McCourt, John. *James Joyce: A Passionate Exile.* New York: St. Martin's, 1999.

———. *The Years of Bloom: James Joyce in Trieste 1904–1920.* Madison: University of Wisconsin Press, 2000.

———, ed. "Joyce and Trieste." *James Joyce Quarterly* 38.3–4 (2001): 309–475.

McHugh, Roland. *Annotations to* Finnegans Wake. 3rd ed. Baltimore: Johns Hopkins University Press, 2006.

Meyer, John A. "Cigarette Century." *American Heritage* 43 (December 1992): 72–80.

Millard, Andre. *America on Record: A History of Recorded Sound.* Cambridge: Cambridge University Press, 1995.

———. *Edison and the Business of Invention.* Baltimore: Johns Hopkins University Press, 1990.

Mink, Louis O. *A* Finnegans Wake *Gazetteer.* Bloomington: Indiana University Press, 1978.

Montaigne, Michel de. *The Complete Works of Montaigne: Essays, Travel Journal, Letters.* Ed. Donald M. Frame. Stanford: Stanford University Press, 1957.

Morely, Patricia A. "Fish Symbolism in Chapter Seven of *Finnegans Wake*: The Hidden Defence of Shem the Penman." *James Joyce Quarterly* 6.4 (1969): 267–70.

Morley, John. *Death, Heaven and the Victorians.* London: Studio Vista, 1971.

Moxon, Joseph. *A Tutor to Astonomy and Geography*. 4th ed. London: S. Roycroft, 1686.

Munich, Adrienne Auslander. "'Dear Dead Women,' or Why Gabriel Conroy Reviews Robert Browning." *New Alliances in Joyce Studies*. Ed. Bonnie Kime Scott. Newark: University of Delaware Press, 1988, 126–34.

Münsterberg, Hugo. *The Film: A Psychological Study*. [1916.] New York: Dover, 1970.

———. *Grundzüge der Psychotechnik*. Leipzig: Barth, 1914.

Murchie, Guy. *Music of the Spheres: The Material Universe—From Atom to Quasar, Simply Explained*. New York: Houghton Mifflin, 1961.

Murphy, James S. *The Condom Industry in the United States*. Jefferson, N.C.: McFarland, 1990.

"Nipper and His Master's Voice." <www2.danbbs.dk/~erikoest/nipper.html>, accessed 2 February 2007.

"Nipper and the Story of 'His Master's Voice.'" <www.nipperhead.com/nipperf2.htm>, accessed 2 February 2007.

Noon, William T., S.J. *Joyce and Aquinas*. New Haven: Yale University Press, 1957.

Norris, Margot. *The Decentered Universe of* Finnegans Wake*: A Structuralist Analysis*. Baltimore: Johns Hopkins University Press, 1976.

———. *Joyce's Web: The Social Unraveling of Modernism*. Austin: University of Texas Press, 1992.

Opie, Iona, and Peter Opie. *The Classic Fairy Tales*. New York: Oxford University Press, 1974.

Oriel, J. D. *The Scars of Venus: A History of Venereology*. New York: Springer, 1994.

Orwell, George. *1984*. [1949.] New York: New American Library, 1977.

Osteen, Mark. *The Economy of* Ulysses*: Making Both Ends Meet*. Syracuse: Syracuse University Press, 1995.

———. "The Intertextual Economy in 'Scylla and Charybdis.'" *James Joyce Quarterly* 28.1 (1990): 197–208.

The Oxford English Dictionary. <dictionary.oed.com/entrance.dtl>, accessed 2 February 2007.

Pais, Abraham. *Inward Bound: Of Matter and Forces in the Physical World*. Oxford: Clarendon, 1986.

Passmore, John. *A Hundred Years of Philosophy*. 2nd ed. Harmondsworth, England: Penguin, 1966.

Pearsall, Ronald. *Popular Music of the Twenties*. Totowa, N.J.: Rowman and Littlefield, 1976.

Pensky, Max. *Melancholy Dialectics: Walter Benjamin and the Play of Mourning*. Amherst: University of Massachusetts Press, 1993.

Petrinovich, Lewis. *The Cannibal Within*. Hawthorne, N.Y.: Aldine de Gruyter, 2000.

Petts, Leonard. *The Story of "Nipper" and the "His Master's Voice" Picture Painted by Francis Barraud*. 2nd rev. ed. Bournemouth, England: Bayly, 1983.

Phillips, Jerry. "Cannibalism qua Capitalism: The Metaphorics of Accumulation in Marx, Conrad, Shakespeare, and Marlowe." *Cannibalism and the Colonial World*.

Ed. Francis Barker, Peter Hulme, and Margaret Iversen. Cambridge: Cambridge University Press, 1998, 183–203.

Picker, John M. *Victorian Soundscapes*. Oxford: Oxford University Press, 2003.

Plato. *Epinomis*. Trans. A. E. Taylor. *Plato: The Collected Dialogues*. Ed. Edith Hamilton and Huntington Cairns. Princeton: Princeton University Press, 1961, 1517–33.

Potts, Willard, ed. *Portraits of the Artist in Exile: Recollections of James Joyce by Europeans*. Seattle: University of Washington Press, 1979.

Power, Mary. "The Discovery of *Ruby*." *James Joyce Quarterly* 18.2 (1981): 115–21.

Price, Merrall Llewelyn. *Consuming Passions: The Uses of Cannibalism in Late Medieval and Early Modern Europe*. New York: Routledge, 2003.

Pridmore-Brown, Michele. "1939–40: Of Virginia Woolf, Gramophones, and Fascism." *PMLA* 113.3 (May 1998): 408–21.

Reynolds, Mary T. *Joyce and Dante: The Shaping Imagination*. Princeton: Princeton University Press, 1981.

Rice, Thomas Jackson. *Joyce, Chaos, and Complexity*. Urbana: University of Illinois Press, 1997.

Riquelme, John Paul. *Teller and Tale in Joyce's Fiction: Oscillating Perspectives*. Baltimore: Johns Hopkins University Press, 1983.

Roitblat, Herbert L., Louis M. Herman, and Paul E. Nachtigall, eds. *Language and Communication: Comparative Perspectives*. Hillsdale, N.J.: Lawrence Erlbaum, 1993.

Sanday, Peggy Reeve. *Divine Hunger: Cannibalism as a Cultural System*. Cambridge: Cambridge University Press, 1986.

Scharnhorst, Gary. *Bret Harte*. New York: Twayne, 1992.

Scharry, John. "The 'Negro Chieftain' and Disharmony in Joyce's 'The Dead.'" *Revue des Langues Vivantes* 39 (1973): 182–83.

Scholes, Robert. "Some Observations on the Text of *Dubliners*: 'The Dead.'" *Studies in Bibliography* 15 (1962): 191–205.

Schutte, William M. *Joyce and Shakespeare: A Study in the Meaning of* Ulysses. New Haven: Yale University Press, 1957.

Schwarz, Frederic D. "Sometimes a Dumb Notion." *American Heritage of Invention and Technology* 22.3 (Winter 2007): 56.

Senn, Fritz. "Righting *Ulysses*." *James Joyce: New Perspectives*. Ed. Colin MacCabe. Sussex: Harvester, 1982, 3–28.

———. "'Stately, plump,' For Example: Allusive Overlays and Widening Circles of Irrelevance." *James Joyce Quarterly* 22.4 (1985): 347–54.

Sherry, Norman. *Conrad's Western World*. Cambridge: Cambridge University Press, 1971.

Shklovsky, Victor. "Art as Technique." [1917]. *Russian Formalist Criticism: Four Essays*. Trans. and ed. Lee T. Lemon and Marion J. Reis. Lincoln: University of Nebraska Press, 1965, 3–24.

———. "Sterne's *Tristram Shandy*: Stylistic Commentary." [1921.] *Russian Formalist*

Criticism: Four Essays. Trans. and ed. Lee T. Lemon and Marion J. Reis. Lincoln: University of Nebraska Press, 1965, 25–57.

Sinclair, John D., trans. *Dante's Inferno: Italian Text with English Translation*. New York: Oxford University Press, 1939.

———. *Dante's Paradiso: Italian Text with English Translation*. New York: Oxford University Press, 1939.

Smart, Robert A., and Michael R. Hutcheson. "The 'Unborn and Unburied Dead': The Rhetoric of Ireland's *An Gorta Mor*." *Ireland's Great Hunger: Silence, Memory, and Commemoration*. Ed. David A. Vilone and Christine Kinealy. Lanham, Md.: University Press of America, 2002, 63–81.

Solomon, Margaret C. *Eternal Geomater: The Sexual Universe of* Finnegans Wake. Carbondale: Southern Illinois University Press, 1969.

Spielberg, Peter. "Addenda: More Food for the Gastronome's *Finnegans Wake*." *James Joyce Quarterly* 3.4 (1966): 297–98.

Spoo, Robert. "Joyce's Attitudes toward History: Rome, 1906–07." *Journal of Modern Literature* 14 (1988): 481–97.

Staden, Hans. *Hans Staden: The True History of His Captivity, 1557*. Trans. and ed. Malcolm Letts. New York: McBride, 1929.

Stoker, Bram. *Dracula*. [1897.] Ed. Nina Auerbach. New York: Norton, 1997.

Strumpen-Darrie, Robert, and Charles F. Berlitz. *The Berlitz Self-Teacher: Russian*. New York: Grosset & Dunlap, 1951.

Strunk, William, Jr., and E. B. White. *The Elements of Style*. 2nd ed. New York: Macmillan, 1972.

Swift, Earl. "The Perfect Inventor." *American Heritage of Invention and Technology* 6.2 (Fall 1990): 24–31.

Swift, Jonathan. "A Modest Proposal." [1729.] *Jonathan Swift*. Ed. Angus Ross and David Woolley. Oxford: Oxford University Press, 1984, 492–99.

"Swiftly, He Said Gamely." *Newsweek* 61 (3 June 1963): 81–82.

Tannahill, Reay. *Flesh and Blood: A History of the Cannibal Complex*. New York: Stein and Day, 1975.

Tennyson, Alfred Lord. "The Charge of the Light Brigade." *The Poems of Tennyson*. Ed. Christopher Ricks. London: Longmans, 1969, 1034–36.

Theoharis, Theoharis C. "*Hedda Gabler* and 'The Dead.'" *ELH* 50 (1983): 791–810.

Thevet, Andrewe [André]. *The New Found Worlde or Antarctike*. [London 1568.] Amsterdam: Theatrum Orbis Terrarum, 1971.

Thomas, Brook. *James Joyce's* Ulysses: *A Book of Many Happy Returns*. Baton Rouge: Louisiana State University Press, 1982.

Thornton, Weldon. *Allusions in* Ulysses. Chapel Hill: University of North Carolina Press, 1961.

Tindall, William York. *A Reader's Guide to* Finnegans Wake. New York: Farrar, Straus and Giroux, 1969.

———. *A Reader's Guide to James Joyce*. New York: Noonday, 1959.

"Tom Swift Carries On—Gamely." *Readers' Digest* 83 (Sept. 1963): 44.

Torchiana, Donald T. *Backgrounds for Joyce's* Dubliners. Boston: Allen & Unwin, 1986.

Tratner, Michael. "Sex and Credit: Consumer Capitalism in *Ulysses.*" *James Joyce Quarterly* 30.4–31.1 (1993): 695–716.

Tysdahl, Bjorn J. *Joyce and Ibsen: A Study in Literary Influence.* New York: Humanities Press, 1968.

Udelson, Joseph H. *The Great Television Race.* University: University of Alabama Press, 1982.

Vickery, John B. *The Literary Impact of the* Golden Bough. Princeton: Princeton University Press, 1973.

Virilio, Paul. *War and Cinema: The Logistics of Perception.* Trans. Patrick Camiller. London: Verso, 1989.

Voraigne, Jacobus de. *The Golden Legend.* Trans. and ed. Granger Ryan and Helmut Ripperger. 1941. New York: Arno, 1969.

Walker, James R. "Old Media on New Media: National Popular Press Reaction to Mechanical Television." *Journal of Popular Culture* 25.1 (1991): 21–29.

Walton, Patricia L. *Our Cannibals, Ourselves.* Urbana: University of Illinois Press, 2004.

Watson, Bruce. "Girls! Boys! It's Edward Stratemeyer." *Smithsonian* 22.7 (October 1991): 50–61.

wbc: "Berlitz: History." <www.berlitz.com/about/history/html>, accessed 2 February 2007.

Weir, David. "Gnomon is an Island: Euclid and Bruno in Joyce's Narrative Practice." *James Joyce Quarterly* 28 (Winter 1991): 343–60.

Weir, Lorraine. *Writing Joyce: A Semiotics of the Joyce System.* Bloomington: Indiana University Press, 1989.

Wells, H. G. *The Time Machine. The War of the Worlds. A Critical Edition.* [1895, 1898.] Ed. Frank D. McConnell, New York: Oxford University Press, 1977.

Whatley, Janet. "Translator's Introduction." *History of a Voyage to the Land of Brazil,* by Jean de Léry. [1578.] Trans. Whatley. Berkeley: University of California Press, 1990, xv–xxxviii.

Wheen, Francis. *Television: A History.* London: Century, 1985.

Whelan, Kevin. "The Memories of 'The Dead.'" *Yale Journal of Criticism* 15.1 (2002): 59–97.

Wikipedia. <www.wikipedia.org>, accessed 2 February 2007.

Wile, Frederic William. *Emile Berliner: Maker of the Microphone.* New York: Bobbs-Merrill, 1926.

Williams, Keith. *British Writers and the Media, 1930–45.* London: Macmillan, 1966.

Williams, Raymond. *Television: Technology and Cultural Form.* New York: Schocken, 1975.

Wilson, Edmund. *Axel's Castle: A Study in the Imaginative Literature of 1870–1930.* New York: Scribner's, 1931.

———. "The Dream of H. C. Earwicker." *The Wound and the Bow: Seven Studies in Literature.* New York: Oxford University Press, 1965, 198–222.

Winthrop-Young, Geoffrey and Michael Wutz. "Translators' Introduction: Friedrich Kittler and Media Discourse Analysis." Friedrich A. Kittler. *Gramophone, Film, Typewriter*, trans. Winthrop-Young and Wutz. Stanford: Stanford University Press, 1999, xi–xli.

Woodward, Llewellyn. *The Age of Reform: 1815–1870*. 2nd ed. Oxford: Clarendon, 1962.

Youssef, H. "The History of the Condom." *Journal of the Royal Society of Medicine* 86 (April 1993): 226–28.

Index

James, William, 133
Joly, Nicholas, 49, 172n6
Joyce, James: conception of art, 5, 14–16, 18,
  23, 25, 27–28, 32–33, 35, 38–44, 100–102,
  103, 160–62, 163–64, 180nn17–18, 181n19,
  185n17, *see also* Creative cannibalism;
  education and intellectual formation,
  xvii, 27; *inquit,* use of, 77, 79, 80, 81,
  82–84; language and style, xiv, xv–xvii,
  27, 31, 32–35, 38–39, 42–44, 48, 54–58,
  78–84, 97–101, 104, 110–11, 112–13, 121,
  129–31, 137, 139, 146, 172n4, 173n9, 173n13,
  180n13; and Paris, 51, 159, 183n6, 183n8;
  political formation and attitudes, xviii, 8,
  70, 85, 102, 103, 104–5, 121, 126, 136, 139,
  159–61, 163–64, 178n7, 180n17; religious
  formation, xviii, 4–5, 14–15, 67, 68, 160;
  responses to technology, xii, xviii, 84–85,
  101, 108–9, 110–12, 115–16, 119, 121, 125–26,
  129, 133, 135–36, 137, 139–41, 148, 149,
  151, 154, 155–56, 157–60, 183n6, 184n16,
  185n17; and Rome, 51, 67, 167n10, 175n9;
  and Trieste, xii, xvii, 27, 44, 47, 51, 52–55,
  57, 95, 136, 173n9, 173n11, 178n7; and Zurich, 51, 101, 180n17
—works of: "Et tu, Healy!" 71; "The Study of
  Languages," xvii, 38, 170n4; *Stephen Hero,*
  13, 15, 39, 165n1, 170n1; *Exiles,* 171n1. See
  also *Dubliners; Finnegans Wake; Portrait of
  the Artist as a Young Man, A; Ulysses*
Joyce, Stanislaus, 51, 64, 173n8, 174n2

Kafka, Franz, 180n17
Kant, Immanuel, 163
Kenner, Hugh, 47, 48, 55, 82, 172n4
Kershner, R. B., xviii, 72
Kittler, Friedrich, 107, 108, 109, 122, 130,
  131–32, 134–35, 136, 163, 181n2

Lacan, Jacques, 108
Landseer, Edwin, 116, 182n6
Larbaud, Valéry, 70, 71
Lawrence, D. H., 89, 90
Lecter, Hannibal, 2
Léry, Jean de, 16, 167n11, 168n15
Levin, Harry, xvii, 138
Lévi-Strauss, Claude, 169n17
Lewis, C. Day, 157–58, 162
Lewis, Wyndham, 128–29, 162, 163–64

Lind, Jenny, 120
"Little Nipper," 109, 112, 113–19, 126,
  181nn4–5. *See also* "His Master's Voice"
  (trademark)
"Little Red Riding Hood." *See* Mythology
  and folklore
Lofting, Hugh, 122
Lortzing, Gustav Albert, 185n19
Lumière brothers (Auguste and Louis Lu-
  mière), 132
Lüsebrink, Hans-Jürgen, xix, 140

Mallarmé, Stéphane, 55
Mandeville, Bernard de, 64
Marconi, Guglielmo, 176n3
Marcuse, Herbert, 162
Marey, Étienne-Jules, xiii–xiv, xv, 131
Marx, Karl, 12, 106, 167n11, 178n7
Mass culture. *See* Popular culture
Mathematics, xvii, 31, 34–35, 38–40, 41–43,
  170n2, 170nn4–5, 171n8, 171n10
Meitner, Lise, 155
Meiwes, Armin, 167n13
Melba, Nellie, 120
Melville, Herman, 4
Mengel, Ewald, 165nn2–3
Milton, John, 137–38
Modernism, xviii, 41, 42, 43, 90–91, 100–
  103, 104–5, 107, 108–9, 121, 140, 178n4,
  180nn17–18, 181n19, 181n2 (chapter 7)
Montaigne, Michel de, 6–7, 15–16, 26, 162,
  168n15
Moxon, Joseph, 37
Mozart, Wolfgang Amadeus, 40, 170n3
Münsterberg, Hugo, 133–36
Music, xvii, 1, 23, 31–35, 37–43, 64, 72, 127,
  162, 170n1, 170n3, 170n6, 171n7, 171n9,
  182n8, 185n19
Music of the spheres, 31, 35, 37–41, 43, 170n3,
  173n6
Mythology and folklore, xi, 65–67, 68, 70,
  102, 177n2; Admetus, 65–66, 67, 174n7,
  176n13; Alcestis, 65–66, 175n7, 176n13;
  Apollo, 65–68, 70, 174n7, 175n8, 175n10;
  Cassandra, 61, 130; Chronos, 3; Fates
  (Clotho, Lachesis, Atropos), 65–68, 70,
  174n7, 175n8, 175n10; Graces, 66; Hercules,
  66; "Jack the Giant Killer," 3; "Little Red
  Riding Hood," 3. *See also* Homer

Thomas Jackson Rice is the author of nine books and over 100 articles and papers on British, American, and world literatures, with primary emphasis on fiction from the nineteenth century to the present. He is best known to the Joyce community for his *James Joyce: A Guide to Research* and *Joyce, Chaos, and Complexity*. He is currently professor of English at the University of South Carolina.

The Florida James Joyce Series

EDITED BY SEBASTIAN D. G. KNOWLES

Zack Bowen, Editor Emeritus

Joyce's Comic Portrait, by Roy Gottfried (2000)

Joyce and Hagiography: Saints Above!, by R. J. Schork (2000)

Voices and Values in Joyce's Ulysses, by Weldon Thornton (2000)

The Dublin Helix: The Life of Language in Joyce's Ulysses, by Sebastian D. G. Knowles (2001)

Joyce Beyond Marx: History and Desire in Ulysses *and* Finnegans Wake, by Patrick McGee (2001)

Joyce's Metamorphosis, by Stanley Sultan (2001)

Joycean Temporalities: Debts, Promises, and Countersignatures, by Tony Thwaites (2001)

Joyce and the Victorians, by Tracey Teets Schwarze (2002)

Joyce's Ulysses *as National Epic: Epic Mimesis and the Political History of the Nation State*, by Andras Ungar (2002)

James Joyce's "Fraudstuff," by Kimberly J. Devlin (2002)

Rite of Passage in the Narratives of Dante and Joyce, by Jennifer Margaret Fraser (2002)

Joyce and the Scene of Modernity, by David Spurr (2002)

Joyce and the Early Freudians: A Synchronic Dialogue of Texts, by Jean Kimball (2003)

Twenty-first Joyce, edited by Ellen Carol Jones and Morris Beja (2004)

Joyce on the Threshold, edited by Anne Fogarty and Timothy Martin (2005)

Wake Rites: The Ancient Irish Rituals of Finnegans Wake, by George Cinclair Gibson (2005)

Ulysses *in Critical Perspective*, edited by Michael Patrick Gillespie and A. Nicholas Fargnoli (2006)

Joyce and the Narrative Structure of Incest, by Jen Shelton (2006)

Joyce, Ireland, Britain, edited by Andrew Gibson and Len Platt (2006)

Joyce in Trieste: An Album of Risky Readings, edited by Sebastian D. G. Knowles, Geert Lernout, and John McCourt (2007)

Joyce's Rare View: The Nature of Things in Finnegans Wake, by Richard Beckman (2007)

Joyce's Misbelief, by Roy Gottfried (2008)

James Joyce's Painful Case, by Cóilín Owens (2008)

Manuscript Genetics, Joyce's Know-How, Beckett's Nohow, by Dirk Van Hulle (2008)

Cannibal Joyce, by Thomas Jackson Rice (2008)